THE CASTLE

'*The Castle* is the first of its kind in its wide-sweeping ambitious chronology presented in an accessible and exciting way. John Goodall uses historical evidence in conjunction with images, architecture, and literary texts to masterfully take the reader on a journey from the earliest origins of the castle to the modern magical castle of Hogwarts and beyond. This book is a must for anyone interested in over 1,000 years of castle history in Britain.' Audrey Thorstad, author of *The Culture of Castles in Tudor England and Wales*

'John Goodall takes the reader on a noble and entertaining walk through British castles, a fascinating and joyful adventure brought eloquently to life!' Martha Lytton Cobbold, President, Historic Houses

'A masterful and erudite companion of the neglected heroes of British architecture.' Simon Jenkins, author of *A Short History of England*

THE CASTLE
A History

JOHN GOODALL

YALE UNIVERSITY PRESS
NEW HAVEN AND LONDON

To Isobel and Edward

For information about this and other Yale University Press publications, please contact:
U.S. Office: sales.press@yale.edu   yalebooks.com
Europe Office: sales@yaleup.co.uk   yalebooks.co.uk

Set in Adobe Caslon Pro by IDSUK (DataConnection) Ltd
Printed in Slovenia by DZS-Grafik d.o.o.

Library of Congress Control Number: 2021952545

ISBN 978-0-300-25190-6

MIX
Paper from
responsible sources
FSC
www.fsc.org   FSC® C106600

A catalogue record for this book is available from the British Library.

10 9 8 7 6 5 4 3 2 1

CONTENTS

CONTENTS

1400–1600 128

1600–1800 202

AFTER 1800 273

CONTENTS

GLOSSARY

Bailey	A fortified enclosure usually defined by ditches and walls. Also sometimes termed a 'ward'
Castlery	A body of estates that supports a castle. Also known as an 'honour'
Dais	A platform or raised area in a great hall reserved for the high table
Gothic	A style of architecture characterised by the pointed arch
Great Chamber	A chamber for the formal reception of guests, usually opening off the hall and by convention the most richly decorated interior in an English great house
Great Tower	A dominating tower of a castle and usually its architectural and residential focus. Also known as a 'keep' or 'donjon'
Honour	A body of estates that supports a castle. Also known as a 'castlery'
Motte	An artificial mound of earth usually surmounted by fortifications to form the centrepiece of a castle
Palatinate	A territory that enjoyed distinct legal privileges and autonomy. In England, Durham, Lancaster and Chester were for periods Palatinates
Privy Lodgings	A group of rooms withdrawn from the public interiors of a great residence to which the head of the household can retire from formal life
Romanesque	A style of architecture that draws inspiration from Roman buildings
Ward	A fortified enclosure usually defined by ditches and walls and normally termed a bailey

INTRODUCTION

As modern visitors enter the great castle at Conwy in North Wales, begun by Edward I in 1283, they pass a small information panel in the rocky ditch. It marks the spot where the naked and frost-covered body of a two-year-old child was discovered by the castle gatekeeper at dawn on 6 September 1303. We will encounter the remarkable story of this toddler, Roger, the son of the castle cook and his wife Dionisia, later in this book. Its details are not presently important. Indeed, some people might regard the event itself as curious but insignificant; a mere human footnote in the long history of this almost overwhelming building. To my mind, however, it helps explain why this book has been written and what it hopes to achieve.

The fact that it is possible precisely to locate an event that took place seven hundred years ago is a reminder that – however remote it may seem – the past took place in the same physical world that we inhabit today. Also, that history is the product of human experience like our own. It doesn't matter that Roger was a figure of no social standing or that he appears and vanishes in the historical record like a flash of lightning. The moment of illumination, however brief, in the midst of so much that is forgotten, adds another layer to our understanding of the castle ruins; they cease to be merely spectacular physical remains and become human ones as well. They are also revealed in a completely unexpected way.

In Roger's case this is because we don't generally associate castles with toddlers. Castles manifestly continue to elicit enormous interest but the way in which they are conventionally understood, discussed and presented remains narrowly focused: they are nearly always treated as a phenomenon of the Middle Ages alone and popular interest in them is almost exclusively focused on their warlike aspects. Indeed, it's scarcely

1

an exaggeration to say that their story prior to 1400 is dominated by discussions of their role and efficacy in warfare. After that date the history of the castle in England is scarcely known except by specialists.

The central purpose of this book, therefore, is to present a short and engaging history of the castle rooted in historical sources that runs from the Middle Ages to the present day. It's intended – like the gatekeeper's shocking encounter with the body of a child – to reveal unexpected aspects to these buildings and challenge the reader's expectations.

Forming its backbone are a selection of quoted texts, arranged in chronological order, from across the whole canvas of English history. They either tell stories about castles or take place against their backdrop, and are drawn from a wide variety of sources including administrative documentation, chronicles, poems, building accounts, letters and sermons. Most relate to real life but the castle also figures large in fiction and some, therefore, describe imagined buildings and events. The texts are all presented in English, though the originals are sometimes written in other languages, including French and Latin. Each is introduced individually and accompanied by explanations and analysis that set them in context.

To put flesh on this skeleton of texts, which constitutes the framework of the book, I have also incorporated a number of illustrations. Through art and architecture we arguably get closer to the physical experience of the past than by any other means. With this in mind, I have treated a selection of these illustrations like the texts and supplied them with an introduction and discursive caption. By this combination of text and image, the intention is to tell a history of the castle through the voices, experience and eyes of the different generations that have contributed to it.

It might be argued that setting up such a huge canvas with such an ambitious purpose dooms a short book to being superficial. That's true but it doesn't necessarily follow, however, that brevity can't be insightful. Implicit in the structure of this book is the idea that the story of the castle needs radical reappraisal. By convention, the castle has been defined as the residence of a knight or nobleman designed to resist attack. As a definition for castles of the eleventh or twelfth centuries, that's reasonably accurate, but even by the thirteenth century, and with growing regularity thereafter, there are buildings that assume the architectural language of defence but can't ever have been powerful fortifications.

INTRODUCTION

For this reason it's still common to find reference to buildings called 'Real Castles'. Real Castles are a specious invention of modern scholarship (informed by nineteenth-century perceptions). The term implicitly acknowledges that there are lots of buildings that were called castles by their builders, or which resemble castles, but it seeks to distinguish from amongst them a particular group that were constructed as fortifications. Put simply, Real Castles – as opposed to all the others, which are by implication fake – were built to be defended.

The architectural trappings of war – battlements, walls, moats, towers and turrets – are inseparable from the story of the castle. What's important to acknowledge, however, is that they assumed significance beyond that of mere function almost from the first. Also, by extension, that they came to be interpreted ever more elaborately in social and aesthetic terms. The secular ruling order of medieval England – knights and nobles – drew their income from land and fought for a living. They wished to live in buildings that made manifest their wealth, advertised their vocation and articulated their power. In this regard their chief residences – castles – were both symbolic and prestigious, characteristics underlined by the appearance of physical strength, scale and magnificence.

To these inextricably related and mutually reinforcing qualities, time added another potent ingredient: from the late twelfth century onwards the greatest castles began to be associated with the foundation myths of the kingdom as well as figures such as Julius Caesar or legendary heroes including King Arthur and Guy of Warwick. In the process they transcended history and became fossilised within the story of the landscape they commanded.

For those fortunate enough to possess major castles – such as Windsor or Belvoir – the antiquity of these buildings was hugely important. Paradoxically, so too was the need to update them and add new buildings in the height of contemporary fashion. Yet while modernisation might compromise their effectiveness as fortifications, they never lost the honorific title of 'castle'. Simply expressed, castles of this kind were – and remain – the most exclusive of possessions, residences beyond the compass of any but inherited wealth.

It was these ancient possessions, meanwhile, that set the architectural standards to which all subsequent builders of castles have consistently aspired. Defence was sometimes an issue for those who commissioned such buildings in the Middle Ages (and afterwards as well, as the reader will discover) but it was rarely the principal focus of their concerns. Much more important was the demonstrative quality of castle architecture. Battlements, walls and towers advertised social standing, wealth and lineage.

So while castles might have begun as fortifications, they very quickly became an enormous amount more. The trappings of war came to be adopted as far down the social scale as propriety would allow and for a small fee it was even possible by the thirteenth century to secure a royal licence authorising the erection of fortifications around a manor, clear evidence that the owner was of the requisite status to live in a castle. They also came to be applied decoratively to any building of architectural pretension, domestic or religious.

From this perspective, what is so astonishing about the architectural trappings of war is that they had such a long existence and wide application, even after they lost their original purpose. Moreover, once they ceased to be functional they could also become fantastical and, therefore, even more magnificent. After all, castles couldn't do without battlements and towers but they could be made infinitely more comfortable and splendid if no one needed to use them for fighting.

The idea that battlements dignified a residence and said something about its owner had an extraordinary longevity. Indeed, arguably, it has never gone away. What has been read into that association, however, has changed enormously over time. That reflects in turn the huge social, political and artistic changes that have taken place over the millennium spanned by this book. After the civil wars of the 1640s, which saw the overthrow of the last vestiges of the medieval social order, the castle was repeatedly reinvented in new and dynamic forms.

The Baroque builders of the late seventeenth century made Classical castles, buildings redolent of history and expressive of Britain's imperial aspirations as a new Rome. To the Enlightenment of the eighteenth century we owe the perception of castles as fantastical architectural creations, a tradition kept alive today in horror films and fiction. The Gothic Revival, meanwhile, fired Britain with an enthusiasm for the Middle Ages and the Romantic rediscovery of its history. It also helps explain the modern story of castles – both ruined and occupied – as public visitor attractions.

INTRODUCTION

What definition, then, would do justice to the full variety of castles in England? I would advocate the following: a castle is a noble residence made imposing through the architectural trappings of war. The advantage of this definition over the conventional one is that it acknowledges the importance of war in shaping the initial form of the castle but it doesn't demand that a castle be a functional building in that regard.

Yet in a book of this kind a definition is not everything. That's because the most honest way of following the story of the castle is to follow the usage of the word itself. After all, if people called something a castle then it is the duty of the historian to explain why they used the term, not to presume to tell them why they got it wrong. So, ultimately, this book is in fact fundamentally about an idea. That's a very complicated thing to chase but it's enormously rich and fascinating.

So for those who find the medieval castle interesting for its warlike associations, rest assured, they can read in the pages that follow accounts of sieges and warfare, of knights, catapults and imprisonment. What I hope they will also realise as they do so is that there is a vast amount more about these buildings to understand besides. Also, that to acknowledge this is not to diminish the castle but to make it infinitely more interesting. In the process, it will also become apparent why the second half of this book relates much more closely to the first than you might expect. There isn't such a thing as a Real Castle – only castles.

In relation to this point it's worth making one observation that has really emerged in the process of compiling this text. That is the recurrent appearance over the full period of time covered by this book of a particular word to describe not only castles and their architecture but also the people who lived within them: noble. That quality in turn implies certain associations that are inextricably interwoven with the story of the castle: landholding (often expressed, incidentally, by the aristocratic privilege of hunting), deep ancestry and military vocation.

This book presents its subject within an overarching chronology, a structure that aims to lend clarity to its narrative as well as force to its argument. Some readers, however, may prefer to dip into the text rather than read through it, or to explore themes – such as construction, warfare, domestic life – within the text. To facilitate this, the texts are prefaced by a thematic index. At the end of the book there is short bibliography for each excerpt. This does not aim to be exhaustive, but simply to point readers in the direction of the books, articles and scholarship that have shaped my own ideas.

It's worth finally saying something about the geographic scope of this book. The reader might reasonably ask why in the pages that follow there is such idiosyncratic coverage of Scotland, Ireland and Wales. That's really because there isn't the space in a book of this kind to examine the story of castles and their distinct histories and architectural traditions across the whole of the British Isles. Nor, however, can this book be limited to England, the history and culture of which is inextricably bound up with those of its immediate neighbours. So the story is focused on England, a decision that can be partly justified with reference to the kingdom's relative size, wealth and long political coherence. It also, however, freely looks beyond it on occasion.

THEMES

THE CASTLE IN ART

1066(b); c. 1300; c. 1320; After 1360; 1375; c. 1450; 1485; 1506; 1520; 1539; 1634; 1648; 1665; 1726; 1777; 1782; 1997(b)

THE CASTLE AS BACKDROP

1141; 1144–9; 1174; 1288; 1303; 1330; 1344; 1381; 1399; 1506; 1520; 1522; 1553; 1559; 1575; 1634; 1635; 1665; 1683; 1770; 1782; 1806; 1839; 1874; 1923; 1969

THE CASTLE BESIEGED

655; 1066(a); 1068; 1095; 1137–53; 1174; 1190; 1215; c. 1300; 1300; c. 1320; 1401; 1403; c. 1450; 1462; 1554; 1645; 1745; 1770; 1940

THE CASTLE UNDER CONSTRUCTION

1066(b); 1081; 1277; 1296; 1344; 1348; 1439; 1474; 1521; 1539; 1540; 1649; 1667; 1669; 1683; 1764; 1770; 1782; 1824; 1844; 1874; 1925; 1930; 1997(a)

THE CASTLE AND DOMESTIC LIFE

1265; 1288; 1303; 1342; 1494; 1522; 1540; 1697; 1824; 1841; 1857; 1874; 1925; 1949; 2009

THE CASTLE

THE CASTLE AND FOOD

1081; 1265; 1323; 1342; 1344; After 1360; 1494; 1506; 1520; 1522; 1539; 1540; 1770; 1824; 1831

THE CASTLE GARRISON

1068; 1215; 1381; 1403; c. 1450; 1462; 1745; 1940

THE CASTLE AND GUNPOWDER

1386; c. 1450; 1520; 1539; 1559; 1598; 1645; 1670; 1715; 1745; 1764; 1770; 1831; 1940

THE CASTLE AND HISTORY

1081; 1375; c. 1450; 1485; 1506; 1598; 1618; 1622; 1648–9; 1665; 1683; 1697; 1726; 1730; 1770; 1790s; 1801; 1819; 1854; 1857; 1874; 1899; 1911; 1921; 1969; 1997(a); 2009

THE CASTLE AND HUNTING

1265; 1342; After 1360; 1375; 1414; 1474; 1506; 1575; 1635; 1670

THE CASTLE AS AN IDEA

1158; c. 1320; 1375; 1539; 1562; 1588; 1670; 1715; 1764; 1801; 1809; 1831; 1841; 1844; 1923; 1930; 1949; 1997(b)

THE CASTLE IN LEGEND

1277; 1290; 1485; 1575; 1618; 1622; 1649; 1697; 1770; 1790s; 1997(b)

THE CASTLE AND LINEAGE

1348; 1485; 1506; 1622; 1649; 1730; 1770; 1790s; 1801; 1831; 1930; 1969; 1997(a)

THEMES
THE CASTLE IN LITERATURE

c. 1150; After 1360; 1575; 1588; 1634; 1678; 1764; 1770; 1831; 1923; 1949; 1997(b)

THE CASTLE AND NOBLE IDENTITY

1141; 1342; 1375; 1414; 1474; 1485; 1506; 1520; 1521; 1540; 1545; 1588; 1649; 1670; 1683; 1715; 1730; 1770; 1801; 1806; 1824; 1831; 1844; 1874; 1923; 1969; 1997(a)

THE CASTLE AS PRISON

1081; 1158; 1241; 1265; 1323; 1522; 1678; 1745; 2012

THE CASTLE RESTORED

1215; 1300; 1342; 1521; 1540; 1649; 1667; 1670; 1683; 1730; 1806; 1857; 1874; 1911; 1921; 1997(a)

THE CASTLE RUINED

1474; 1540; 1648–9; 1649; 1665; 1667; 1726; 1777; 1782; 1790s; 1806; 1874; 1899; 1911; 1921; 1949

THE CASTLE AND TOURISM

1265; 1485; 1545; 1598; 1697; 1777; 1782; 1801; 1819(a); 1839; 1854; 1899; 1921; 2009

A NOTE ON THE TEXTS

My aim has been to render historic texts included here in a way that is both true to the original and comprehensible to an interested, modern reader. The rules I have applied are few and simple:

- All the texts, regardless of the language in which they are originally written, are rendered in modern English spelling.

- Texts are punctuated according to modern English usage unless the original punctuation is integral to the sense.

- In some cases I have trimmed texts to clarify meaning or focus description. Missing words are indicated with ellipses . . .

- Any words inserted by me to simplify or explain a reading are enclosed in square brackets, for example: in the first year of Edward III [1327–8]

- Where particular words in the original text are significant they are written in *italics* and enclosed in square brackets after the translation. For example: castle [*chastel*]

- Where texts are originally in English I have not removed arcane words or simplified eccentric constructions.

- Where I have used a published translation of a text in Latin or French I have put the name of the translator in brackets at the end of each quotation. For example: Orderic Vitalis (trans.

A NOTE ON THE TEXTS

Marjorie Chibnall). If no translator is named, the translation is unattributed or my own.

- Full references for the sources of each text, along with further reading for each section, are supplied at the back of the book and are arranged by year according to the chronology.

THE WORD 'CASTLE'

The story of the castle properly begins not with archaeology, a place or even a person but with the word itself. The modern English word 'castle' ultimately derives from the Latin word for a fort or encampment castrum *and its diminutive form* castellum, *literally meaning 'a little fort'. It is a word commonly applied today as if it had a specific and consistent meaning but the following three short extracts, all taken from texts a thousand years old or more, make apparent the historical depth and potential variety of its usage.*

Caesar disembarked his army and chose a suitable spot for a camp [*castris*] . . . he left ten cohorts and 300 cavalry on the coast to guard the fleet, and marched against the Britons shortly after midnight.

> Around 50 BC, *The Conquest of Gaul* (trans. S.A. Handford)

Now it came to pass as they went, that he [Jesus] entered into a certain town [*castellum*]: and a certain woman named Martha, received him into her house.

> Fourth century, *Vulgate Gospel of Luke* 10:38
> (Douay-Rheims translation, 1611)

Then the King sent for all his council . . . The foreigners had then built a castle [*castel*] in Herefordshire in Earl Swein's province, and inflicted every injury and insult they could upon the king's men thereabouts.

> 1051, *Anglo-Saxon Chronicles*, E version (trans. M. Swanton)

The first of these three short passages describes the landing of Julius Caesar on British soil in 54 BC. As the account of the invasion makes clear, this encampment – we know nothing securely of its physical form – was a fortified base that secured the connection of the Roman army with its invasion fleet. The second text, by contrast, is not concerned with warfare at all. It comes from the Vulgate translation of the Bible, the standard Latin biblical text of the Middle Ages. Here the word *castellum* is rendered in early English translations as 'town', and its use has no obvious warlike connotations.

Both these texts would have been familiar to educated people throughout the Middle Ages and beyond. They demonstrate how deeply rooted in linguistic terms the word 'castle' is. Also that it had both biblical and Classical resonances and that in origin it might have had widely divergent application. Such breadth of association is vitally important to remember both when reading historical texts and when considering how the word has passed into common currency today.

The third quotation takes us closer to the familiar modern usage of the word. It comes from the *Anglo-Saxon Chronicles* and was written more than a millennium after Caesar's commentary. It's a particular curiosity because this is perhaps the first known use of this Latinate word in an Old English text. That said, it forms one in a small group of similar references in the *Anglo-Saxon Chronicles* of the early 1050s. In every case the word appears in connection with the activities of a group of foreigners in the realm.

The English king at the time, Edward the Confessor, had spent twenty-five years in Continental exile before his accession to the English throne in 1042. It was an experience that deeply coloured the character of his reign and exposed his kingdom to a number of foreign favourites as well as new ideas and cultural currents. One of these was a new type of fortification long familiar on the Continent: the castle.

This building type seems to have first emerged during the breakdown of civil order that accompanied the collapse of the Carolingian Empire in the tenth century. The magnates in modern-day France and Belgium who seized control of the fragmenting empire began to fortify their houses to create what we would term castles. Crucially, these buildings were also associated with a new system of land ownership, whereby each lord parcelled out his estates by 'fee', or *feodum*, to support a following of soldiers. These followers, moreover, were not just people who could fight as the need arose but specialists. Their landed income allowed them to follow a martial vocation, requiring long training, expensive weapons, armour and horses; they were knights. Castles, in other words, were the architectural expression of a new type of 'feudal' society that physically embodied lordship, landholding and military might.

It's clear from fragmentary archaeological and documentary evidence available that castles on the Continent during the tenth century were usually characterised by a dominating tower. Very occasionally this was constructed of stone, a highly prestigious material vastly time-consuming to fashion, expensive to move and explicitly evocative of the monumental architecture of the Roman past (see 1081 below). A common alternative, only fractionally less demanding in terms of resources, was to construct a timber tower on a high mound or 'motte' of earth (see 1066b below).

Man-made fortifications were to be found across Anglo-Saxon England encircling its major settlements and also the houses of noblemen or thegns. There is no evidence, however, that the Anglo-Saxons attempted to construct towers of the kind associated with Continental castles. The most plausible interpretation of this 1051 chronicle entry, therefore, is that the writer wanted to identify a new and unfamiliar type of fortification built by these troublesome foreigners, probably a motte with a surmounting tower of timber.

If so, this *castel* was a harbinger of the future. In the decades following the Norman Conquest in 1066, huge numbers of buildings with dominating towers of stone or earth and timber (as well as in other forms, such as a circular ditched enclosure termed a ring-work) appeared across the kingdom. They were built by a largely new and foreign ruling class, who were distinguished from the English they had conquered by language, dress and habits. Their castles, moreover, now assumed a prominent role in everyday life. In peacetime they served as centres of lordship and administration, and in war as powerful strongholds.

Just to confuse matters, however, these buildings were never consistently described. In Latin alone they are referred to by many names including *turris* (tower), *mota* (motte), *firmitas* (fortress) and *munitiones* (stronghold). These four words, indeed, all occur in one passage from the Treaty of Westminster in 1153 as descriptions of respectively the castles of London, Windsor, Lincoln and Southampton. Simply expressed, the word 'castle' is properly an umbrella term in modern English for buildings that might be referred to by many different words in the Middle Ages.

655
BAMBURGH
Anglo-Saxon Fortifications

The great plug of volcanic rock occupied by Bebba's burgh, now Bamburgh Castle, Northumbria. St Aidan's hermitage is thought to have stood on Inner Farne, the island visible to the left.

Anglo-Saxon England possessed fortifications that may have resembled later castles in physical terms but were different from them. When the pagan king of Mercia, Penda, for example, tried to seize the stronghold of Bamburgh in 655, the defences created around this spectacular coastal site with its sheersided plug of volcanic rock defeated him.

Penda and his enemy army of Mercians spread ruin far and wide throughout the land of the Northumbrians and reached the very gate of the royal city [*urbs* (and elsewhere *civitas*)], which takes its name from Bebba, a former queen. Unable to enter it either by

15

force or after a siege, Penda attempted to set fire to it. Pulling down all the neighbouring villages, he carried to Bamburgh a vast quantity of beams, rafters, wattle walls, and thatched roof, piling it high around the city wall on the landward side. Directly the wind became favourable, he set fire to this mass, intending to destroy the city. Now, while all this was happening, the most reverend Bishop Aidan was living on Farne Island, which lies nearly two miles from the city, and which was his retreat when he wished to pray alone and undisturbed. Indeed, his lonely hermitage can be seen there to this day. When the saint saw the column of smoke and flame wafted by the winds above the city walls, he is said to have raised his eyes and hands to heaven, saying with tears: 'Lord, see what evil Penda does!' No sooner had he spoken than the wind shifted away from the city, and drove back the flames on those who had kindled them, so injuring some and unnerving all that they abandoned their assault on a city so clearly under God's protection.

Bede, *Ecclesiastical History of the English People* (trans. L. Sherley-Price)

THIS account of the siege of Bamburgh was written in 731, some eighty years after the event, by the father of English history, the Venerable Bede. It's impossible to reconstruct very much about Bamburgh's defences in the seventh century but the site must have been defined by the rock that has been occupied since the eleventh century by a castle. This has an area sufficient to accommodate a small settlement. That, indeed, might explain Bede's use of the word 'city' to describe Bamburgh, as well as the Old English word 'burgh', meaning a fortified enclosure, in the name.

It's worth saying, however, that for Bede, familiar with literary descriptions of Rome or Jerusalem, the term 'city' might have seemed appropriate not because Bamburgh was populous but because it was defined by walls and gates. In this regard, the particular association with Queen Bebba is fascinating. Is this 'royal city' in fact a royal citadel rather than a settlement?

Modern scholarship has emphasised the private nature of castles as fortified residences. In this quality of privacy, it is argued, castles distinguish themselves from the public or communal defences of earlier towns or forts. Yet, given the paucity of evidence, perhaps this distinction – as applied, for example, to Bamburgh – sacrifices truth for clarity.

Certainly, from at least the ninth century it seems clear by inference that the word 'burgh' was not just being applied to communal defences but also the fortified residences of Anglo-Saxon noblemen or 'thegns'. Among the defining architectural features of such buildings were large-scale timber gate towers and halls. In England both types of structure were the object of particular aggrandisement. It's suggestive of how Norman architecture borrowed from Anglo-Saxon precedent that architecturally ambitious halls (see 1204 and 1290 below) and gateways also dignified English castles in the aftermath of the Norman Conquest.

While the fortified houses of thegns may have resembled later castles in physical terms, however, it is not common to read of sieges in the warfare of the Anglo-Saxon period. This fact alone strongly implies that prior to the Norman Conquest in 1066, the various types of fortification that existed in England were used strategically in a quite different way from castles (which appear everywhere in narratives of conflicts in the late eleventh and twelfth centuries).

That's an interesting detail to bear in mind when reading this account. As Bede describes it, there was no planned assault, nor did Penda make use of catapults or other engines of war. After being frustrated in an attempt to force a way in, his simple hope was that a huge bonfire might consume Bamburgh itself. Nor were his enemies active in their own defence. Indeed, if we take the account at face value, there was no actual fighting at all while the bonfire was constructed. In comparison to the narratives of castle sieges we will read later, the whole undertaking seems almost improbably passive.

It would only make sense of Penda's attempt to burn Bamburgh if the buildings within the fortifications were substantially built of timber and other combustible materials. That would perfectly agree with what we know of the archaeology of domestic buildings from this remote period. It's probable that the fortifications themselves were also of timber, though it's just possible that a stone wall existed and the intention was that the flames would overleap it and consume the buildings beyond.

Whatever the physical form and nature of Bamburgh, this account of its escape from Penda through the intercession of St Aidan speaks of a different military and social world from that which came to England at the Norman Conquest of 1066.

1066
PEVENSEY AND HASTINGS
The Norman Landing

The death of the childless king Edward the Confessor at Westminster on 5 January 1066 precipitated perhaps the most important – and certainly the most celebrated – dispute over the succession to the throne in English history. William, Duke of Normandy, determined to assert his claim to the English crown by force of arms against his English rival, Harold. This passage comes from an account of the Norman invasion written in about 1070 by a chronicler supportive of William. Here the landing of the Norman army is described, as well as its movements prior to its fateful confrontation with the English at the Battle of Hastings, on 14 October 1066. The narrative sheds a fascinating light on the Norman use of castles in this military campaign.

When the Duke, William, who by right should have been crowned with the royal diadem, observed how Harold daily grew in strength, he had a fleet of up to 3000 ships hastily put together and anchored, full of vigorous horses and very strong men armed with hauberks and helmets. Thence with favourable wind and sails billowing aloft, he crossed the sea and landed at Pevensey, where at once he built a strong entrenched fortification. Leaving a force of knights in that, he speedily went to Hastings, where he quickly raised another one. Harold, hastening to take him by surprise, gathered in innumerable English forces and, riding through the night, arrived at the battlefield at dawn.

William of Jumièges, *Deeds of the Norman Dukes* (trans. E. M. C. van Houts)

GIVEN the risks attached to William's invasion, the landfall of the Norman fleet at Pevensey, Sussex, cannot have been a coincidence. This was the site of a natural harbour (now drained), which was commanded by the ruins of a Roman fort. Even as ruins, Roman buildings were amongst the largest man-made structures in the landscape of eleventh-century Britain and their forts in particular had a long and complex afterlife following the withdrawal of the legions. A considerable number were planted with castles by the Normans.

The Norman army made an unopposed landing at Pevensey and it was presumably within the protection of the Roman walls and towers that it spent its first night on English soil. The account mentions the creation of earthworks here and the traces of a ditch dividing the interior of the Roman fort have been tentatively associated with this operation. Another description of the campaign by the writer Wace, written about a century after the Conquest, says that the Norman army brought with it materials that were used to erect a castle at Pevensey (for portable fortifications see 1386 below).

Having landed safely, the Normans then moved a short distance along the coast to Hastings and constructed a second castle there. Again, it's likely that this objective had been predetermined but the reason for this short move along the coast is not entirely clear. Some accounts associate it with the need to gather supplies, which might explain why the *Anglo-Saxon Chronicles* describe Hastings as a 'market-town'.

Another authoritative account of the Norman Conquest, written in the 1070s by William of Poitiers, describes the delivery of a letter to the duke, waiting at Hastings, written by a Norman, called Robert, living in England. It recommended that William remain in his defences and avoid battle. William responded defiantly, 'I shall not seek the shelter of ditch or walls but do battle with Harold as soon as possible.' The episode underlines the eleventh-century perception of the Norman invasion as a trial by battle for the English Crown. Confident in the justice of his cause, William needed to abandon his newly built fortifications so that an open encounter could unambiguously demonstrate divine approval for his claim.

The Battle of Hastings provided exactly the decisive victory William desired. In its aftermath he expected the English to submit. When they didn't he went on to seize Dover (the site of a possible pre-Conquest castle) and strengthen its defences, again securing an important harbour link between England and the Continent. He then marched to London, where his entry to the city was contested. Having burnt the suburb of

Southwark he retired and marched around the city in a great predatory arc before receiving the submission of the English at Little Berkhamsted, Hertfordshire. At no point in this campaign is any further mention made of castle building.

In other words, the first three Norman castles at Pevensey, Hastings and Dover were really built to secure lines of communication with Normandy (much like Julius Caesar's encampment referred to above). Events would prove, however, that while William might win the English crown on the battlefield, resistance to Norman rule demanded the creation of a second generation of castles to subdue the kingdom and then a third to bind it into an Anglo-Norman realm.

1066

HASTINGS CASTLE
A Campaign Castle

The Bayeux Tapestry is an eleventh-century embroidery that famously depicts the events of the Norman Conquest. Almost everything about this celebrated work of embroidery is contested: where it was made, who commissioned it, how it was displayed and what the later stages of its narrative – now lost – depicted. Nevertheless, looking at it the modern viewer can see the world through eleventh-century eyes.

THIS scene shows the construction of the castle at Hastings; its Latin text reads: 'He ordered a castle to be dug at Hastings.' The man in question, who holds a banner, appears twice, once just off the left of this detail, presiding over a gang of workmen, two of whom are fighting with spades, and again in the centre as they cast up earth onto the castle motte. Whether the labourers are Norman or English is not clear, nor is the subject of their quarrel recorded. Castle earthworks, however, required enormous quantities of labour to create and the demands

21

imposed on local populations to dig them were deeply resented. Whatever the nature of their dispute, the implication is that it has been resolved or overcome by the man with the standard. It may be significant, therefore, that in the next scene (not shown here) a very similarly dressed figure with a standard is specifically identified as William.

The castle at Hastings is very plain by comparison with some of the others depicted on the Bayeux Tapestry. In every other case, for example, the summit of the castle motte supports a central tower and is approached up a bridge with steps. The absence of the bridge and the simplicity of the structure on the motte (possibly a ring of timber) may reflect its character as a hurriedly erected campaign castle. It is not clear whether the stripes in the motte are merely decorative or intended to suggest a layered system of construction.

1068
YORK, WARWICK AND NOTTINGHAM CASTLES
The Subjugation of England

Lincoln Castle is unusual for possessing two artificial mounds or mottes, visible here to the centre and left. They were probably erected as a mark of the twelfth-century division of lordship over the castle between the king and the Earl of Chester. One hundred and sixty-six houses in the upper city were destroyed to create the castle here.

The coronation of William the Conqueror at Westminster Abbey on Christmas Day 1066 brought the Norman Conquest of England to its conclusion within the tidy span of a single year. Norman rule, however, was fiercely opposed by the English. In response William began to construct a second generation of castles in major towns. These he garrisoned and handed over to reliable followers as a means of enforcing his authority. According to the monk chronicler Orderic Vitalis, writing in about 1080, the English were unfamiliar with castles and their construction both frustrated their resistance and terrified them into submission.

a general outcry arose against the injustice and tyranny which the Normans and their comrades-in-arms had inflicted on the English. They sent envoys into every corner of Albion to incite men openly and secretly against the enemy. All were ready to conspire together to recover their former liberty, and bind themselves by weighty oaths against the Normans. In the regions north of the Humber violent disturbances broke out. The rebels prepared to defend themselves in woods, marshes, and creeks, and in some cities. The city of York was seething with discontent . . .

To meet the danger the King rode to all the remote parts of his kingdom and fortified strategic sites against enemy attacks. For the fortifications [*munitiones*] called castles [*castella*] by the Normans were scarcely known in the English provinces, and so the English – in spite of their courage and love of fighting – could put up only a weak resistance to their enemies. The King built a castle at Warwick and gave it into the keeping of Henry, son of Roger of Beaumont . . . Next the King built Nottingham Castle and entrusted it to William Peverell.

When the men of York heard this they were terrified, hastened to surrender less worst befell, and sent the King hostages and the keys of the city. As he was very doubtful of their loyalty he fortified a castle in the city and left trustworthy knights to guard it. Then Archill, the most powerful of the Northumbrian nobles made peace with the King . . . When this was done the King retired, building castles in Lincoln, Huntingdon and Cambridge on his way and garrisoning them strongly.

Orderic Vitalis, *Ecclesiastical History* (trans. M. Chibnall)

SUSTAINED English resistance in the late 1060s prompted William the Conqueror to adopt a new approach to controlling the kingdom and its populace. While campaigning he began to construct castles in strategic locations and install loyal garrisons. We know from other sources, notably the Domesday survey (see 1086 below), that the construction of these castles was often extremely intrusive. At Warwick, for example, it resulted in rent from four houses being lost. Presumably they were flattened to accommodate it. Likewise, twenty-seven houses were lost in Cambridge, twenty in Huntingdon and 166 at Lincoln. Such associated destruction may in part explain why the English were so frightened by the prospect of a castle being constructed.

What is less immediately obvious is why – according to Orderic – the English found themselves unable to respond effectively to castles. After all, large-scale fortifications did exist prior to the Conquest, as for example those systematically constructed around settlements by King Alfred in the ninth century as protection against the Danes. Part of the explanation may lie in the fact that, hitherto, the English preferred fighting in the field and simply didn't possess expertise in the management of sieges (see 655 above). Hence the comment that many went to remote places – woods, marshes and creeks – to resist Norman rule. No less important, perhaps, was the fact that the garrisons of these fortifications were foreigners and had no connection with the communities they were imposed upon. In effect, they ruled – and were solely ruled by – the edge of the sword.

The castles of the 1060s, constructed under the exigencies of war, must all have been rapidly constructed from timber and earth. It's unlikely that they were architecturally ambitious and, indeed, they might subsequently have vanished altogether but for another change of policy on William's part.

In 1069 William's patience with the English finally snapped and over the ensuing winter he devastated a great swathe of northern England. The 'Harrowing of the North' shocked even contemporary commentators and began a process whereby the Anglo-Saxon nobility was completely dispossessed and England was redistributed to a new circle of rulers both secular and ecclesiastic.

Land redistribution on a grand scale was only really possible from the 1070s onwards following the death or disinheritance of so many English families. It permitted the constitution of new estates – usually termed honours – that were focused on great castles. By this means castles were made permanent fixtures in the administration of the realm. They absorbed its wealth and resources and stood as testimony to the authority of its new owners. In the process, for the first time, English castle buildings began to be erected in that most imposing and unyielding material redolent of Rome: stone.

1081
TOWER OF LONDON
Building in Stone

The Tower of London – also known since the thirteenth century as the White Tower – is a building of such ambition and prominence that it has bequeathed London Castle its familiar name. It stands a short distance from the Thames just within the line of the Roman city wall (the ruined stub of masonry visible in the central foreground marks its line). Work to this great tower or keep began sometime after 1077, when William the Conqueror placed the building operation under the direction of Gundulf, Bishop of Rochester, and was certainly under way by 1081.

THE Tower of London was probably only completed in about 1100, a reminder of the practical challenges of constructing such a vast masonry building in the eleventh century. It was evocatively described in the

26

1170s as 'a fortress, palatine, massive and strong, its walls and its floors rising from the deepest foundations and its mortar tempered with the blood of animals'. This building instituted an English tradition of massive, rectangular towers, which became the architectural mark of the greatest castles (see 1141, 1439 and 1649 below).

The tower is rectangular in plan and outline and comprises three storeys set over a basement level. As originally completed the roof of the building was countersunk within the top storey (today there is a flat lead roof), giving it a distinctive rectilinear outline. There are turrets with Tudor domes and weathervanes at each corner. A spiral stair occupies the round turret to the right and the near angle of the tower swells out to accommodate the altar of a vaulted chapel. The external expression of internal planning by such means is a commonplace of medieval English architecture. Likewise, the size, number and ornamentation of windows hint at the relative importance of the middle storey. That said, nothing is certainly known about the original function of the tower's chambers. They are generally interpreted as spacious domestic interiors. Certainly, they were warmed by fires and comfortably appointed with built-in latrines. The thick walls open out internally with passages, an arrangement also found in major church buildings of the period.

Just visible to the top left of the tower are small windows with central columns. In 1100–1 Rannulf Flambard, Bishop of Durham, was imprisoned in the tower. Having feasted his guards and made them drunk he escaped by climbing down a rope while clutching his bishop's staff or crozier. It's specifically reported that he tied one end of the rope to a column in the centre of a window, presumably, therefore, an opening at this level. Keeps were commonly used as places of incarceration, particularly for socially significant prisoners, throughout the Middle Ages and beyond (see 1265 and 2012 below).

When work began to the Tower of London no building comparable to it had ever been seen in England. Its immediate source was almost certainly the lost tower of the ducal castle at Rouen, Normandy, which was demolished in the thirteenth century and likewise commanded the river approach to the town. This was one of several buildings created by the Dukes of Normandy on a similar plan. Some sense of the prestige attached to these gigantic towers is suggested by a story in circulation around 1100 that the architect, Lanfred, responsible for building one at

Ivry-la-Bataille, was executed by Albereda, wife of the Count of Bayeux, so that he could never build another. In stylistic terms the tower – constructed of stone on a monumental scale with round arches – spoke the language of Roman architecture, hence the term Romanesque to describe Norman architecture. Even by the thirteenth century the White Tower was believed to have been built by the Romans and has long enjoyed a special place in the national consciousness (see 1559 below).

1086
RICHMOND CASTLE
Interpreting Domesday

Richmond Castle, Yorkshire. The building to the right is a hall that probably dates to the 1080s, making it one of the earliest domestic buildings to survive in Britain. The keep to the left was raised over the original castle gateway in the 1160s.

William the Conqueror spent Christmas 1085 at Gloucester. There, after nearly two decades of war, rebellion and strife, he set in motion an astonishingly ambitious survey of the kingdom. As the Anglo-Saxon Chronicles *expressed it:*

the king had great thought and very deep conversation with his council about this land, how it was occupied, or with which men. Then he sent his men all over England into every shire and had them ascertain . . . what or how much each man had who was occupying land here in England, in land or in livestock, and how much money it was worth. He had it investigated so very narrowly that there was not one single hide, not one yard of land, not even (it is shameful to tell – but it seemed no shame to him to do it) one ox, not one cow, not one pig was left out, that was not set down in his record.

1085, *Anglo-Saxon Chronicles*, E version (trans. M. Swanton)

THE resulting Domesday Survey of 1086 – an exhaustive description of more than thirteen thousand places and including about 45,000 personal names, recorded in two massive volumes on the skins of some thousand sheep – is the most complete record of an eleventh-century society to survive anywhere in the world. Overall it documents the largest single transfer of property in English history. As the Anglo-Saxon nobility were reduced by war and rebellion, their land passed to a new and foreign ruling circle, concentrating the lion's share of the resources of the kingdom in the hands of about seventy individuals, lay and ecclesiastic. For all its detail, however, Domesday incorporates reference or allusion to just fifty castles (a further twenty-one are referred to in other sources prior to this date). It would be perfectly possible to imagine from this evidence that castles were not in fact very important to the new political order.

What it really proves, however, is the distorting insufficiency of the documentary evidence. That's because Domesday was really concerned with answering questions that looked straight through castles. Its compilers were charged with discovering the ownership of property on the last day of the reign of Edward the Confessor (5 January 1066), its ownership when the survey was undertaken in 1086 and changes in value of property between these two dates. As a result, castles only get a mention when their construction changed land values, most commonly by the destruction of property in cities to accommodate them (see 1068 above).

Take the example of Alan Rufus, Count of Penthièvre in Brittany, the leader of a Breton contingent at the Battle of Hastings. He acquired numerous grants of land including the property of Earl Edwin in Yorkshire after his rebellion in 1069 and that of Ralph de Gael in East Anglia after 1075. Cumulatively he became one of the largest landowners in the kingdom. Besides listing his possessions Domesday simply says:

Count Alan has in his castellany [*castellarium*] two hundred manors less one . . . Besides the castellany he has 43 manors

It's only by looking at later documentary material that it's possible to unpack the full significance of these two short sentences. Expressed another way, they tell us that three-quarters of Count Alan's property – 156 of the 199 manors he owned – had been constituted as a castellany, or group of estates that generated the resources and manpower necessary to build, maintain and garrison a castle. Such estates – also variously referred to as honours, castleries and rapes – were attached to every major castle foundation of the period. In this particular case the castle in question was built by Count Alan on a greenfield site at a place named in passing by Domesday (but with no reference to its new-found significance) *Hidrelaghe*, now Richmond, Yorkshire.

The Honour of Richmond – as the castellany later came to be known – is one of a small group of such castle estates that had relatively coherent landholdings in a geographic sense; the core of the estate derived from Earl Edwin's lands, though there were outlying properties as far afield as Lincolnshire and London. Such coherent honours, all established by about 1100, were ranged around the borders of the kingdom facing north to Scotland, west to Wales and south (the so-called Rapes of Sussex) and east (Holderness) towards the Continent. Elsewhere castle estates tended to follow complex and inherited patterns of landholding. The idea of constituting an estate to support an institution is of course prefigured in monastic foundations and also in the maintenance of important bridges, as at London and Rochester, arrangements that may date back to the late Roman period.

Alan in turn distributed the lands of his castellany to his followers, many of them fellow Bretons, in return for both military and household service. His steward, Wimar, for example, received land sufficient to support fifteen knights; the castle constable, Enisant Musard, land for thirteen knights; and his butler, another Alan, land for two knights. There are the earthwork remains of castles on the properties known to have been owned by several of these men. From this evidence it has been deduced that the lands attached to two or more knights' fees gave an individual follower the financial resources to build their own castles. In this way a great castle spawned offspring. These followers – and their descendants; the appointments were hereditary – also assumed responsibility for garrisoning Richmond Castle. Possibly from the first, and certainly by the 1190s, each took charge of a section of the defences (see *c.* 1450 below).

Richmond Castle was integrally planned with a fortified settlement and marketplace. The plantation of new towns beside castles was a widespread phenomenon in the decades following the Norman Conquest. So too was the foundation of new religious houses, which were often endowed out of the castle estate, their service of kind being prayer. At Richmond the Chapel of St Nicholas was gifted to St Mary's Abbey, York, in 1088 or 1089, which implies that the circuit of the walls (which include the chapel tower) was complete by then.

Properly understood, therefore, these two sentences in Domesday speak of a fundamental reordering of the kingdom and the imposition upon it of a new social, economic, religious and political order. Castles were becoming permanent and also architecturally ambitious.

BAMBURGH AND TYNEMOUTH
Early Baronial Castles

Self-serving, belligerent and ambitious, the great barons of the Anglo-Norman realm were, for the successors of William the Conqueror, no more dependable than the Anglo-Saxon nobility they replaced. And they knew all about castles. By the assessment of one contemporary, Orderic Vitalis, Robert de Mowbray was a tall, strong-built soldier, swarthy and bearded. In character he was silent, crafty and proud, disdainful of his equals and superiors. His severe countenance was rarely enlivened by a smile. Well connected in Normandy, he became Earl of Northumbria with authority over a huge swathe of north-east England in the late 1080s. Events reveal that he quickly secured this territory with castles.

Robert quarrelled with all his most powerful neighbours and he particularly annoyed the monks of Durham by granting the headland at Tynemouth – with its church and shrine of St Oswin – to the great Benedictine Abbey of St Albans, Hertfordshire. Durham coveted the site and the saint for itself. In 1093 he also successfully ambushed Malcolm III, King of the Scots, who was killed by the hand of his nephew, Morel. Two years after this ambush Robert plundered four trading vessels and their owners turned to the English king, William Rufus, for redress. Robert was summoned to Windsor but was refused promise of safe passage and his failure to appear was interpreted as rebellion:

the king therefore summoned his army and went to Northumbria against the earl, and immediately he came there he conquered many, and well-nigh all the best men of the earl's court inside one fortress [probably Morpeth], and put them in captivity, and besieged the castle at Tynemouth until he conquered it, and in there the earl's brother and all those who were with him, and afterwards travelled to Bamburgh, and besieged the earl in there.

But then, when the king saw that he could not conquer it, he then ordered a castle to be made in front of Bamburgh, and called it in his language *Malveisin*, that is in English 'bad neighbour', and set it strongly with his men and afterwards went southward . . .

Then immediately after the king had gone south, the earl travelled out one night from Bamburgh towards Tynemouth; but those who were in the new castle [the *Malveisin*] became aware of it and went after him, and fought against and wounded and afterwards captured him, and of those who were with him, some killed, some took alive . . . [Then the king] ordered Robert the Earl of Northumbria to be seized and led to Bamburgh, and both eyes put out unless those who were inside would give up the castle. His wife and Morel, who was his steward and also his relative, held it. Through this, the castle was then given up.

1095, *Anglo-Saxon Chronicles*, E version (trans. M. Swanton)

IN this account Robert's surprising decision to leave the relative safety of besieged Bamburgh is not explained. Other sources, however, suggest that he aimed to capture Newcastle and, thereby, turn the tables on his opponents. If so, the plan went awry. They also reveal that his party numbering thirty knights was finally overwhelmed at Tynemouth after a six-day siege. Having been wounded in the leg, Robert took sanctuary in St Oswin's church but was dragged out on the king's orders and ignominiously returned to Bamburgh for the surrender of the castle.

Robert lost everything as a result of this rebellion. He was taken to Windsor, where he began a period of upwards of twenty years as a prisoner. His wife was granted an annulment and remarried. Shortly before he died (either in 1115 or 1125) he may have become a monk of St Albans, where he was buried. Durham never forgot the slight of Robert's behaviour over Tynemouth and one of its chroniclers, the monk Symeon, smugly recorded the testimony of a Yorkshire knight, Arnold de Percy, who claimed to have witnessed the fallen earl's passage through Durham in 1095. Arnold stated that Robert asked his guards if he could pray at St Cuthbert's shrine in the cathedral priory. When they refused he burst into tears and said, 'Oh, St Cuthbert, justly do I suffer these misfortunes, for I have sinned against thee and thine . . . Saint of God have mercy on me.' But St Albans kept hold of Tynemouth nevertheless and established a junior monastic cell here, Tynemouth Priory. It has an unexpected subsequent history.

Tynemouth Priory was constituted as the heart of a territorial liberty, within which it exercised legal rights normally reserved for the king. Malefactors could also claim sanctuary from the law within the *grith* of the priory, an area extending a mile around the church and demarcated by stone crosses. From its headland site the priory also controlled trade on the River Tyne, which set it in conflict with Newcastle. Added to which, in the Anglo-Scottish Wars of the fourteenth century, it served as an important fortress, with a permanent garrison of over eighty men maintained by the priory. This latter function in turn led to a bizarre legal dispute in the 1340s that hinged on whether Tynemouth was a monastery – and therefore under the control of its ruling monk, the prior – or a castle, and therefore technically a possession of the king and his officers. Even in the Middle Ages there might be disputes as to what was, or was not, a castle.

1137–53
HEREFORD CASTLE
Castle Building in the Anarchy

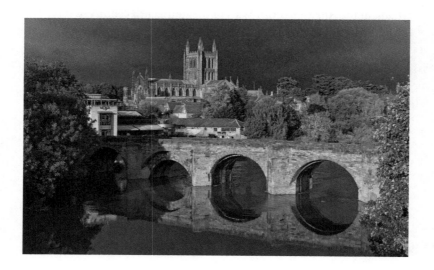

Hereford Cathedral was occupied as a castle during the Anarchy. The central tower, which was used to mount siege engines, has since been rebuilt. These siege engines were fired towards the castle, which occupied a site – now a park – beyond the trees to the right.

On 25 November 1120, a boat full of men and women born to greatness in the Anglo-Norman realm foundered in the Channel. Henry I's only legitimate son was among the drowned and the king demanded, therefore, that the throne pass to his surviving daughter, Matilda. His barons reluctantly agreed but on condition that they be given a say in whom she married. It was, however, without their consent that in 1128 Matilda was secretly wedded to Geoffrey, Count of Anjou, an arch-enemy of Normandy. When Henry I died in 1135, therefore, the alienated barons supported the succession of the king's nephew, Stephen of Blois. Matilda and Stephen (as well as his wife, another Matilda) now proceeded to fight for the crown in a civil war that spanned the Channel. Their dispute, familiar today as the Anarchy, was only finally resolved in 1153, when both sides agreed that Matilda's son, Henry II, should succeed Stephen. The two following texts respectively give a flavour of the experience of the civil war. The Anarchy was in part a castle war, as this famous description of it makes clear:

> every powerful man made his castles and held them against the king; and they filled the land with castles. They greatly oppressed the wretched men of the land with castle-work; then when the castles were made, they filled them with devils and evil men. Then both by night and by day they seized those men whom they imagined had any wealth, common men and women, and put them in prison to get their gold and silver, and tortured them with unspeakable tortures . . . These things we suffered for nineteen long years for our sins and they said openly that Christ and his angels slept.
>
> 1137, *Anglo-Saxon Chronicles*, Peterborough
> Manuscript (trans. M. Swanton)

WHAT this passage describes was the attempt by the two sides to assert control of a place or an area using castles. At the height of the conflict Stephen and Matilda began supporting the rival claims of their followers to the same territorial prizes. In practice this meant that one side occupied an existing castle and the other built one or more new castles nearby to contain the enemy garrison (like William Rufus's *Malveisin* or 'bad neighbour' castle at Bamburgh in 1095 above). Both, meanwhile, extorted what they could from their surrounds. Without a supporting army neither side had a decisive advantage, leading to long and destructive stalemates. These hastily erected fortifications were sometimes new-built earth and timber castles – a good example, known as The Rings, survives as an earthwork about 320 yards south-west of Corfe Castle, Dorset – but they could equally make use of churches, fortifying them where necessary. That was the approach of Geoffrey Talbot, a long-standing supporter of Matilda, at Hereford:

Geoffrey Talbot undertook to besiege the troops that the king had left in the castle of Hereford as defenders of the country and servants and guardians of his rights. Entering the church of the Mother of God, the Cathedral Church of the episcopal see, and impiously driving out the ministrants at God's table, he recklessly brought in a throng of armed men . . . Everywhere the townspeople were uttering cries of lamentation, either because the earth of their kinsfolk's graveyard was being heaped up for a rampart and they could see, a cruel sight, the bodies of parents and relations, some half-rotten, some quite lately buried, pitilessly dragged from the depths; or because at one time it was visible that catapults were being put up on the tower from which they had heard the sweet and pacific admonition of the bells, at another that missiles were being shot from it to harm the King's garrison [in the castle].

Anon., *Deeds of Stephen* (trans. K. R. Potter)

The Romanesque tower of Hereford Cathedral was rebuilt in the fourteenth century and the castle motte has since been levelled. Nevertheless, it's perfectly possible from the modern topography of the city to grasp what this confrontation must have been like (the 200 yards between them was evidently the range of a siege engine). The gruesome emphasis on the exhumation of bodies underlines once again the suffering of ordinary people. In the prosecution of war, medieval armies, like their modern successors, could be pitiless.

Most of the hastily built castles constructed during the Anarchy came and went with the fighting. In some cases, however, the breakdown in royal authority allowed the beneficiaries from this conflict to build masonry castles on an unprecedented scale. They were often inspired by the example of local royal buildings and used resources usurped from the Crown. In doing so, they followed in the footsteps of a trusted royal servant to both Henry I and King Stephen, Roger of Salisbury.

1139
ROGER OF SALISBURY
Castle-Building by Royal Favour

The gatehouse of Sherborne Castle, Dorset, built by Bishop Roger and faced with beautifully squared blocks of stone, an unusual extravagance in a mid-twelfth-century castle building. Roger also encrusted his buildings with carving, even treating chimneys as works of abstract sculpture.

While on campaign in Normandy in the late 1090s, the future Henry I stumbled across a small church on the outskirts of Caen. He and his companions asked the poor parish priest there to celebrate Mass for them. This the priest did with such remarkable speed that Henry's knights declared he would make a perfect military chaplain. Henry, therefore, took the man,

Roger, into his service. This at least is how William of Newburgh, writing in the 1190s, sought to explain the first step to power of a man who became one of the greatest builders of his generation. What is certainly known is that Roger became Bishop of Salisbury in 1102 and grew by degrees in authority until King Stephen imprisoned him in 1139. This hostile account of his fall accuses him of promising to support Stephen against 'the children of Henry I', by which he means in particular Matilda and her illegitimate brother, Robert, Earl of Gloucester, and of turning the resources of the realm to the benefit of himself and his relatives. His castle building is singled out for particular criticism, expressing both opulence and military ambitions completely at odds with his role as a churchman.

[Roger, Bishop of Salisbury] was reckoned next to the king in the whole government of the kingdom. So he, though he enjoyed the king's [Stephen's] strong affection, and though he was given particular charge of all the business of the kingdom, yet he showed more affection and friendship [for the] . . . children of King Henry. He promised, but in secret . . . that he would most loyally keep faith with them and grant them zealous aid, and his castles, which he had built most elaborately, he was filling on a very lavish scale with weapons and supplies of food, shrewdly combining service to the King with waiting till the time . . . he could help them with the utmost vigour and speed . . . everywhere he went, and especially to the king's court, he was encircled by a large and numerous bodyguard of troops . . . His nephews too, who bore the titles of Bishop of Lincoln and Bishop of Ely, men who loved display and were rash in their reckless presumption, agreed with this policy, and disregarding the holy and simple manner of life that befits a Christian priest, they devoted themselves so utterly to warfare and the vanities of this world that whenever they attended court by appointment they aroused general astonishment on account of the extraordinary concourse of knights by which they were surrounded on every side . . . [Their jealous enemies said] that those bishops owned the primacy of the kingdom, all the splendour of their wealth, the whole force of men, not for the King's honour; that they had built castles of great renown, raised towers and buildings of strength, and not to put the king in possession of his kingdom, but to steal his royal majesty from him and plot against the majesty of his crown.

Anon., *Deeds of Stephen* (trans. K. R. Potter)

IN the course of his career, Roger built or reworked five important castles, each associated with great landed estates, major religious foundations and towns. These were at Old Sarum, Wiltshire, the seat of his bishopric and the predecessor town to Salisbury; Sherborne, Dorset, where the abbey had been the former seat of the bishopric; Devizes and Malmesbury, Wiltshire; and Kidwelly, Carmarthen. The buildings he created at these places, both castles and churches, were regarded as architectural prodigies by contemporaries. One, William of Malmesbury, a monk writing in the 1130s, declared that Roger:

never spared expense towards completing his designs, especially in buildings. This is to be seen above all at Salisbury and Malmesbury; for there he erected buildings large in scale, expensive and very beautiful to look at; the courses of stone being laid so exactly that the joints deceive the eye and give the whole wall the appearance of a rock-face.

William of Malmesbury, *Deeds of the Kings of England* (trans. R. A. B. Mynors, R. M. Thomson and M. Winterbottom)

Accurately cut stonework was vastly expensive and technically demanding to create. It had, therefore, hitherto been the almost exclusive preserve of church buildings, the senior branch of architectural practice throughout the Middle Ages (the eleventh-century great towers of Corfe, Dorset and Norwich, Norfolk are the earliest surviving English castle buildings of cut stone). Roger, however, adopted it throughout his castles. As an additional opulence he also encrusted his buildings with ornamental sculpture. In the case of Old Sarum he even decorated the chimney pots with carved, abstract patterns. It's possible that the later medieval English tradition of embellished chimneys in grand residential buildings – outward advertisements of inner comfort and wealth – stems from this astonishing experiment.

At least two of Roger's castles also had domestic apartments formally arranged around a courtyard, a sophistication of planning presumably borrowed from monastic design. And at Devizes, Roger constructed a keep on an immense scale. These, in short, were revolutionary buildings, unparalleled in sophistication and effectively funded from the royal coffers.

Roger's fall was dramatic. He was summoned to the court at Oxford in June 1139 after Stephen had been warned of his activities. He arrived with his nephews (also significant builders; see 1726 below) and a large armed following. Following a violent scuffle the king demanded that the bishops surrender their castles to him. They demurred and were imprisoned (though the Bishop of Ely briefly escaped to Devizes). Roger died within the year.

1141
CASTLE HEDINGHAM, ESSEX
The Mark of an Earl

The principal interior of the keep or great tower of Castle Hedingham, Essex, built by Aubrey de Vere, Earl of Oxford, in the 1140s. Given the cost and difficulty of building in stone, this building was clearly not a response to the needs of war (timber and earth being the architectural materials of urgency). Instead, the sheer grandeur of this interior, with its fireplace, windows and decorative carving, suggests luxury. How can the character of this building be explained given the wider political chaos of the period?

AS part of the intense competition to attract support for their cause, Stephen and Matilda not only backed rival claims to territory, they were also generous with titles. The Anglo-Saxon title of earl was invested with

43

enormous prestige and had often been assumed – rather than conferred – as an honorific by the most powerful nobles. It was always associated with a place, a county or town, that was its notional seat. During the Anarchy, however, the title began to be touted as a reward for support and the number of earldoms in England consequently swelled dramatically from about seven to nearly forty. The new earls sought to assume the architectural trappings appropriate to their new-found status. Abbeys and priories were particular beneficiaries of their largesse, but so too were castles. For reasons of sheer expense, great towers or keeps of stone – buildings redolent of wealth, power and dominion – had hitherto been the preserve of the king and his favoured circle. So now new earls began to erect them as well.

By a unique grant of 1141, Aubrey was offered an earldom by Matilda with a choice of title: either Cambridgeshire, Oxfordshire, Berkshire, Wiltshire or Dorset. He chose the second and almost certainly began the great tower at Hedingham – in a region where he and his brother-in-law enjoyed particular authority – to celebrate his new-found status. By every measure this was a prodigy building. It comprises five storeys and stands over 100 feet high, the benchmark of a medieval skyscraper. This room, the principal interior within it, is conceived on a scale to match: the arch spanning the room is one of the widest to survive from the twelfth century in England, far exceeding the span of many great church arches. The room is comfortably appointed with a fireplace and its flat ceiling was originally boarded, possibly to create a surface for painted decoration. There were no kitchens or small domestic chambers in the building, which may imply that it was intended only for ceremonial use. That would accord with the fact that the gallery running round the upper storey of the room is entered through a door carved with decoration only on one side, a detail that implies a correct direction of circulation within the building. The latrines that served the room discharged into the basement, a surprising arrangement that must have demanded intense management if the whole building was not to stink.

The association of great towers with noble titles persisted far beyond the end of the Middle Ages (see 1649 below), and the distribution of peerages as a reward for the support of a government remains a feature of British political life to the present day.

1144−9
DURHAM CASTLE
A Castle Described

The monumental juxtaposition of castle and Cathedral at Durham. The tower on the motte, rebuilt in stone in the fourteenth century and subsequently truncated, is visible to the extreme left.

Composed between 1144 and 1149 by a monk – and later prior – of Durham, Laurence, this verse offers us a rare glimpse of a great castle as it appeared to twelfth-century eyes. The Latin is florid, which makes it hard to translate, but repays careful reading. It forms part of a description of the whole city of Durham, which, at the time of writing, was still scarred by the events of the Anarchy. As if in the opening of a film, Laurence sets the scene and then leads us from the gate up to the citadel and then back down to the castle enclosure or bailey with its buildings and bustle:

the castle [*arx*] is seated like a queen; from its threatening height it holds all that it sees as its own. From its gate, the stubborn wall rises with the rising mound, and rising still further, makes towards the comfort of the citadel [*arcis*]. The citadel, however, rising into a crown strong within and without, well fitted for its work. For within it stands three cubits higher than without, ground made firm by solid earth. Above this a stalwart house springs yet higher than the citadel, glittering with splendid beauty in every part; four posts are visible, on which it rests, one post at each strong corner. Each face is girded by a beautiful walkway [*ala*], which is fixed into the war-like wall. A bridge gives a ready ascent to the ramparts, easy to climb; starting from them, a broad way makes the round of the top of the wall, and this is the usual way to the top of the castle . . . Hence into the castle the bridge looks down bringing also an easy return. The bridge is divided into easy steps, no headlong drop, but an easy slope from the top to the bottom. Near the bridge a wall descends from the citadel turning its face westward towards the river. From the river's lofty bank it turns away in a broad curve to meet the field. It is no bare plot empty of buildings that this high wall surrounds, but one containing goodly habitations. There you will find two vast palaces built with porches, the skill of whose builders the building well reveals. There the columned chapel stands out, not too large but fair enough to view. Here chambers are joined to chambers, house to house, each suited to the purpose that it serves. Here are fine costumes, there shining vessels and flashing arms, here money, meat and bread. Here is fruit, there wine, here beer, there is a place for fine flour. Since house joins to house, building to building, no part lies empty. There is a building in the courtyard of the castle which has a deep well of abundant water . . . The haughty and powerful gate faces out to the south, easily held by the hand of a feeble woman. The bridge of the gate is extended as a way out, and thus the way goes out across the broad ditch. It goes to the plain [Palace Green] which is protected on all sides by a wall, where the youth often held their joyous games.

Laurence, *The dialogues of Laurence,*
monk and prior of Durham

FOR all the changes that it has undergone, Laurence's description of Durham Castle is easy to relate to the building today. The mound or motte still survives, though now surmounted with the truncated remains of a fourteenth-century stone keep, and so too does the chapel (or at least the lower part of it). What is striking about the description is the degree to which Laurence's account emphasises the comfort, activity and luxury of the building as a whole. Its defensive qualities are both important and beautiful but the implication is that this castle is so magnificently strong that no one would dare presume to attack it anyway. Who would attack a queen?

One curious detail to which Laurence does not allude is that the See of Durham and all its temporal possessions were understood in the Middle Ages to belong to St Cuthbert. His incorrupt body in the neighbouring cathedral priory is perhaps the only corpse that has ever held property under English law. In expression of this, the key of the castle formerly hung over his shrine. The reality, however, was that the bishop controlled the castle and the prior the shrine and monastery. Relations between them, moreover, could be strained.

c. 1150
THE PRINCIPLES OF CASTLE DESIGN
A Sermon

*In the century after the Norman Conquest we know frustratingly little –
beyond an occasional name – about the professionals who actually conceived
and erected castles. This sermon preached by Aelred, abbot of the Cistercian
monastery of Rievaulx, Yorkshire, from 1147 to 1167, however, offers an
unexpected insight into the defensive principles on which they were designed.
It draws an analogy between the elements of a castle and religious virtues. It
was preached on the feast day of the Assumption of the Virgin, the day on
which the mother of Christ, Mary, was assumed into heaven. The listener is
enjoined to imitate Mary and build a castle spiritually in their heart as a
devotional womb to receive Christ.*

> Therefore let us prepare this castle. Three things make up the
> castle so that it might be strong, namely a ditch, a wall and a
> tower: first the ditch [for humility], and after that a wall [for
> chastity] over the ditch, and then the tower [for charity] which is
> stronger and better than the others. The wall and the ditch guard
> each other, because if the ditch were not there, men could by
> some device get in to undermine the wall; and if the wall were not
> above the ditch, they could get to the ditch and fill it in. The
> tower guards everything, because it is taller than everything else.
> So let us enter our minds, and see how all things should be
> brought into being spiritually within ourselves
>
> St Aelred, *Sermon 17: On the Assumption of the Blessed Mary*
> (trans. A. Wheatley)

THE complementary role of the ditch, the wall and the tower in defence
summarise the essential theory of fortification as understood in the
mid-twelfth century. It's clear from castle buildings (and, indeed, other

sermons) that the principle of concentric lines of defence – in which layers of defence were organised like the skins of an onion, one within the other – was also understood in the same period.

Aelred was recognised as a saint by his order in 1476 and might seem an unlikely figure to offer observations on castles. In reality, however, his early career was spent in the service of David I, King of Scots. Consequently, like many prominent ecclesiastics of the period, he was completely at home in both the court and the cloister. It's just one illustration of this that in addition to his devotional writings he also produced an account of the Battle of the Standard fought between the Scots and the English near Northallerton, Yorkshire, in 1138.

There was, in fact, a close connection between castle-building and the monastic revival associated with church reform of the late eleventh century. From the 1070s onwards, religious foundations were repeatedly established (or existing ones regularised) in the shadow of new castles and endowed out of their estates. Rievaulx was no exception. The site of the abbey was first colonised in March 1132 with monks from Clairvaux Abbey in Burgundy on land granted by Walter Espec, lord of nearby Helmsley. Aelred, its second abbot, presided over an extraordinarily vibrant and well-connected institution. From 1150 he not only began the wholesale reconstruction of his monastery in stone, including an enormous church (Helmsley Castle was likewise acquiring masonry fortifications from about the same period), but also the steady expansion of its community. In the 1160s it possessed about 140 monks beside an army of lay brothers, a workforce of unlettered labourers that lived under vows as servants of the abbey. That these men saw their vocation in a quasi-military light is illustrated by the eleventh-century statues of the Cistercian order, which called the monks 'the new knights of Christ'. It was this militant spirit that launched the crusades and also underpinned the foundation of fighting orders including the Knights Hospitallers, Templars and the Teutonic Knights.

Throughout the Middle Ages and far beyond, the idea of a castle was used as an intellectual conceit in devotional writing (see *c.* 1320 and 1678 below). It also had many other applications besides, as reflected in book titles such as *The Castle of Helthe* (1541), *The Castle of Memorie* (1561) and the *Castell of Courtesie* (1581).

1158
CARDIFF CASTLE
Injustice and Hostage-Taking

Not every attack on a castle involved large numbers of men and war machines, as this case of a dispute between the Welshman, Ivor the Little, and his overlord, the Earl of Gloucester, reveals. This account comes from the writings of the Anglo-Welsh cleric, Gerald, who toured through Wales in 1188 and wrote his Itinerary through Wales, *based on his experiences. He undertook the tour in company with Baldwin, Archbishop of Canterbury, who was seeking volunteers for the crusade following Saladin's dramatic victories and his entry into Jerusalem on 2 October 1187.*

An extraordinary circumstance occurred likewise at the castle of Cardiff. William, earl of Gloucester, son of earl Eobert, who, besides that castle, possessed by hereditary right all the province of Glamorgan, that is, the land of Morgan, had a dispute with one of his dependants, whose name was Ivor the Little, being a man of short stature, but of great courage. This man was, after the manner of the Welsh, owner of a tract of mountainous and woody country, of the whole, or a part of which, the earl endeavoured to deprive him. At that time the castle of Cardiff was surrounded with high walls, guarded by one hundred and twenty men-at-arms, a numerous body of archers, and a strong watch. The city also contained many stipendiary soldiers; yet, in defiance of all these precautions of security, Ivor, in the dead of night, secretly scaled the walls, and, seizing the count and countess, with their only son, carried them off into the woods, and did not release them until he had recovered everything that had been unjustly taken from him, and received a compensation of additional property

THE scale of the Cardiff Castle garrison described by Gerald is a reminder of its importance in the control of South Wales, also of the deep hostility between the Anglo-Normans and the Welsh. Curiously, it's possible that the son of the Earl of Gloucester who was carried off in this raid – or alternatively a yet younger member of the same family – is mentioned again by Gerald in the same book as the victim of another castle misadventure:

> A circumstance happened in the castle of Haverford during our time, which ought not to be omitted. A famous robber was fettered and confined in one of its towers, and was often visited by three boys, the son of the earl of Clare; and two others, one of whom was son of the lord of the castle, and the other his grandson, sent thither for their education, and who applied to him to make arrows, with which he used to supply them. One day, at the request of the children, the robber, being brought from his dungeon, took advantage of the absence of the gaoler, closed the door, and shut himself up with the boys. A great clamour instantly arose, as well from the boys within, as from the people without; nor did he cease, with an uplifted axe, to threaten the lives of the children, until indemnity and security were assured to him in the most ample manner.
>
> Gerald of Wales, *The Itinerary through Wales* (trans. Sir Richard Colt Hoare)

It's interesting that in both stories Gerald notes that each man got what he demanded and something extra, as if they were being rewarded for what they had done. The addition suggests admiration for their cunning.

Castles clearly were regularly used as prisons, a function that continued unbroken into the early twenty-first century (see 2012 below). The modern reader might imagine that the freebooter was held in a vaulted dungeon but medieval prisoners could be held in almost any secure castle building and notably great towers (see 1265 below). A stone salvaged from one of the internal galleries of William Rufus's palatial great tower of the 1090s at Norwich, for example, bears a neat French inscription in a fourteenth-century hand that proclaims pathetically: 'Bartholomew. Truly, wrongfully and without reason I am shut in this prison.'

1174
BROUGH AND ALNWICK CASTLES
Capturing a King

In 1174 William the Lion, King of Scotland, mounted an invasion of England. All the fighting was focused on castles, as this contemporary French poem by one Jordan Fantosme – who writes from an English perspective – makes clear. William's first target was Wark, Northumberland, where he was humiliatingly rebuffed after a misfiring catapult nearly killed one of his own men. He moved on to Carlisle, Cumberland, and negotiated unsuccessfully for its surrender. From there he moved on to Appleby Castle, Westmorland, which was without a garrison. Having received its surrender he continued to Brough, Cumberland, where he was stoutly resisted. William's followers therefore:

mount a fierce attack and on the first day they have captured the bailey, the defenders having abandoned it and taken to the tower . . . the attackers set fire to it and they will burn them up inside it . . . They are at the end of their resistance and have surrendered themselves to the king . . . But a newly dubbed knight has come amongst them that day. Now hear of his deeds and his mighty acts! After his companions had all surrendered, he remained in the tower and took two shields and hung them over the battlements. He held out for a long time and hurled three sharp javelins at the Scots and killed one of them with each of the javelins. Having no more of these, he picked up pointed stakes and hurled them at the Scots and did much mischief . . . When the fire consumed the shields he had hung for his defence, he cannot be blamed for surrendering then.

Presumably the stakes thrown by this enthusiastic young knight were torn from the building itself, which sounds as if it was entirely constructed of timber. It was presumably the predecessor of the ruined stone tower that survives at Brough today. The detail of the knight hanging the shields over the parapet is important as well. Clearly these afforded protection but they also symbolised defiance. In the late twelfth century the art of heraldry, the insignia of an exclusive knightly class, was already in development and it subsequently became subsumed into castle architecture with carved coats of arms appearing particularly over gates. William went on to overrun Harbottle and Warkworth Castles, Northumberland, but had to raise the siege of Prudhoe when news came of an approaching English army. On his way home he determined to attack Alnwick, dispersing his army to devastate the surrounding countryside in the meantime. What he didn't know was that a group of English knights led by Randolph de Glanville had pressed forward to catch him unawares and sent out a scout to find him. Arriving on a hot summer morning, 13 July, with a small party of knights beneath the walls of Alnwick Castle in what he believed to be complete safety, he surveyed the scene:

> And the King of Scotland said: 'let us await our army and then we shall launch a powerful attack on the castle. As it is getting very hot, my lords, let us break our fast'. He takes the helmet off his head . . .
>
> Our knights [the English] have gone into a copse, where they find their scout who gives them all possible information. Said Randolph de Glanville: 'Thanks be to God! Take up your arms and fear nothing!' Then you would have seen knights in action like a flash, leaping to horse and snatching up their arms . . .
>
> The King of Scotland was a valiant knight and prodigiously bold. There he stood unarmoured in front of Alnwick. I relate no fable as one telling from hearsay, but as one who was on the spot, for I saw it all myself. When some have cried out de Vesci's battle-cry, others 'Glanville, knights!', and others 'Balliol!' Odinel d'Umfraville raised his war-cry as did the Stutevilles, those doughty knights . . .
>
> Immediately the king has himself speedily armed, and sprang on his swift horse, and rides into the fray with exceeding boldness. He throws down the first man he smote. The king and his companions put up a tremendous fight. All might have gone well, so I reckon, had it not been for a sergeant who rushes at him and thrusts the lance he held into his horse . . .

> The King lay felled to the ground . . . between his thighs the horse lay on him . . . He was at once captured – this I saw with my own two eyes – by Randolph de Glanville to whom he later surrendered; the boldest of his knights are made prisoners too. There was no love lost between the two sides, they were enemies to a man . . . Randolph was overjoyed when he perceived and understood that the war as far as the King is concerned is truly finished. England is at peace and her worthy inhabitants will fear William no more, nor will the Scots do them any further mischief.
>
> Jordan Fantosme, *Chronicle* (trans. R. C. Johnston)

WHEN Glanville's triumph was reported to the King of England, Henry II, in London, it assumed a completely new and miraculous significance. Four years earlier, on 29 December 1170, in response to an outburst of royal rage, a group of knights had broken into Canterbury Cathedral and murdered the Archbishop of Canterbury, Thomas Becket. Henry II had borne the opprobrium of Christendom for this terrible deed. On 14 July, the morning after William the Lion's capture, Henry II had performed an astonishing act of repentance for it: having prostrated himself in the chapter house of Canterbury, he had been publicly whipped by the monks, every one of the eighty-strong community laying on three strokes.

To Henry II it was clear from the capture of the Scottish king that God and Thomas Becket had pleased to signal their acceptance of his extraordinary penance. William the Lion was brought to Henry II as a common miscreant, his feet bound beneath the horse he rode. Castles were not the immediate cause of his humiliation but they shaped every stage of his unhappy invasion and served as the backdrop to his fall. The episode was long remembered at Alnwick (see 1770 below).

1181
DOVER CASTLE
A Pilgrimage Route

In 1180–1 Henry II began a new keep or great tower within the huge enclosure of the cliff-top fortifications at Dover, Kent. The timing of this project was not coincidental. Following the murder of Thomas Becket, the miracles worked by the murdered archbishop began to attract pilgrims including, in 1179, the King of France. In the meantime, following a fire in 1174, a new setting was created for the saint's shrine at Canterbury Cathedral. Dover, commanding the shortest sea crossing between England and the Continent, was the landfall for international pilgrims to England and the new castle looks like a reaction to the development of Becket's cult. Indeed, one of the two chapels in the great tower is known to have been dedicated to the saint and precisely borrows architectural details from the new work at Canterbury Cathedral. Dover remained in military use until the late twentieth century and its medieval buildings have been heavily reworked over time.

THE progress of Henry II's work to Dover Castle is recorded in a series of royal accounts known as the Pipe Rolls. Its design and construction was overseen by a mason and *ingeniator*, or 'engineer', in royal service called Maurice. The latter term was also applied to the specialists involved in constructing and operating siege engines. After four years the incomplete tower was victualled and garrisoned, suggesting that it was already several storeys high. Work to it continued, however, for a further three years. As it was drawing to a close, in 1185–6, a wall or 'girdle' was built around the tower to create an enclosure or bailey around it. Shown here is the north end of the girdle. Its three towers – the pair to the right creating a twin-towered gate – echo the form of the great tower with its triple turrets. Enclosing this composition is a fortified outwork termed a barbican that was in turn approached up a long bridge-like ramp, the medieval remains of which are encased in the foreground structure.

As originally completed, the exterior of the keep was faced with broad bands of striped masonry, possibly in conscious evocation of the banding of materials in Roman architecture. In the later Middle Ages the tower was believed to have been constructed by Julius Caesar and was repeatedly remodelled as a royal residence (see 1520 below). The building incorporates a vast well about 350 feet deep ('Big Ben' at Westminster stands 315 feet high). Water from this supplied a complex system of lead pipes laid into the fabric of the building, clear evidence of the very sophisticated domestic arrangements it was originally intended to accommodate.

1190
YORK CASTLE
The Massacre of the Jews

A riot in London during the coronation festivities of Richard I in September 1189 precipitated a wave of violence against Jews in cities across England. The Jews were popularly represented as the murderers of Christ but were additionally disliked because – unlike Christians – they were able to lend money at interest under royal protection. This was seen as a useful evil but deeply resented by those in their debt. To compound their perceived error in rejecting Christianity, moreover, wild and horrific stories circulated about their supposed religious practices.

One shocking episode in this cycle of violence in 1189–90 occurred at York Castle in March 1190. This account is composed by a local cleric, William of Newburgh, and we take up his narrative after the Jews of York have put themselves in the care of the governor of the castle, a representative of their protector, the king. This follows killing, rioting and looting in the city by a sworn 'confederacy' motivated by a desire for plunder. For some reason, there is a subsequent misunderstanding with the governor, who is denied access to the castle by the terrified Jews. Understandably angry, he is persuaded by the confederacy to order an attack on the castle. He immediately regrets what he has done. A mob gathers and while many of the well-to-do refuse to get involved, the castle is surrounded by a great concourse baying for blood, including a handful of knights and some clergy, notably a Premonstratensian hermit.

Thus were the Jews besieged in the royal castle; and in consequence of the want of a sufficient supply of food, they would, without doubt, have been compelled to surrender, even if no one had attacked them from without, for they had not arms sufficient either for their own protection, or to repel the enemy. Nevertheless, they kept off the besiegers with stones alone, which they pulled out of the wall . . . That hermit of the Premonstratensian order, whom I have

mentioned, urged onward the fatal work more than any one else . . .
To such an extent had he persuaded himself, by his mental blindness,
that he was employed on a religious matter, that he laboured to
persuade others of it; and when the [siege] engines were moved
forward, he fervently helped with all his strength. Whence it came
to pass, that, approaching the wall incautiously, and not observing a
large stone which was falling from above, he was crushed by it . . .

The engines being brought up, the capture of the castle was
certain; and it was no longer doubtful that the hour fatal to the
besieged was come . . . the Jews strong and unbending through
desperation alone, had but little rest, and debated among
themselves what was to be done in such an emergency.

There was among them a certain elder, a most famous doctor
of the law, who had come from countries beyond the sea to
instruct the Jews in England, as it is said . . . When his advice was
asked, he replied, 'God, to whom we ought not to say "Why dost
Thou this?" commands us to die now for His law – and behold
our death be at the doors . . . we ought to prefer a glorious death
to an infamous life . . . for if we should fall into the hands of the
enemy, we should die according to their pleasure, and amidst their
mockery . . .' When he had said this, many embraced the fatal
advice; but to others this discourse seemed hard . . . Soon after, at
the suggestion of that mad old man, to prevent their enemies from
being enriched by their wealth . . . [they burnt] their precious
vestments . . . Then it was decided that the men whose minds
were more firm, should kill their wives and children . . . When all
were killed, together with the leader of the crime, the fire which
(as it was said) they had lighted when they were about to die,
began to burn the interior of the castle. Those, however, who had
chosen life, contended as well as they could against the flames . . .

In the morning, when a large multitude of people had assembled
together to storm the castle, they found the wretched Jews who had
survived standing on the battlements, announcing, in melancholy
voice, the massacre of their people . . . [they throw the bodies
over the wall as proof of their story and ask to be baptised as
Christians] . . . While they thus spoke, with tears in their eyes,
many of our people looked with deep horror and astonishment

upon the madness of those who were dead, and pitied the survivors; but the chiefs of the confederacy (among whom was one Richard, truly surnamed Malbeste [evil beast], a most daring fellow) were unmoved by pity for these miserable wretches. They deceitfully addressed kind words to them, and promised the favour they hoped but, as soon as they came out, those cruel swordsmen seized them as enemies, and slaughtered them in the midst of their continual cries for the baptism of Christ . . .

When the massacre was complete, the confederates proceeded immediately to the cathedral church, and, by violent representations, compelled the terrified wardens to deliver up the acknowledgements of the debts . . . [which] they solemnly committed to the flames in the midst of the church.

William of Newburgh, *A History of English Affairs* (trans. J. Stevenson)

IT's implicit from this account that William of Newburgh strongly disapproves of religiously motivated violence both by Christians and the Jews. Also, that he believes many of those Christians acting against the Jews are motivated by greed and a desire to escape debt. Indeed, his overall disgust and ambivalence are striking. It's important to understand, however, the degree to which his narrative is coloured by historical episodes narrated by the first-century AD historian of the Jews, Josephus, such as the Roman siege of Masada. Also, that in some details his story must be invented: William can't really have known, for example, what the Jews debated amongst themselves in the castle. To some extent, therefore, his narrative is a literary construction projected as an explanation onto a shocking event.

It has usually been assumed that the Jews in this episode took refuge on the surviving castle motte in York. Also, that the tower here in 1190 was built of timber, hence the final fire. That's a perfectly reasonable assumption but it arguably sits at odds with the detail supplied by William that the Jews tore stones from the walls to protect themselves. Possibly the whole castle, therefore, actually featured in this terrible drama. The motte itself is now the site of Clifford's Tower, erected in the 1240s by the royal mason Henry of Reyns, also the designer of Westminster Abbey. Much of the castle site is today a car park.

1204
DUBLIN CASTLE
Mandates for a New Castle and a Royal Hall

The Anglo-Norman Conquest of Ireland began almost by accident in the late 1160s. In 1170, however, the marriage between Richard de Clare, second Earl of Pembroke, alias Strongbow, to the daughter of the King of Leinster offered such alarming evidence of its gathering pace that Henry II visited the following year to assert his lordship over the Irish. In the decades that followed, Ireland's experience in some ways closely mirrored that of England under the Normans a hundred years earlier. A series of Anglo-Norman landholdings was quickly staked out along the eastern seaboard, each one with a castle as its focus. There was, however, no seat of royal authority on this coastline. Hence this very unusual mandate or written order from King John in 1204 to the Justiciar or viceroy of Ireland to build a castle in Dublin:

The King . . . to his trusty and well-beloved Meiler, son of Henry, Justiciar of Ireland, greetings. You have given us to understand that you have no safe place for the custody of our treasure and, because for this reason and for many others we are in need of a strong fortress [*fortilecia*] in Dublin, we command you to erect a castle [*castellum*] there in such a place as you may consider to be suitable for the administration of justice and if need be for the defence of the city, making it as strong as you can with good ditches and strong walls [*cum bonis fossatis et fortibus muris*]. But you are first to build a tower [*turrim*], to which a castle and bailey [*castellum and baluum*] and other requirements may be conveniently added: for all these you have our authority. At present you may take and make use of 300 marks from Geoffrey fitz Robert, in which he stands indebted to us.

August 1204, mandate of King John

TO judge from this mandate, John recognised that he needed a castle in Dublin to store treasure securely and to serve as a place for the administration of justice (see 1288 below). If appropriate, he also notes, the castle could strengthen the fortifications of the city. Intriguingly, he evidently anticipated that the building would be completed in stages with the construction of a tower – presumably for the treasury – to which a fortified and ditched enclosure termed a bailey could be added later. It was clearly assumed that the Justiciar would determine the location of the castle and possessed the power to clear the site.

The sum of 300 marks or £200 made available for the task was generous for a tower but not a whole castle. Pledging money in the form of a transferred loan, moreover, probably made it less generous still. By way of comparison, the construction of Orford Castle, Suffolk, on a greenfield site, from 1165 to 1173, cost Henry II over £1,400. That said, castle building in Ireland may have been cheaper than in England: an earth and timber fortification at Clones, Co. Monahan, in 1212, for example, cost the Justiciar just £19 4s 10d ha'penny (including £8 for 'Irishmen to dig ditches').

One tower may indeed have been erected at Dublin after this order was issued, but doubtless the shortage of money explains why building operations to the castle as a whole only got under way some ten years later, between 1213 and around 1230. In this period a four-square castle with corner towers and a twin-towered gatehouse came into being at one angle of the city walls. Such buildings as were erected inside the castle do not sound particularly ambitious. A castle chapel, for example, existed by 1225 and was supplied with glass windows in 1242. Then, quite unexpectedly, the castle became the focus of an architectural project that must have dwarfed everything else accomplished here to date.

In 1243, in anticipation of a visit by Henry III, the king directed that a hall be constructed in the castle. The mandate for it sets a budget of 3,000 marks (£2,000) at the least. It makes sense of this huge sum, ten times the amount proposed for the original castle, that the building was to be modelled on the hall of the Archbishop of Canterbury at Canterbury (one of the most ambitious buildings of its kind in thirteenth-century England). It was to accommodate a rose window and a monumental painting:

a hall should be made in Dublin castle 120 feet in length and 80 feet in breadth and with windows and glazing in the manner of the hall of Canterbury as much as they think appropriate; and to be made in the gable above the dais a round window 30 feet broad. They should make a painting, moreover, above the dais of the king and queen seated with their barons. They should make moreover at the entrance of the said hall a great porch. So should the hall be made in its entirety for the lord king before his arrival.

24 April 1243, *Close Rolls of the Reign of Henry III*

Henry III's careful directions for his new hall at Dublin Castle – he always gave exceptionally detailed directions for the alteration and decoration of buildings – suggest that he saw it as a physical embodiment of his power and authority in Ireland. That was also the message of the wall painting in the room, which made his presence, along with the queen and the barons of the realm (in effect, what would later constitute the core of a medieval parliament), a dominant and permanent feature of the interior. Presumably, he intended the room to serve as a centre for the royal administration and ceremonial events (see 1635 below). The huge expenditure also suggests that to Henry III the hall of the castle was of much greater significance than its fortifications.

1215
THE FALL OF ROCHESTER CASTLE
The Fat of Forty Pigs

On 15 June 1215, King John was forced by a powerful party of barons to assent to the charter of liberties famously known as Magna Carta. He had no intention of observing its terms and immediately called on the pope to quash it. Within three months the kingdom was embroiled in civil war. Both sides looked to the Continent for help. The rebels seized London in September and appealed to the French King, Philip Augustus, while John sent for mercenary reinforcements from Flanders and Brabant. As the king awaited his army in Kent, a force of rebel knights marched south from London to surprise him. Warned of each other's approach, however, both forces ended up running away, the king to Dover and the rebels to Rochester on the Medway. John's mercenaries finally arrived on 26 September, their numbers much depleted by a storm, and the royal army marched on Rochester. The town fell immediately and the rebels scattered, some fleeing to London and others into the castle. John then broke the bridge to isolate the town from reinforcements and settled down to besiege the castle for seven weeks, bombarding it with siege machines. With the outer defences broken down the garrison withdrew to the 1120s keep or great tower of the castle, a vastly ambitious structure laid out on a rectangular plan with a spine wall dividing the building into two through its full height.

When all the other defences were broken down, the great tower [*arx*] alone stood intact, though it too was damaged by the barrage of stones; it was older than the other buildings but constructed more soundly. Then miners were sent in. One side of the building was brought down, but the defenders took up a strong position in the other half, for the great tower was built in such a way that a very thick wall separated this part from the side which had fallen. Never in our age has a siege been driven so hard, or resisted so bravely. But after days without respite, the men in the tower, besieged there alone and without assistance, were struck by terrible hunger; they had only the flesh of horses to eat and water to drink (which was particularly hard for them, being accustomed to finer food). At last the end came. First they threw out all the men who seemed least able to fight on: the King took some of them and cut off their feet. Then, soon afterwards, all the rest were captured and except those who claimed Benefit of Clergy, they were put in chains. The King kept the knights and most eminent prisoners for himself, and granted the remainder to others. From the enormity of his rage, it seemed that he was going to have the whole army put to the most terrible death, but in fact he only ordered the hanging of one man, a crossbowman; they say that John had fostered him from childhood. All the other rebels were desperate at this news; some fled in fear back to London, others took refuge in monasteries, and now there were few who cared to put their trust in castles.

The Memorials of Brother Walter of Coventry

THE collapse described in this account is still visible as a great V-shaped gash in the masonry at the south corner of the tower at Rochester. From the evidence of this it's clear that the miners did not tunnel under the tower but quarried into its base at ground level, presumably under some kind of protective covering. The likelihood is that they cut away the masonry and shored up the structure with timber props, which they then burned away. Certainly they used fire because a royal writ dated from Rochester on 25 November demands:

We direct that with all haste by day and night to send us forty pigs, and those of the kind that are less good for eating, to create and maintain fire beneath the tower.

25 November 1215 mandate of King John

This collapse was repaired after the siege by Henry III in the 1220s (see *c.* 1300 below). He must also have restored the floors of the building, which shows extensive evidence of fire damage, another legacy of the forty pigs.

All those who fought against the king did so at the hazard of their lives. The treatment of the garrison, however, highlights some interesting distinctions within it. It's likely that the first group expelled from the castle were all socially insignificant and the act of cutting off their feet was an act of demonstrative justice intended to terrify the remaining defenders. When these eventually surrendered they clearly included some knights of wealth, hence their being used to good food and something better than water to drink (by chance the well in the tower faced away from the side of the building that collapsed). These prisoners were reserved by the king, probably for ransom. Likewise, for smaller ransoms, the more humble figures whom the king distributed to his followers. There were clergy too but the king was careful not to meddle directly with them beyond loading them with chains. Crossbowmen were mercenaries and the rank and file of professional garrisons. There must have been a number of them but John hanged only one, a personal act of retribution for his disloyalty.

Walter of Coventry's final comment about the failure of trust in castles is noteworthy. In absolute terms it's not true; over the next two years castles, and in particular the conduct of major sieges at Dover, Windsor and Lincoln, played a crucial role in determining the accession of John's son, Henry III, to the throne. Rather, Walter's observation should probably be read as a reflection on the increasing organisation of sieges and the almost irresistible might of royal resources; John's siege of Rochester is worlds away from the attacks of Penda and William Rufus on Bamburgh, Northumberland (see 655 and 1095 above).

1241
TOWER OF LONDON
Fighting Royal Tyranny

Caerphilly Castle, Glamorgan, begun in 1268. The form of this castle with its water defences, double circuit of masonry fortifications laid out on a regular plan and great gatehouses was probably inspired by Henry III's work to the Tower of London.

In 1238 or 1239 Henry III began to expand the fortifications of the Tower of London. His intention was to create around the castle a new circuit of walls and a tidal moat of immense size. Londoners were nervous as to the king's intentions in rebuilding the castle. Was he planning to strengthen his grip on the city by force? Their suspicions were vindicated when the murdered Archbishop Thomas Becket, the nemesis of tyrants, born on Cheapside, the main thoroughfare of the City, was seen to intervene from beyond the grave in the building project.

At about this time, a night-time vision appeared to a certain wise and godly priest, in which an archbishop, wearing his full vestments and brandishing a cross in his hand, came up to the walls which the king had then raised next to the Tower of London, and looking at them with an angry expression, he boldly struck the walls hard with the cross in his right hand and said 'to what end are you being rebuilt?' Suddenly the walls collapsed as if they had been struck by an earthquake, although they were only recently built.

At this a clerk appeared following the archbishop. The priest, terrified by what he had seen, asked him 'who is this Archbishop?' He replied 'This is the Blessed martyr Thomas, a Londoner by birth, who sees these buildings as an insult and a danger to the Londoners; that is why he has destroyed them irreparably'. The priest replied 'but what about the cost and effort of the workmen? He has ruined it all'. The clerk answered him 'if the poor needy workmen were able to buy food with the wages they earned, that is indeed a good thing, but these walls were built not for the defence of the realm but to harm innocent citizens and if the Blessed Thomas had not destroyed them, his successor Saint Edmund the Confessor would have uprooted the foundations even more violently'.

. . . Early next morning, a rumour spread through the whole city of London, that the walls which had been built around the Tower, on which the king had spent more than twelve thousand marks, had collapsed irreparably. Many people wondered at this and declared it was an evil omen, because at exactly the same time, that is to say, Saint George's night [23 April], but in the previous year [1240], the same walls fell down together with their outworks. The citizens of London were completely amazed at this and not at all sorry. The walls were like a thorn in their eye. They had heard people taunting that . . . if anyone dared to stand up for the rights of the city, they could be clapped in irons and imprisoned inside. Many cells could be seen in the buildings for the imprisonment of large numbers separately, so that none of them could speak with another.

Matthew Paris, *Chronica Majora* (trans. Jeremy Ashbee)

THIS story nicely captures the nervousness ordinary people might have felt at the sight of major works to a castle. It's a response that is intermittently documented in England until the Civil Wars of the mid-seventeenth century. Castles were a tool of political control and the powers of the officials who managed them were often openly abused. Certainly, Londoners were right to fear the arbitrary exercise of royal authority from the Tower. In the late thirteenth century, for example, many Jews were imprisoned and executed here on what were later revealed as trumped-up charges.

This whole story might sound like an invention but archaeological excavation in 1995–6 unexpectedly revealed the truth of Matthew Paris's chronology. This exposed the rectangular foundation of a tower to the west of the castle, presumably the outworks of Henry III's gatehouse, which had been reinforced after structural failure with beechwood piles. The timbers dated neatly to 1240/1, the period between the two collapses.

Henry III's gatehouse probably looked very similar to that which survives today at Tonbridge, Kent, owned by the powerful de Clare family. Another of their castles, at Caerphilly, Glamorgan, probably gives an impression of what Henry III wished to create in London. Work to it was subsequently abandoned and Henry III's son, Edward I, overbuilt the site with what is known today as the Beauchamp Tower, completed in 1281. He also reduced the size of his father's moat in this area, testimony to the immense scale of the original.

1265
DOVER CASTLE
The Barons' War

*In 1264 a civil war broke out in England between Henry III and a party of
barons under the leadership of Simon de Montfort, 6th Earl of Leicester. The
capture of Henry III and his heir, Prince Edward (later Edward I), at
the Battle of Lewes on 14 May 1264 put Simon in effective control of the
kingdom. A year later Prince Edward escaped from custody and the fighting
resumed. The prince surprised a rebel force mustering outside Kenilworth
Castle on 2 August 1265. Then, at the Battle of Evesham on 4 August,
Simon de Montfort and his son were both killed.*

*One fascinating sidelight on these dramatic events is supplied by a short
surviving sequence of household accounts for Simon's wife, Eleanor, a sister of
Henry III.*

*The accounts – among the earliest of their kind to survive from an English
noble household – were a working document with distinct records of regular and
occasional costs, each noted down in chronological order as it was made. They
show that Eleanor was residing at Odiham, a small castle with excellent hunting,
when news of Prince Edward's escape reached her. In response, on 1 June 1265,
she moved by night to Portchester and then via Bramber Castle to the strategically
crucial castle of Dover. These select entries show that she facilitated diplomatic
negotiations from here and strengthened the defences with a catapult:*

Paid to Sir Matthew of Hastings, for the passage of Sir Dromo de
Noviomo and Brother Boniface, messengers of the Lord the King
of France, at the Feast of St Peter in Chains [1 August] 12 shillings
    Hired, for one boat, for seeking a machine, at Pevensey by
Thomas Saleqim 40 shillings

ON 11 August, a week after the Battle of Evesham – probably in direct
response to the news of the earl's death – she dined the whole garrison in

69

the castle hall at her own expense and sent the master of the Hospital of God's House at Dover to the king, presumably with instructions to intercede for her. He was generously rewarded, as was the departing engineer, whom she must have hired to operate her catapult:

> Delivered to the Master of God's House, Dover, going to the King, on the morrow of St Lawrence [11 August] 40 shillings
> On the same day delivered to master William *machinatori* [elsewhere *ingeniator* or engineer] by the gift of the Countess 40 shillings

From 11 to 20 August she did not dine in public in the hall, presumably a mark of mourning, and then made a bequest or oblation for the soul of her deceased husband. The subsequent payment to Prince Edward's messenger perhaps suggests that he brought welcome promise of clemency from her victorious nephew:

> For the offerings of the Countess by John Scot, from Wednesday before the Feast of St James [22 July] to Wednesday after the Assumption [19 August], with 12 shillings and nine pence for the soul of the Earl [of Leicester] 22 shillings 4 pence
> Given to the messenger of the Lord Edward, coming with letters to the Countess, for his wages 2 shillings
> *Household Roll of Eleanor de Montfort* (trans. L. J. Wilkinson)

By September it's clear from the accounts that there is a shortage of supplies in the castle because the accounts speak of animals being foraged for food. Then the sequence ends. Sadly, therefore, we do not have accounts to flesh out our understanding of the dramatic culmination of Eleanor's occupation of Dover. For this we must turn to a chronicle account.

Probably in the light of changing political circumstances, a group of royalist prisoners incarcerated in the great tower of the castle persuaded two of their guards to release them and fortified their prison against the garrison:

> about 14 nobles of the realm, who were being held in the tower of the castle of Dover, their feet chained, having plotted with two

guards – unless I'm mistaken a third had been sent out wisely to the town to buy food for the nobles; which having been obtained, they defended in a military manner, at once fortifying the door from the inside to exclude those within the castle, who began vigorously to attack in their desire to break in. The defenders constructed a strong wall against the inside of the door to block it against entrance from the hard-fought assaults that they were continuously receiving and only with difficulty repelling. When he heard the news, the Lord Edward flew from London to Dover without even sleeping. Having gathered a not inconsiderable force, he boldly attacked the aforesaid fortress from the front. Those within the tower were well provisioned and began to press from there upon those without, hurling down from above spears and crossbow bolts with great forcefulness, of which they had an abundant supply in the tower. The garrison, who were being indefatigably attacked from both within and without, could not continue to resist this divided assault. They were compelled hastily to give to the eldest son of the king this copiously provisioned castle, only just saving their lives and arms.

Thomas Wykes, *Chronicle*

After this fiasco Eleanor went into exile in France, where she took the veil and became abbess of Montargis, Loiret.

It's worth adding that Henry III had recently spent large sums of money repairing Dover in the 1220s. The pride he took in the building is apparent in a very unusual instruction he gave to the constable of the castle when an important visitor, Gautherus de Chastillun, came to see it:

lead him into the castle of Dover and show him the aforesaid castle in such a way that the nobility of the castle is apparent to him and that he can see nothing defective in it.

23 November 1247, *Close Rolls of the Reign of Henry III*

The use of the word 'nobility' in this context is very striking and underlines the interconnected qualities – at least to a medieval eye – of a castle's fortifications and social status.

1277
CASTLE BUILDING
Pressing Labour for the King

The ruins of Flint Castle, begun in 1277 when the site was a camp and staging post for the thousands of workmen involved in constructing Edward I's Welsh castles. As we shall see later, Richard II spent his last hours of liberty in 1399 in the unusual drum-shaped keep to the left.

At Westminster on 17 November 1276, Edward I, together with a large council of peers and prelates, considered the failure of Llywelyn ap Gruffudd, Prince of Wales, to answer three royal summons to perform homage. As the Calendar of Close Rolls notes, the king determined to march against Llywelyn as a 'rebel and disturber of the peace' and declared that those who 'owe him service shall be summoned to be at Worcester at Midsummer next with horses and arms and with all their service, to set out with the king into Wales'. So began the first of three major campaigns fought by Edward I in Wales.

While Edward I's feudal army prepared itself, the king set in train another much less glamorous muster. This was for an army of craftsmen and

*labourers intended to support the army. In mid-June 1277, copied amidst a
mass of other official documentation are two short notes:*

> Master William de Perton, king's clerk, sent to the counties of
> Lincoln and Leicester to provide, with the counsel of the sheriffs,
> masons and carpenters, as many as he can get, and in whose-
> soever works or service they may be, and to conduct them whither
> he has been enjoined.
>
> The like for Master Robert de Belvero, sent to divers parts of
> the realm for the same purpose.
>
> 16 June 1277, *Calendar of Patent Rolls*

THESE two clerks, and possibly others besides, enlisted hundreds of
specialist workmen and compelled them to serve the king in his war.
Their recruits converged on Chester in July, where the royal army had
just advanced from Worcester. Five days later they were moved on to a
camp, now known as Flint. By the end of July about 1,750 men,
including 330 carpenters, two hundred masons and twelve smiths, were
assembled here. This constituted an enormous concentration of expert
labour. And yet more followed. On 9 August, Master William of March
brought three hundred ditchers (*fossatores*) to Flint from Cambridgeshire,
the Fens and even Holland. They were accompanied by three mounted
serjeants to prevent desertion on the road, clear evidence that not
everyone answered the king's summons willingly. By the end of the
month there were nearly 2,300 ditchers in the camp.

With this enormous force of labour, the king supplied a series of
major building projects on his first Welsh campaign, notably at the new
castles of Flint (on the site of the camp) and Rhuddlan. These were
ambitious projects set a day's march apart along the coast. By September,
968 of the ditchers were employed at Rhuddlan alone, canalising a
three-mile stretch of the River Clwyd so as to make it navigable and
connect the castle with the sea.

Edward I's advance forced his opponent to sue for peace and perform
homage in September 1277. Five years later, in 1282, however, Llywelyn
joined a rebellion led by his brother and Edward I's response was
overwhelming: he marched three armies into Wales simultaneously and,
following Llywelyn's death in a skirmish, built three new castles to

command the former heartland of the prince's power in Gwynedd. The most important of these initially was Conwy, built on the site of Llywelyn's razed seat and largely completed between 1283 and 1287 at the vast cost of £15,000. The walled town beside it was populated with an imported English population.

In 1283, however, Edward I's focus of attention shifted in response to the most remarkable circumstances. The ruins of the Roman town of Segontium about 20 miles from Conwy yielded up a body identified as that of Magnus Maximus, 'father of the noble Emperor Constantine'. What the king made of this discovery is not clear but he had the body reburied and, presumably in order to appropriate the legendary associations of the place to himself, immediately began to build a new capital of Wales nearby at Caernarfon. The third royal castle in the group was at Harlech.

Meanwhile, the king also encouraged the construction of castles such as Denbigh, Holt and Chirk in lordships carved out of newly conquered territory. All these projects are interrelated architecturally and probably employed craftsmen brought to the region by royal order. It is hard to find even European parallels for such an intense and coherent episode of castle building. Finally, in 1284 North Wales was divided up into counties after the model of England. The Conquest, however, left deep tensions that would explode into violence a decade later, as we will discover.

1288
MONTGOMERY CASTLE
Trying on a New Cloak

Court cases occasionally shed light on daily life in castles. In this instance one Matilda Vras lent a metal cooking pot termed a kettle to the sub-constable of Montgomery Castle, William of St Albans. When she came early one winter morning – around the fifth hour on 1 January 1288 – to collect it, William was in the chamber above the gatehouse with his tailor choosing a new cloak. Constables or their deputies often lodged over gates, where they could control access to the castle. On the ground beside William was a stone, presumably stored here as a missile to throw down on attackers. As Matilda stood beneath, it somehow fell through the portcullis slot and killed her.

Mabel, Matilda's daughter, accused William of murder and the case came to court nine years later at Montgomery Castle itself, on 27 April 1297. According to the record of the court, William responded by claiming to be a clergyman, effectively removing the case from the arbitration of the royal judges present, named as Justice Mallore and Justice Guildford. A senior cleric, the local dean, confirmed William's status as the most junior rank of clergyman, a clerk, and asked on what charge William should be presented, therefore, to the bishop for judgement. To determine this a jury of twelve men was called and delivered judgement on the charge.

Twelve jurors from the town of Montgomery thereupon said upon oath that, on the date and year aforesaid [1 January 1288], the aforenamed Matilda Vras had gone to Montgomery Castle to fetch her kettle back; that at the time she stood in the great gateway under the portcullis, the aforesaid William was in a room over the gate with his tailor, choosing and trying on a new cloak; and that this cloak chanced to touch a large stone thereby causing it to fall through the middle of the portcullis onto Matilda's head, the blow from the stone causing Matilda to die on the same day.

When asked whether William had feloniously as a felon and by premeditated felony, thrown the stone on to the aforementioned Matilda's head, the jury said no, that the aforesaid stone had been touched by the cloak of the aforesaid William and fallen by misadventure, not by any premeditated felony . . . William was committed to custody in the gaol of the aforesaid castle of the lord king of Montgomery.

Court Roll (trans. A. J. Taylor)

READING the bald statements of this case more than seven centuries after the event it's hard to imagine that a cloak could cause a large stone to fall through a portcullis slot. Nevertheless, the jury thought differently. Perhaps there was some personal vendetta to take account of or simply a desire on the part of locals to forget this long-running dispute. Whatever the case, two months after the trial a pardon was issued to William from Westminster on the grounds that Matilda had been killed 'by misadventure' – a clear acquittal.

As well as recording a human tragedy, this record illuminates the role of castles in the administration of justice. The royal judges were on circuit, travelling from place to place to hear cases. By long convention, castles accommodated both royal and local courts, offering comfortable lodgings for the judges, space for hearings and prisons for the accused. For this reason, there are still courts operating today in some medieval castles, such as Lincoln. The case described here would certainly have been heard in the castle hall. It speaks of the centralisation of the medieval judicial system that William's pardon was issued from Westminster.

In the ruins of Montgomery Castle it's still possible to visit the spot on which Matilda Vras died, see the base of the portcullis slot through which the stone fell and a window of William's chamber.

1290
WINCHESTER CASTLE
The Great Hall and King Arthur's Round Table

Hanging above the dais in the thirteenth-century great hall at Winchester Castle is the top of a large, circular oak table about 18 feet in diameter and weighing just over a ton. Since about 1520 it has been painted with the text and images visible today. These show the figure of a king enthroned above a Tudor Rose. Round this central emblem is an inscription that reads, 'This is the Round Table of King Arthur with 24 of his named knights.' The names – Sir Galahad, Sir Lancelot du Lac etc. – appear on the outer rim of the table with the space for each figure demarcated alternately in white and green, the Tudor livery colours. The scientific dating of timbers from this remarkable object suggest that it was made in the decades around 1300. Possibly it was created, therefore, for a joust at Winchester in 1290.

THE legend of King Arthur, the once and future king, as well as the adventures of his knights, enjoyed European popularity in the Middle Ages. It's no coincidence, therefore, that this table is hung in this architecturally splendid great hall, built between 1222 and 1236. Such rooms were universally familiar in great residences across England for more than a thousand years. They were public interiors used for formal gatherings and the exercise of justice. The internal arcades dividing the interior into three unequal aisles – here of polished Purbeck marble – are a throwback to the design of Anglo-Saxon halls. They support a high, open, timber roof, rebuilt in its present form in the fifteenth century. Originally this space was heated by an open fire on a central hearth, another conscious archaism (even by the twelfth century fireplaces were a widespread feature of domestic interiors). Henry III decorated many of his halls with didactic images (see 1204 above). Here the interior was painted at his instruction with a map of the world and a Wheel of Fortune, but no trace of this decoration now survives.

The table has probably hung in the hall since 1344, when preparations were made to carry it to Windsor as the centrepiece of a new building called the Round Table (see 1344 below). In the event, it never made the journey but its legs were possibly cut off at this time to facilitate movement. The table is described by the historian John Rous around 1480 as a copy of King Arthur's original, which he states was made out of silver.

As well as illustrating the extraordinary power and popularity of the legend of King Arthur, the Winchester table is an early surviving example of the use of great halls as places for the display of castle heirlooms. Most commonly these were the swords of legendary chivalric heroes, as can still be seen at Warwick (Guy of Warwick; see 1697 below) and Arundel Castle (the giant Bevis). Such relics illustrate the way in which castles, within two hundred years of their first foundation, came to be viewed as buildings with a history that stretched back time out of mind to the foundations of history. Close inspection of the table has revealed about fifty bullet holes concentrated on the Tudor Rose and the figure of King Arthur. These date from the seventeenth century and were probably fired by Parliamentarian soldiers to disfigure this royal image.

1296
BEAUMARIS CASTLE
A Progress Report

Beaumaris Castle, Anglesey, begun in 1295 to create a secure landing-point on the island. It was built at great speed starting with the outer, apron wall but left unfinished because money ran out. The inner circuit of walls and towers was intended to stand a full storey higher.

English rule in North Wales following Edward I's overthrow of Llywelyn ap Gruffudd proved harsh and in 1294 the whole region rose in revolt. All the new royal and baronial castles were overwhelmed but over the ensuing winter Edward I crushed the rebellion. His campaign culminated in an attack on Anglesey, made possible by the construction of a bridge of boats across the treacherous waters dividing it from the mainland. To secure the island a new castle was laid out at Beaumaris, a low-level site on the seashore that could be supplied by ship. Work to it was driven forward with astonishing speed under the direction of a master mason from Savoy, James of St George. He was a leading figure in Edward I's castle-building projects in Wales, some technical details of which reflect his foreign training. Within six months alone an incredible £6,000 was spent on the project. On 27 February 1296, James wrote to explain what had been achieved and his needs. He offers an exceptionally vivid impression of the site, the ambition of the enterprise and the pressures under which he worked:

As our lord King has commanded us, by letters of the exchequer, to let you have a clear picture of all aspects of the state of the works at Beaumaris . . . we write to inform you that the work we are doing is very costly and we need a great deal of money.

You should know:

1) That we have kept on masons, stonecutters, quarrymen and minor workmen all through the winter, and are still employing them for making mortar and breaking up stone from lime; we have carts bringing this stone to the site and timber for erecting the buildings in which we are all now living inside the castle; we also have 1,000 carpenters, smiths, plasterers and navvies, quite apart from a mounted garrison: 10 men accounting for 70 shillings a week, 20 crossbowmen who add another 47 shillings 10 pence and 100 infantry who take a further £6 2 shillings and sixpence.

2) That when this letter was written we were short of £500, for both workmen and garrison. The men's pay has been and still is very much in arrears, we are having the greatest difficulty in keeping them because they simply have nothing to live on.

3) That if our lord the King wants the work to be finished as quickly as it should be and on the scale on which it has been commenced, we could not make do with less than £250 a week throughout the season; with it, this season could see the work well advanced . . .

As for the progress of the works . . . We can tell you that some of it already stands about 28 feet high and even where it is lowest it is 20 feet. We have begun ten of the outer and four of the inner towers, i.e. the two for each of the two gatehouse passages. Four gates have been hung and are shut and locked every night, and each gateway is to have three portcullises. You should also know that at high tide a 40 ton vessel will be able to come fully laden right up to the castle gateway; so much we have been able to do in spite of all the Welshmen. In case you should wonder where so much money could go in a week, we would have you know that we have needed – and shall continue to need – 400 Masons, both cutters and layers, together with 2,000 minor workmen, 100 carts, 60 wagons and 30 boats bringing stone and sea coal, 200 quarrymen; 30 smiths; and carpenters for putting in the joists and floorboards and other necessary jobs. All this takes no account of the garrison mentioned above, nor of purchases of materials, of which there will have to be a great quantity.

As to how things stand in the land of Wales, we still cannot be too sure. But, as you well know, Welshmen are Welshmen, and you need to understand them properly; if, which God forbid, there is war with France and Scotland, we shall need to watch them all the more closely . . .

P. S. And, sirs, for God's sake be quick with the money for the works, as much as ever our lord King wills; otherwise everything done up to now will have been of no avail.

James of St George, letter (trans. A. J. Taylor)

UNFORTUNATELY for James, the royal exchequer could not satisfy his wants and over the next two years expenditure on Beaumaris declined. The castle remains incomplete but is imposing testimony, nevertheless, to what about £11,500 spent over roughly three years and a small army of labourers could achieve in the 1290s.

c. 1300
SEAL OF ROCHESTER
The Image of the Castle

'Seal of the city of Rochester', as the self-explanatory inscription reads. The seal matrix, from which this modern impression is taken, probably dates to about 1300 and remained in use until the 1880s. It shows a recognisable, if stylised, view of the castle on a disc three inches (7.5 cm) across.

THE great tower of the castle shown to the left was begun in 1127 by William of Corbeil, Archbishop of Canterbury. Kent was unique in England for possessing two cathedrals – Canterbury and Rochester – and the tower was a predatory assertion of authority by the former over the latter. To the tops of its corner turrets it is the tallest surviving Romanesque great tower in Europe. By the time it was depicted on the seal the tower had been damaged by King John (see 1215 above) and then repaired by Henry III. In 1240, when this work was complete, the king also ordered that it be whitewashed. Henry III clearly liked this finish and a similar order at London gave the White Tower its familiar name. A royal standard flutters above the entrance to the tower and the heads of the walls are shown with sockets and projecting timbers, supports for temporary fighting galleries termed *hourdes*. Such galleries might be assembled and dismantled at need, transforming the outward appearance of the castle in war. From the twelfth century there is physical evidence at castles such as Framlingham, Suffolk, for wooden shutters being hung between battlements as an additional protection.

The east side of the castle with its gateway, wall and towers is depicted across the bottom of the seal. There are likewise hourde sockets in the upper stage of the gatehouse. This building is approached across a bridge and entered through an arch with a portcullis. On the upper battlements a trumpeter plays an imaginary welcome. The wall towers have flanking arches that span the angle with the adjacent wall. This might either be a defensive arrangement – allowing the garrison to overlook the base of the wall – or a means of incorporating latrines with a drop into the castle ditch. All the castle buildings are shown as being constructed of cut blocks of stone. In reality, they are of rubble. The artist's depiction of the masonry – with double vertical joints and single horizontal ones – is precisely paralleled in decorative wall-painting schemes of the period.

Water is shown washing the base of the castle wall on the seal. Rochester commands the Medway crossing of Watling Street, a Roman road that connected London with Dover and the Continent. The Medway is actually on the opposite side of the castle but this clearly didn't trouble the artist. Nor did the fact that the keep windows are in fact round-headed rather than pointed in the more up-to-date Gothic manner. On the reverse of the seal is an image of St Andrew, the patron of Rochester Cathedral.

1300
CAERLAVEROCK CASTLE
Edward I's Subjection of Scotland

A view of Caerlaverock Castle, Dumfries. The castle has been rebuilt since the siege of 1300 but preserves its original triangular plan with the gatehouse at one corner. The trees conceal a view of the Solway Firth.

In March 1286 Alexander III of Scotland was accidentally killed falling from his horse. His death was the opening incident in a dispute over the succession to the Scottish throne that drew England and Scotland into three centuries of conflict. Edward I of England arbitrated over the succession, asserting thereby his feudal overlordship of Scotland. The resulting friction culminated in his launching an overwhelming invasion of Scotland and deposing the Scottish king. The trouble continued, however, and further English invasions followed. One of these, in the summer of 1300, began with Edward I marching up the western seaboard to Caerlaverock Castle. The events of the ensuing siege are recorded in a French poem thought to have been written by a friar, Walter of Exeter (also the author of a life of Guy of Warwick, a hero of medieval chivalric romance). The poem begins with the royal summons to Carlisle and describes the army's march northwards in four squadrons (eschieles) during glorious July weather. There follows a long list of the knights present and the heraldry of their banners. When they arrive at Caerlaverock, Dumfriesshire, the poet describes the setting and form of this triangular or 'shield-shaped' castle:

Caerlaverock was so strong a castle, that it did not fear a siege, therefore the king [Edward I] came himself, because it would not consent to surrender. But it was furnished for its defence, whenever it was required with men, engines and provisions. Its shape was like that of a shield, for it had only three sides all round, with a tower on each angle; but one of them [the towers] was a double one, so high, so long, and so large, that under it was the gate with a drawbridge, well made and strong, and a sufficiency of other defences. It had good walls, and good ditches filled to the edge with water; and I believe there never was seen a castle more beautifully situated, for at once could be seen the Irish sea towards the West, and the north a fine country, surrounded by an arm of the sea . . . And in that place by the king's commands his battalions were formed into three, as they were to be quartered . . . and then might be seen houses built without carpenters or masons, of many different fashions, and many a cord stretched, with white and coloured cloth, with many pins driven into the ground, many a large tree cut down to make huts; and leaves, herbs and flowers gathered in the woods, which were strewn within; and then our people took up their quarters.

Soon afterwards it fortunately happened that the navy arrived with the engines and provisions, and then the foot-men began to march against the castle; then might be seen stones, arrows, and quarrels to fly among them.

Walter of Exeter, *The Siege of Carlaverock*
(trans. N. H. Nicolas)

THE accuracy of this description suggests that the author had seen Caerlaverock. It's interesting to have the form of the tented royal encampment described, as well as its implied splendour and comfort. There follows a long and slightly formulaic description of the siege itself in which heraldry figures very largely. It concludes with the surrender of the garrison, apparently in the face of 'engines, very large, of great power and very destructive' being erected by the besieging force. The poem concludes with the king sparing the lives of the garrison and giving each 'a new garment' (presumably their arms and armour were spoils of war). Another account, *The Chronicle of Lanercost*, however, grimly notes that 'many of those within the castle were hung'.

Time and again the resources of the English Crown, and in particular its ability to field huge siege machines, determined that it could capture any Scottish castle held against it. Documentation relating to the siege of Stirling in 1304 offers an insight into the associated logistics of such sieges. Securing the lead necessary for the counterweights of the catapults in this case proved a particular problem, and on 12 April Edward I instructed the Prince of Wales:

> to take as much lead as you can about the town of St John of Perth and Dunblane, and elsewhere, as from the churches and from other places where you can find it, provided always that the churches be not uncovered over the altars.
>
> 12 April 1304, Letter from Edward I to the Prince of Wales

Meanwhile, Robert Bruce, Earl of Carrick (who later fought against the English and became Robert I of Scotland), was on the coast at Inverkip supplying Edward I with catapults for the siege. He wrote to say, however, that he could not find a cart big enough to move the throwing arm or beam of a 'great engine' or catapult, which had presumably arrived by ship. The king wrote back to urge its immediate delivery:

> We charge you especially that on no account that you desist from using all the pains and deliberation possible to cause the said beam to be carried to us with stones and all other things pertaining to this engine, and to the other engines, as far as you can procure them; and for want of lead do not on any account desist from expediting the dispatch.
>
> 16 April 1304, Letter from Edward I to the Earl of Carrick

Stirling duly capitulated but Edward I refused to accept the proffered surrender of the garrison before he had tried out his pride and joy, an engine of prodigious size called the 'The War Wolf'.

Increasingly conscious that they were locked in an unequal war, Edward I's Scottish opponents began razing castles to the ground, rather than occupying them. That approach, the impoverished state of the English royal exchequer and the nature of the contest for Scottish territory, determined that no chain of castles to match those in Wales came into being in Scotland. Caerlaverock today, indeed, is almost entirely a creation of the fourteenth century onwards, though it preserves the plan and form of its thirteenth-century predecessor.

1303
CONWY CASTLE
A Miracle in a Moat

The site of Roger's accident at the gate of Conwy Castle. He fell from the medieval carriageway at the level of the modern, timber balcony between the turrets into the rock-cut ditch, where a railed path now runs. The stump of masonry to the right is what remains of the approach ramp from the town that he must have scrambled up.

At sunrise on 6 September 1303, John of Gyffin, the gatekeeper of Conwy Castle in North Wales, discovered the body of a two-year-old boy in the moat beneath the main gate. He found the child 'completely stiff and cold, for there had been a frost, and he was completely undressed . . . His mouth was closed, his spittle was frozen all around his mouth, and his eyes had rolled up so that nothing could be seen of his pupils.' The toddler, called Roger, the son of the castle cook, appeared to have fallen accidentally into the ditch, the drawbridge to the castle having been raised during the night. It was a lethal drop of 28 feet onto rock and everyone judged the boy to be dead. A bystander, however, offered a prayer to Thomas Cantilupe, a former Bishop of Hereford, and soon afterwards, to universal astonishment, the boy recovered in his mother's arms. The episode was minutely investigated four years later when Thomas was proposed for canonisation as a saint. The depositions of witnesses preserve names, details and circumstances that would otherwise long ago have been lost and offer an impression of the interrelationship of a castle with its local community. Here is that offered by Roger's mother, Dionisia, a free woman aged thirty. On the night of the accident she left her children for a vigil in the parish church. Notice that she measures time in terms of distance walked. The clerk narrates her deposition in the third person:

she had left the said Roger her son, then aged two years and three months, bound in his cot as children are, and sleeping in a single bed nearby her daughters Isolda, six years old, and Agnes, five, in the house where she lived in the town of Conwy a stone's throw from the castle. At twilight she went out of the house together with Wenthliana, a serving woman of the said castle, and pulled the door closed behind her but did not shut it from the outside because there was no closer on the outside of the door, nor was the said door shut from the inside because her aforesaid son and daughters were asleep. After leaving, she went straight to the parish church of the said town with the said Wenthliana, to keep vigil for the funeral of Cecilia, lady in waiting to the wife of Sir William de Cycouns, constable of the said castle, since Dionisia had nursed Cecilia in the illness from which she died, and also to keep vigil for the funeral of Gerard, servant of the said castle.

Item, she said that when she and the said serving woman, together with others, had been in the said church for as long as she would have taken to walk two English miles, as she judged, her said husband left the church holding a lighted candle, looking to go back to the house. When he had been outside for as long as it would take her to walk a mile, as she judged, he came back into the church and told the said Dionisia that he had been unable to find the said Roger in the house, nor in the neighbourhood, where he had looked for him, and that he thought that one of the neighbours must have taken him in. The said Dionisia believed him, and did not think to go looking for him.

Item . . . she finally left the church to go home before matins were said, and before dawn, together with her said husband and the serving woman and did not find the said Roger at home, but her daughters asleep, and the cot, bound up with the sheets in which the said Roger had been wrapped. She was so upset by this and so weighed down with tiredness from the previous vigils that she fell asleep until full day, as she judged, for the time it would take to go a mile, until it was dawn. At that time, John of Gyffin [the castle gatekeeper] came to the house to ask where the said Roger was. When the said Dionisia answered that she did not know, the same John told her that he was lying dead in the ditch of the said castle. She fell to the ground in grief, almost out of her mind, at which her neighbours took her and restrained her to stop her leaving her said house. She stayed there until the time when, as she thought, the said Roger was brought to her in the house, when he seemed to her to be dead. She could feel no breath, and when she placed her tongue inside the said Roger's mouth, his mouth was so cold that she could not hold her tongue there without injury. And so tearing her upper clothes down to her girdle, the said Dionisia placed the said Roger in her lap for warmth, and after holding him in this way for a long time, she carried him to the parish church of the said town, and sat with him before the cross: she judged that there were more than 200 in the congregation. And when the said Anian, former bishop of Bangor, had finished saying Mass in the said church, he came to the said Roger and with his thumb, made the sign of the cross on his brow, at which the said Roger looked at him in terror. Dionisia felt the said Roger move a little in her lap for the first time, and his heart was beating so fast that she shouted out in fear that he would die a second time. But seeing that he was alive, she gave praise to God and the sweet Saint Thomas of Hereford, giving thanks, at which all the other onlookers did the same. On the same day he could stand up, and around vespers time, he could suckle and on the third day could walk, though it was three weeks before he was completely recovered as before.

Dionisia, court deposition (trans. Jeremy Ashbee)

IN conclusion, the clerk notes that Dionisia 'gave her evidence in English because she could not speak French nor, as she said, in letters [Latin]'. Depositions were given in all these languages (but not Welsh) and her husband gave his in French. The differences imply an association of language and social status.

Apparent in Dionisia's narrative is the close interrelationship between the life of the castle and the town. Not only is she the wife of the castle cook but she has nursed the constable's wife and is a friend of Wenthliana, a castle servant. In effect, the community of one is an extension of the other. Quite possibly the accident itself merely resulted from the child taking a familiar walk – from his house to his father's place of work, the castle kitchen – at an unfamiliar time.

This is one of several miracles performed by Thomas Cantilupe investigated in such detail and which won him canonisation as a saint. His cult enjoyed brief but intense popularity in Wales and the Marches. Roger himself later travelled to the bishop's tomb in thanksgiving for his revival.

c. 1320
THE CASTLE OF LOVE
Court Entertainment

An illustration of the Castle of Love from the Luttrell Psalter of about 1320–40, one of the most sumptuously decorated English manuscripts of the period. Illuminations depicting devotional, profane or absurd imagery were a popular (and expensive) way of enlivening books, adding to their interest, beauty and curiosity. Here women defend the battlements of a castle using flowers to drive away a host of attacking knights.

THERE are descriptions of court pageants and entertainments in which scenes of exactly this kind were enacted from at least the early thirteenth century. On such occasions it seems that the entire protocol of a siege might be enacted with an assault, a parley and the final triumphant entry of the knights into the stage-fortification to claim their partners. The depiction of the scene here is almost certainly informed by the imagery of such sieges on valuable ivory caskets made in Paris. It can be read in playful relationship to the text on the page. This comes from two consecutive Psalms. Shown here is the opening of Psalm 38, in which there is a plea that 'I will take heed [*custodiam*] to my ways: that I sin not with my tongue'. The figure of King David, believed to be the author of the Psalms, appears in the initial and points to his tongue, while the castle illustrates a pun on the word *custodiam*, which also means to guard or watch. Further up the page is the end of Psalm 37 which includes a plea for help from God: 'But my enemies live, and are stronger than I'. That also clearly relates to this scene, in which the fully armed knights have such an obvious advantage. To those familiar with images of this subject there is one striking omission: the figure of Love, who is usually shown as presiding over the scene. Added to which, the image incorporates the oddity of one knight with his visor raised, who has run from his fellows and is knocking on the gate. This perhaps relates to devotional texts of the period which speak of the Castle of Love as a place that holds out against the evils of the world. It's at the gate of this fortress that the devout Christian must knock for admission. Images of this kind illustrate the way in which the Middle Ages delighted in the imagery of the castle and deployed it for the purposes of devotion and entertainment.

1 3 2 3
TOWER OF LONDON
St Peter in Chains

On 1 August 1323 Roger de Mortimer, a baron in the Welsh Marches and Ireland, escaped from imprisonment in the Tower of London. The escape took place on the feast of St Peter ad Vincula, the celebration of that apostle's divine release from King Herod's imprisonment on the eve of his trial. Since Roger had been condemned for treason on 2 August 1322, the feast was also the eve of the calendar year since his own trial. Such symmetry is too perfect to be coincidental.

Far away and five days later at Kirkham Priory, Yorkshire, Edward II – by the timing of Roger's escape implicitly characterised as a second Herod – heard the news. His response, recorded in a flurry of orders all dated 6 August from the priory, speaks of his fear. Here is a selection of these orders. The first incidentally reveals that Roger escaped by poisoning his captors and instructs the trusted Walter, Bishop of Exeter, urgently to secure the Tower of London, entering by deception. The king goes on in multiple letters to every sheriff (the royal officer in each county) to forbid all tournaments, which might serve as a cover for massing a rebellious army, and issues a general order to capture the malefactor. There follows an instruction seeking for news in every harbour of Roger's whereabouts and a warning to constables across the kingdom to guard their prisoners and their castles.

To Walter, Bishop of Exeter, the Treasurer. As the king understands for certain that Roger de Mortimer of Wigmore, the king's enemy and rebel, who was imprisoned in the Tower of London, has broken the prison and escaped from the Tower by night, and that during the perpetration of this sedition Stephen de Segrave, late constable of the Tower, and many others in the Tower were poisoned by artifice, and that Stephen in consequence is so seriously ill that he is now insufficient for the safe custody of the Tower, and as the king fully confides in the fidelity and circumspection of the Treasurer, he has caused a commission to him of the custody of the Tower and its appurtenances to be sent to him, and enjoins and requests him to go to the Tower with his household and others whom he wishes to take with him under the pretext of visiting the treasure or other pretext, and when he has entered the Tower, to shew his commission and to receive the custody of the Tower according to the commission, and to cause it to be kept safely by himself or another in whom he can confide fully.

To the sheriff of York. Order to cause proclamation to be made prohibiting the holding of tournaments without the king's special licence, and to certify the king of the names of any presuming to exercise feats of arms after this prohibition. The like to all the sheriffs of England.

To the sheriff of Kent. Order to cause proclamation to be made that all and singular who are in the king's peace shall pursue with hue and cry Roger de Mortimer of Wigmore, the king's rebel, who has escaped from prison in the Tower of London by night . . . that they shall arrest him alive or dead. The like to all the sheriffs of England.

To Edmund, Earl of Kent, constable of Dover Castle and Warden of the Cinque Ports . . . to appoint spies in all the said ports and to cause diligent search to be made for the aforesaid Roger, and to take him alive or dead if he come thither, and to enquire, in case Roger have crossed the sea from those ports, who have taken him out of the realm, in what ship they have taken him . . . The like to the bailiffs and mayors [of ports across the kingdom].

To the constable of Pontefract castle. Order to cause all the prisoners in his custody in that castle to be kept safely and securely at his peril, so that he can answer for the bodies of all of them at the king's order, and to cause the castle to be kept and guarded so that damage or peril may not arise to it. The like to the constables of eighty castles.

To the justice of Wales, or to him who supplies his place. Like order concerning the castles in that land.

6 August 1323, *Calendar of Close Rolls*

THESE orders show how royal authority at a moment of crisis depended on castles and the officers who controlled them. They were gaolers and police and guardians of treasure.

Despite all these efforts – and more besides – Roger did escape to France. There he was welcomed in Paris by the King of France, Charles IV, who was then at war with Edward II and delighted to succour his enemies. Two years later, Isabella of France, the wife of Edward II and sister of Charles IV, also arrived in Paris. Her relations with Edward II were extremely strained and, having been joined in Paris by her son, the future Edward III, she increasingly consorted with English exiles. By the following March Isabella and Roger were rumoured to be lovers and they began to plan an invasion of England. They landed on 24 September 1326 at Orwell, Suffolk, and Edward II's unpopular regime collapsed almost without resistance. His circle of favourites, meanwhile, including the elder and younger Hugh Despenser, were executed, the latter with gruesome theatre: he was clothed with his reversed coat of arms, crowned with stinging nettles and hung from a 50-foot scaffold before being eviscerated alive and then decapitated. Edward II was informed at Kenilworth Castle of a decision by Parliament that he should no longer reign and less than a year later, on 21 September 1327, he was murdered in Berkeley Castle, the possession of Roger Mortimer's son-in-law (see 1618 below).

Roger and Isabella now began a three-year rule in the name of the latter's son, Edward III. With unfettered power Roger behaved with much the same arrogance as the favourites of Edward II, whom he had deposed. In 1328 he elevated himself to the dignity of Earl of March and, probably at this time, began a new chapel in his castle at Ludlow. It was dedicated to St Peter, the saint who had presided over his momentous escape from the Tower of London.

1330
NOTTINGHAM CASTLE
A Palace Coup

The brief rule of Queen Isabella and her lover Roger Mortimer came to a dramatic close at Nottingham Castle in October 1330. Having called a parliament in the city, rumours began to circulate that the seventeen-year-old Edward III, in whose name the couple administered the realm, as well as his circle of friends, were at risk of falling victim to Roger's ambitions. To add to the tension, Roger was fearful of his life. He took control of the castle with Isabella and refused Edward III entry with his entourage.

The king and his followers therefore decided to seize Mortimer; as one of them is reported to have commented, 'It is better to eat the dog than have the dog eat you.' On 19 October Edward III and his companions left the city, only to return secretly after dark. With inside help they entered the castle covertly at night. The dramatic ensuing encounter was widely recorded and grew in the telling. This version by Geoffrey le Baker of Swinbrook, a clerk connected to Osney, Oxford, is probably not independently authoritative but it is immediate.

In AD 1330, the fourth year of King Edward III, on the first Friday after the feast of Saint Luke [19 October], a parliament was held in Nottingham, at which Roger Mortimer, Earl of March, glittered in all his transient glory as the principal advisor of Queen Isabella, at whose nod everything is arranged [attended] . . . Murmurs of criticism, which flew to the ears of the people, now arose among the nobles from those who said in secret that Mortimer, the lover of the Queen and the King's master, was panting to overthrow the royal blood and usurp his royal majesty. Such murmurings brought terror to the King's ears and to such friends of the King as William Montague, Edward de Bohun and others. These now formed a conspiracy to save the King. They considered, and justly, that they would be saving their

97

country and doing it a service, if they put that Mortimer to death. The conspirators were joined by . . . [William Eland], who had been keeper of the castle for many years and knew well all its most secret winding ways. They discussed with him how the King and his friends, without the knowledge of the doorkeepers, might get access from outside the castle to the Queen's bedroom.

With lighted torches the keeper led his master the King into the castle by a secret underground passage, which began from far outside the castle and ended in the middle of the kitchen or of the hall of the main tower, where the Queen was lodged. Springing from the depths of the underground pathway, the friends of the King armed with drawn swords made for the Queen's bedroom, which by the grace of God they found open. They left the King outside the door so that his mother should not see him and entered the room. They killed the knight Hugh Turpington who tried to stop them, the blow being dealt by Lord John de Neville of Hornby. Then they found the Queen Mother apparently prepared for bed and sleep and the Earl of March, the man they wanted. They seized him and took him away into the hall, with the Queen crying aloud, 'Dear boy! dear boy! Have pity on gentle Mortimer'. For she suspected that her son was there, even if she could not see him. The conspirators speedily sent for the keys of the castle so that the complete control of the castle had now passed into the King's hands. But they did this so secretly that no one outside the castle knew of it . . .

At dawn the next day, amid a terrifying hue and cry, with the Earl of Lancaster who was now blind himself joining in the shouting, they took Roger Mortimer and some other friends of his, who had been seized with him, through Loughborough and Leicester to London. He was committed to prison in the Tower, as had happened to him once before, and, by the verdict of the parliament of the realm sitting at Westminster, on the following eve of the feast of St Andrew [29 November] he was drawn and hung on the common gallows of thieves at the Elms, and thus by his death brought to an end the civil wars.

Geoffrey le Baker of Swinbrook, *Chronicle* (trans. E. Preest)

THE seizure of Roger Mortimer launched Edward III's majority rule. As described here, the return to London made possible the parliamentary trial of Mortimer. His execution at 'the Elms' or Tyburn, as Geoffrey le Baker notes, turned him into a common criminal. He was not permitted to appear at his own trial, his crimes being described as notorious.

After this episode, Queen Isabella was soon comfortably retired to Castle Rising in Norfolk. She later travelled freely as a dowager queen consort and died at Hertford Castle in 1358. Considering how unhappy the consequences of her marriage to Edward II were, it's curious that she chose to be buried in her wedding mantle.

It's worth adding that Nottingham is one of a small group of major medieval castles – along with Windsor, Knaresborough, Winchester and Dover – that possessed a substantial network of subterranean passages. These could only be created where a castle sat on living rock that could be easily worked. Such passages usually opened into the moat and were constructed to allow the garrison to mount surprise attacks in the event of a hard-pressed siege. Longer passages connecting distant buildings, such as that described at Nottingham, are very rare but have become a defining feature of castles in the popular imagination (see 1764 below).

1342
BERKELEY CASTLE
The Noble Life

In 1618 the long-standing steward of the Berkeley family, John Smyth, completed A Relation of the Lives of the Lord Berkeleys of Berkeley Castle in the County of Gloucester. *He aimed to create a celebratory history that would instruct and inform the behaviour of future generations of the family. The account of the life of Thomas, third Lord Berkeley (d. 1361) – who inherited Berkeley Castle in 1327 during the upheavals of Edward II's deposition and had custody of the king there when he was murdered – is illuminated using medieval household accounts. From these Smyth not only constructs an account of Lord Berkeley's campaigning as a soldier, a reminder that medieval nobles lived for war, but of his continuous travels between many residences as well as to tournaments and to Parliament.*

In the course of his whole life I seldom observe him to continue one whole year together at any one of his houses, but ... [he travelled to many] as Berkeley and Beverston castles, Awre, Wotton, Portbury, Bedminster, Bradley Wendon and others; and I generally observe that at such times as he was in wars abroad, as often and long he was, or did with reason to wander continue at tilts, tournaments or other hastiludes, as often whole months together at Worcester, Coventry, Dunstable, Stamford, London, Winchester, Exeter and other places he did: Or was at the parliament at London, York, Lincoln, or the like places, his good and frugal lady withdrew herself for the most part to her houses of least resort and receipt; whether for her retirement or frugality, or both, I determine not.

TO illustrate Lord Berkeley's agricultural wealth, Smyth cites accounts to show that he had flocks of sheep numbering hundreds or thousands on scores of manors (the largest was at Beverston, where 5,575 sheep were sheared in 1333), besides dovecotes (that at Hame supplied 2,151 young pigeons in one year) and huge numbers of geese, ducks, peacocks, hens, capons and chickens. For his agricultural work and pastimes, the accounts record his ownership in 1346–7 of 15,381 horses.

On a daily basis, his kitchens provided food – by Smyth's estimate – for a household of more than three hundred people. These included twelve knights and twenty-four esquires, each one accompanied by a page. All these men were liveried in a garment of ray and crimson (a type of woollen cloth with stripes), lined with different kinds of fur depending upon their degree: miniver, coarser miniver, coney and lambskin termed *budge*. His household bills in 1346–7 totalled a staggering £1,309 14s 6d ha'penny.

Lord Berkeley also built across his estate, including improvements to several residences and additions both to Berkeley Castle in 1342–6 and Beverston Castle in 1348–50 (counterintuitively, while his estates were being devastated by the Black Death). The former included:

In the 16th of King Edward III [1342–3] this lord new built, (then ruinated,) the great high Tower of the north part of the keep in Berkeley Castle, called at this day Thorps Tower . . . which cost him £108 3s 1d, fetching most of the stones by boat from [the River] Severn. And the Tuft stone from Dursley by land

Perhaps most illuminating of all, however, are Smyth's listings of Lord Berkeley's 'recreations and delights', which essentially concern the two long-standing obsessions of the medieval (and later) nobility: hunting and martial exercise:

Touching the delights of this lord Thomas; he much enlarged Whitcliffe Park. And instead of the hedge which each three years was with excrescence of thorns there growing, new made, and the old fold, he first paled it. And therein put certain white deer, which he had of William de Montecute, Earl of Salisbury.

For the hounds which this lord kept for several chaces, let their number be estimated by one kind of meal they eat, being forty four quarters and one bushel of oats [about 7 tonnes] from the manor of Hame in the 23rd of King Edward III [1349–50]; And as many from Alkington and four other several manors . . .

And as it seemeth this lord was so much delighted with this sort of recreation, that he and his brothers have kept out 4 nights and days together, with their nets and dogs, in hunting of the fox.

As for this lord's falcons and other hawks, his reeve's accounts of Hame, Portbury and Wotton do tell us, that they have eaten five and six of their hens in a night and day, while this lord and his falconers stayed with them in those manors.

For this lord's other delights in martial jousts and tournaments, let it suffice, that in the first year of Edward III [1327–8] he went to Blyth, York, and Northampton. And there at jousts and tournaments spent at those places £53 7s

And in the second year [1328–9] to Hereford. And there at jousts and tournaments spent – £29 6s 4d

And the same year at Coventry spent – £5 14s 3d

And the same year at Exeter £50 4d ha'penny. And that his armour for his body that year cost him £11 8s 11d

And therin exercised his menial esquires also; given to his esquires to play at spearplay at Bristol 26s 8d

And so in diverse other years till age grew on

John Smyth, *The Lives of the Berkeleys*

Such accounts underline the scale, efficiency and organisation of great medieval estates and the peripatetic households they supported. They also illustrate the character of the medieval nobility as pleasure-loving, which is something that can be hard to rescue at this distance of time. Castles were an essential adjunct to their lifestyle, celebrating in architecture the martial responsibilities that were so crucial to noble identity.

WINDSOR CASTLE
Arthur's Round Table and the Order of the Garter

The heads of lions or leopards – royal beasts and also heraldic emblems of England – set in one of the gatehouse vaults built by Edward III in the Tower of London. These sculptures could be removed and the openings used to drop missiles on the passage beneath. There are traces of gilding on the ribs, possibly a medieval survival.

During the early part of his reign, Edward III showed little interest in his birthplace, Windsor Castle. That changed suddenly in January 1344, when he announced his intention of establishing a Round Table in the castle after the famous example of King Arthur. King Arthur reputedly adopted a circular table in order to avoid quarrels over precedence between his honour-hungry followers; each knight held an equal place at it. Edward III's intention seems to have been that his new order of chivalry would comprise three hundred knights and that its round table would be physically represented by a great circular building in the castle, where it could meet annually. He launched his project on a suitably regal scale.

Edward III ordered a great tournament to be held on the nineteenth day of January in the place of his birth, that is, in the castle of Windsor . . . He invited to this by his own letters all the ladies of the south of England and the wives of the citizens of London. There assembled in the said castle on Sunday, January 20, earls, barons, knights, and very many ladies. There the king provided the customary banquet so that the great hall was filled with the ladies, not a single man being present excepting only two knights who had come from France for this occasion. At this banquet there were present two queens, nine countesses, wives of the barons, knights, and citizens, who could not easily be counted, and who had been placed by the king himself in their seats according to rank.

The Prince of Wales, the Duke of Cornwall, the earls, barons, and knights ate together with the people in a tent and other places where food supplies and all other necessaries had been prepared freely for all without murmur; and in the evening there was dancing. For the three following days the king with nineteen other knights kept a joust against all who came from without; and the king, not on account of royal favour but because of great skill which he showed and because of the good fortune which he had, for three days gained the palm among those at home . . .

On the following Thursday, after the esquires had jousted, the king gave a banquet at which he founded the Round Table, and under a certain form belonging to the said Round Table he received the oaths of certain earls, barons, and knights whom he wished to belong to this said Round Table; and he fixed the day for holding the Round Table for the next day of Pentecost following, giving to all present the right of returning home with their badges of honour. Afterwards he ordered a very fine building to be erected there, in which the said Round Table could meet at the designated time. For the erection of this building he brought in stonecutters, carpenters, and other workmen, ordering wood as well as stone to be procured, sparing neither labour nor expense.

Adam of Murimuth, *The Continuation of the Chronicle*

EDWARD III was fascinated by King Arthur, whose spirit hovers behind this whole project at Windsor. He inspected the reputed remains of the Once and Future King at Glastonbury Abbey in 1331 and three years later he appeared at a tournament in Dunstable bearing the arms of King Arthur's companion, Sir Gawain, under the assumed name of 'Sir Lionel'. The latter made a punning reference both to his martial prowess and the arms of England, with its three lions (termed leopards). For the same reason, Edward III kept a number of these royal beasts in the entrance to the Tower of London and also ornamented several of his castle buildings with images of lions' heads.

The Round Table at Windsor made him, by implication, a second Arthur and promised to constitute a highly motivated force of noblemen and knights who could help him realise the hugely ambitious claim he made to the throne of France. For this reason the creation of the order needed to be well witnessed and dignified by oaths of loyalty, the distribution of marks of membership – or 'badges of honour' – and also a permanent home in Windsor Castle.

The Round Table was laid out on a circular plan with an outer wall of stone and probably possessed internal galleries of timber, like a Shakespearian theatre. The encircling range was covered in tiles. In 2006 part of the building was revealed during an archaeological dig in the upper ward of Windsor Castle. It had a diameter of 200 feet and was doubtless intended to serve as an enclosed ground for tournaments and martial games, termed *hastiludes*, in which competing teams might appear in glorious costume. It was to this building that Edward III presumably intended to remove the round table at Winchester Castle (see 1290 above). By the end of November 1344 a large sum of £507 had been expended on the work. Then, rather mysteriously, the project was abandoned. Nevertheless, it undoubtedly formed the inspiration for another initiative at Windsor Castle a few years later.

Following his military triumph at Crecy in August 1346, Edward III established the Order of the Garter. This chivalric order was much smaller than the Round Table and comprised two connected elements. The first was a group of twenty-four knight companions along with the king and his son; a total of twenty-six. This was twice thirteen, the number of Christ and the apostles; it also neatly furnished two teams for a hastilude. In counterpart to this martial body was a college dedicated to the soldier St George, who henceforward became the patron saint of England. It was founded in 1348 with a corresponding community of twenty-four clergy (augmented four years later to comprise twelve priests or canons and thirteen deputies or vicars under the authority of a Warden; also a total of twenty-six) and an attached community of twenty-four 'poor knights', effectively almsmen.

The enigmatic motto of the new order, 'Honi soit qui mal y pense' – shame on him who thinks evil of it – almost certainly refers to Edward III's claim to the French throne and the companions assumed a livery of blue, the French royal colour (rather than English red). Its emblem was a garter and the order was provided with a permanent home in the form of a sumptuous new church and college in the Lower Ward of Windsor Castle. Here the knight companions possessed their own stalls in the choir, each one overhung by a sword and helm (and latterly by a plate bearing their coat of arms). The king subsequently went on to rebuild his own residence in the castle on the most enormous scale, henceforth unequivocally establishing Windsor as the principal seat of England's kings.

Chivalric societies like the Order of the Garter came into being across Europe in the late Middle Ages. All of them were highly exclusive and possessed strange badges. It is, however, the only one to survive to the present and its members gather annually on Garter Day in Windsor Castle.

1348
STAFFORD CASTLE
A Castle-Building Contract

The motte of Stafford Castle preserves the remains of the rectangular castle, which was contracted to be built by Master John in 1348 on the eve of the Black Death. He agreed to convey all the building materials from the foot of the motte to the summit.

The earliest legal contracts to survive for the construction of castles in England by professional masons date to the fourteenth century and conform in format and language (French) to those of any legal agreement of the period. The following document was an indenture. To create this, two identical copies of the text were written out on a single sheet of parchment. This was then 'indented' or cut in two with a wavy or zigzag line. Both halves were affixed with the seals of the two parties impressed in wax, the equivalent of a signature, and a copy reserved by each. In the event of a dispute, the document could be authenticated by laying the two counterparts against each other to see that the line of the cut between them matched.

This contract only survives in a sixteenth-century copy. It relates to the construction of a 'chastelle', or castle, on the summit of the substantial mound or motte of Stafford by a mason called Master John de Burcestre (perhaps Bicester, Oxfordshire) for the lord of the castle, Ralph, Lord Stafford. Only the foundations of this building survive. They show that it was compactly laid out on a rectangular plan with five projecting towers and incorporated a complete suite of domestic chambers. Confusingly, while the contract lists both the architectural features of the buildings and the responsibilities of the two parties in the construction process, it doesn't set out a meaningful design. That would undoubtedly have been expressed in an accompanying 'device', a drawing, now lost. As was common in this period, the masonry was to be paid for at 5 marks for each perch (24 feet) erected. To avoid any ambiguity in calculating cost by this linear measurement, the contract states that the walls should be 7 feet wide at their base. Also that voids created by doors and windows would not count in the computation of each perch.

This indenture is made between Monsieur Ralph, Baron of Stafford, on the one hand, and Master John of Burcestre, mason, on the other part. Witness that it is settled between them that the said Master John will build a castle on the motte [*un chastelle sur le moete*] in the manner of length and breadth and height, with towers, halls, chambers, chapel, privies, chimneys, vices, windows, doors, and gates, together with vaults, according to the device and ordinance [*de deuys et lordinaunce*] of the said Monsieur Ralph, and that all the towers shall be 10 feet higher than the hall and chambers, and that the base of the wall shall be seven royal foot wide, without plinths or string courses, taking 5 marks for each perch of royal feet, and the perch is 24 feet; and that the vices, vaults, windows, chimneys and doors should be measured by all the surfaces within the walls. And that the said Monsieur Ralph will transport stone, sand and lime as far as the foot of the motte. And the said Monsieur Ralph will find scaffolding, ladders, hurdles, barrows, buckets, gins, cables and vessels necessary for the work, fuel for his [Master John's] lodging, and that of his people, and hay for his horse.

And the said Master [John] will transport the stone, sand and all other things necessary pertaining to the work, from the foot of the motte to the summit at his own cost until the work of the said castle is complete. In witness of which, the aforesaid parties have interchangeably set their seals to these indentures. And because Monsieur Ralph's seal is not at hand, the seals of Master William of Colton and of John of Pikstoke are affixed. Written at the castle of Stafford on St Hilary's day, the 21st year of the reign of King Edward the third after the Conquest.

13 January 1348, indenture (trans. M. J. B. Hislop
and A. M. Hislop)

MASTER John's castle was largely destroyed on the order of Parliament in 1643–4, which makes it hard to relate this contract to the building. What remains, however, bears stylistic comparison with the roughly contemporary castle of Maxstoke, Warwickshire, and the list of chambers suggests that it was intended to comprise all the rooms appropriate to a grand domestic residence. That's an impression confirmed by a survey of 1521, which gave an enthusiastic description of the castle and deemed it suitable for use by Henry VIII: it enjoyed fabulous views, overlooked a good park, and was built in a 'uniform fashion' with a hall and great chamber at first-floor level, services beneath and numerous chambers.

No other building by Master John is documented and he may have died soon afterwards during the pandemic known as the Black Death. Whatever the case, it's quite likely – indeed the contract explicitly suggests this – that he was merely a local executant mason realising a design created by someone else, probably a senior mason retained by a major local church or someone in royal employment. Senior masons were highly paid and by this date can be shown to have worked like modern architects, producing designs on paper remotely. They then visited building sites to check the quality of the work or to corroborate costs. These working practices are most fully documented in the late fourteenth-century career of the King's Mason Henry Yevele, who managed an architectural practice and tomb-making business across the south-east of England from London.

Such a division of labour helps explain the focus of the contract on the practical division of responsibilities between the patron and the mason. In essence, all the materials had to be delivered by the former to the bottom of the motte, along with all the tools to construct the building and lodging and necessaries for the workforce. Master John, by contrast, had to find the team of builders, convey the materials to the top of the motte and create the building in accordance with a design he was given. The concluding description of the sealing of the document is a curiosity. Both Master William of Colton and John of Pikstoke were local figures, who might plausibly have been in the following of Ralph. Here, however, they appear to be standing as surety for Master John. Perhaps the latter was an up-and-coming figure sealing his first contract. If so, the text could also be understood to describe his seal as 'not yet ready' (*nest pas preste*).

The timing of the work to the new castle is significant, Ralph having just returned triumphant from campaigning in France. His new castle was an expression of his martial prowess and new-found wealth (through two advantageous marriages). It also anticipated the award three years later, in 1351, of the earldom of Stafford. Curiously, the association thus established between the castle, its estates and this noble title had an unexpected postscript.

In 1806 one Edward Jerningham repaired and then occupied the ruins of Stafford Castle on behalf of his brother, a claimant to the Barony of Stafford. As Edward explained in a letter of about 1813, 'possession of the castle would be part of a strong case we would . . . be able to bring forward for the restitution of the barony'. Their efforts were rewarded and the barony was restored in 1824. Unfortunately, however, Jerningham's castle was largely demolished in 1961 to save the local council the expense of maintaining it.

AFTER 1360
A PAPER CASTLE
Sir Gawain Seeks Hospitality

A party of noblemen and women, hunting simultaneously with hawks and hounds, ride out from the gates of a castle. Two women watch from the battlements. Hunting was both a beloved aristocratic pastime and an enactment of lordship over land. The scene is depicted on an ivory panel made in Paris in the mid-fourteenth century as part of a valuable casket.

Sir Gawain and the Green Knight *is an English poem in the tradition of alliterative verse stretching back to the Anglo-Saxon period. It's written in a north-western dialect but nothing is securely known about its writer or the exact date of its composition between about 1360 and 1410. The modern translation from which this excerpt is taken recreates the original verse structure with a natural pause in the middle of each line and the repeated letter sounds.*

The story opens at Camelot at the Christmas feast of King Arthur. Festivities are interrupted by the arrival of a giant, green knight. He gruffly issues a challenge to the assembled company. Is there anyone willing to strike him a single blow with his great axe on condition that he will receive one in return a year hence? Gawain puts himself forward and strikes off the giant's head. To universal amazement the giant picks up his severed head and orders Gawain to come and find him a year hence for the return blow. All he must do to find his monstrous challenger is ask for the chapel of the Green Knight. Gawain sets out a year later accordingly on his horse Gringolet. On Christmas Eve, while still engaged in his search, and in desperate need of shelter, he glimpses a moated castle:

He saw in that wood a home in a moat,
Above a plain, on a knoll, locked under boughs,
Of many brawny boles about by the ditches;
The comeliest castle [*castel*] that knight had ever seen,
Perched among pastures, a park all about,
Within a spiked palisade pinned full thick,
That tied in many trees for more than two miles.
Our horseman surveyed that homestead on that side,
As it shimmered and shone through the sheer oaks;
Then he hoists his helm highly and honourably thanks
Jesus and Saint Julian that are both most gracious,
Who had cared for him courteously and heard all his cries.
'But I beseech', said the noble, 'pray grant me good hostelry.'
Then he urges on Gringolet with his gilt heels,
And by good chance he chose to take the chief road,
That brought brightly that noble quick to the drawbridge at last.
The bridge was up, not laid,
The gates were all shot fast,
The walls were well arrayed;
That place feared no wind's blast.
The knight bided on his horse and beheld from the bank
Of the deep double ditch that defended that place,
That its walls rose from water wonderfully deep,
And thus a huge height it seemed heaped upon high
Of hand-hewn stones right up to the corbels [*tabyl ʒ*],
In a band under the battlements [*abataylment*], in the best manner;
And then guard towers [*garyte ʒ*] full gay all geared between,
With many lovely arrow loops [*loupe*] that locked full clean;
A better barbican [*barbican*] that noble had never looked upon.
And within he beheld a hall full high,

All tucked between the towers, battlemented [*trochet*] full thick,
With fine, fair finials [*fylyole ʒ*] all tall and full fixed,
With carved conical caps, craftily skilled.
Many chimneys he chances upon, pale as chalk [*chalkwhyt*],
Upon bold tower [*bastel*] roofs that blinked full white;
So many painted pinnacles [*pynakle*] were peppered everywhere,
Among the castle's crenellations [*carnele ʒ*], clustered so thick,
That place purely, it seemed, to be pared out of paper [*papure*]
      Anon., *Sir Gawain and the Green Knight* (trans. M. Smith)

THIS passage offers us a medieval aesthetic response to a castle and its setting. The castle is viewed initially from a distance, hence the impression in the first verse that it rises above an enclosing wood. There is pasture amidst the trees, suggesting husbandry, but much more significant is the pale of an encircling park intended to protect game for the jealously guarded aristocratic pleasure of hunting (which is later crucial to the story). The walls of the building stand out in the half light. They also shimmer by reflection in the dark water of the surrounding moat. When Gawain arrives he finds the drawbridge raised and the gates shut; the castle is closed to the world outside. Not even a chink of light is mentioned.

In the second verse we are given a close-up look at the building. It's protected by deep double ditches filled with water. One possible reading of the description is that the earth cast up from these has created the castle knoll, which accentuates the height of the fortifications. The pale walls are revealed as being of cut stone and rise to battlements projected on corbels – what would today be termed a machicolation – in the best defensive manner and punctuated by towers. There are arrow loops and a 'noble' barbican, an adjective implying both strength and status. In time-honoured English tradition, however, one domestic building makes its presence apparent within all this martial array: the hall. This is 'tall' presumably because it is covered by a high roof and its outline is visually differentiated from the battlemented walls and towers by an array of pinnacles. Inner luxury and domestic comfort are also suggested by the white chimneys that rise above the parapets and roofs. So fantastical is the outline of the building that it seems to Gawain to be made out of paper, possibly a reference to table decorations (curiously, in the eighteenth century a similar comparison of materials was famously drawn by Horace Walpole, an early enthusiast for medieval architecture, between paper and the Gothic complexities of his 'castle', Strawberry Hill, Middlesex).

Gawain clearly admires this castle because it appears to be strong and well built. The building, however, has a context – its wider landscape and park – that is clearly important as well. A medieval estate was very different in many ways from that of a country house today but the essential relationship between architecture and setting applies to both.

1375
BISHOP WYVILLE
Symbols of Lordship

A rubbing by Derrick Chivers of the funerary brass of Bishop Wyville of Salisbury, who died in 1375. The engraved metal plates of the original brass are inset within a slab of Purbeck marble over 7 feet 6 inches (228 cm) long. This created a strong visual contrast in the newly completed monument between the engraved, golden image and its dark polished ground. The brass originally lay in the centre of the choir of Salisbury Cathedral. It shows the bishop at prayer inside a castle arrayed with battlements, turrets, arrow loops and square gun ports. At the gate stands a figure armed with a shield and battle pick and around the walls are tiny rabbits emerging from holes in the ground. An epitaph in Latin, now partly lost, ran around the whole rim of the backing slab to explain this striking image.

Here lies Robert Wyville, of happy memory, bishop of the church of Salisbury, who ruled that church peaceably and laudably for more than forty-five years; he prudently gathered together the dispersed possessions of the church, and they having been collected, he maintained them as a vigilant pastor. And amongst the least of his other gifts he recovered in the manner of an intrepid champion the castle of Sherborne, which for two hundred years or more had been withheld from this church by hand of military might, and he also obtained restitution to the same church of the chase of Bere; who on the 4th day of September in the year of Our Lord 1375 and the 46th year since his consecration, as the Most High pleased, he rendered his debt of human nature in the said castle. May He, in whose power he hoped and believed, have mercy on his soul.

THE loss of Sherborne Castle, to which the inscription referred, occurred over two centuries earlier (see 1139 above). Wyville ostensibly recovered it by judicial combat (though, in reality, money changed hands), hence the figure at the gate, who is identified as the bishop's champion by his curious shield and battle pick, the conventional armaments for trials by combat. The rabbits in their warren presumably refer to the chase of Bere; one expression of lordship was the so-called 'right of warren', or the permission to hunt.

The castle and warren were trappings of medieval lordship, distinct from the bishop's ecclesiastical office but essential to its prestige and authority. Indeed, most historic English bishoprics had castles associated with them into the twentieth century, as for example Rose, Cumbria with Carlisle; Hartlebury with Worcester; and Farnham with Winchester.

A number of other episcopal effigies made in the fourteenth century incorporate castle imagery both in England – as for example, that of Bishop de Braose, Hereford – and beyond. The lost effigy of Bishop Henry III of Hildesheim (d. 1363), for example, depicts him surrounded by images of four castles he had built or acquired, and in Cologne the posthumous tomb of Archbishop Philipp I von Heinsberg (d. 1191) is magnificently encircled by the miniature walls and gates of the city.

1 3 8 1
TOWER OF LONDON
Kissing a Queen and Beheading an Archbishop

The gatehouse of Saltwood Castle, Kent. Archbishop Courtenay of Canterbury added this grand frontage to an earlier gate as an expression of feudal authority. It was here that he passed judgement on his recalcitrant tenants who conveyed straw to him in sacks 'for their own convenience', not in carts 'for his glory'.

In 1381 the levy of a heavy poll tax was the immediate cause of the Peasants' Revolt, one of the most serious popular uprisings in English history. A large army of rebels entered London and the city lay at its mercy for two days. Richard II, a boy of fourteen still in his minority, retired with his councillors to the Tower of London and is described as surveying the destruction of property by the mob from a turret of the castle. On Friday, 14 June, he rode out to parley with the rebels at Mile End. We take up the story as told by Thomas of Walsingham, a monk of St Albans writing in the tradition of his great thirteenth-century historian predecessor, Matthew Paris.

By that time the squads of the peasants had split up into three parts. One of them, as I have described, was intent on destroying the estate at Highbury. Another was waiting near London, at a place called Mile End. A third had actually seized Tower Hill. This crowd near the Tower showed itself to be so out of control and lacking in respect that it shamelessly seized goods belonging to the king that were being conveyed to the Tower. And besides this, it was driven to such a pitch of madness that it forced the king to hand over to them the archbishop [of Canterbury], the Master of the Hospital of St John and the others hiding inside the Tower itself . . .

At that time, there were present in the actual Tower 600 soldiers equipped with weapons, all strong, experienced men, and 600 archers. The amazing thing was that all of these were so lacking in fight that you would have thought them more dead than alive. For all memory of their former famous military career was dead among them, they had completely forgotten their previous strength and glory, and, in a word, in the face of those peasants from almost all of England all their military boldness had withered away.

For who would ever have believed that not just peasants, but the lowest of them, and not several of them together, but individuals on their own, would have dared with their worthless staves to force a way into the bedroom of the king or of his mother, scaring all the nobles with their threats and even touching and stroking with their rough, filthy hands the beards of some of the most eminent of them? Or that they would have begun chatting about future socializing . . . And besides all this, several of them, who, as I have said, had gone on their own into the various rooms, had the effrontery to sit and lie on the bed of the king joking merrily, with one or two even asking the king's mother for a kiss.

Yet it is a remarkable fact that the several knights and esquires that were there did not dare to summon a single one of the rebels from such impropriety, or to lay hands upon them to stop them, or even to mutter about it beneath their breath . . . Now let me write about what happened to the archbishop . . . They found one of his servants and furiously commanded him to lead them to the place in which the holy father (whom they called 'traitor') was hiding. The servant did not dare to disobey their command, and led them to the chapel, in which the archbishop having celebrated mass and received holy communion, was busy with his prayers . . . they dragged the archbishop by his hands and his hood through different places until they came to their fellow accomplices outside the gates on Tower Hill.

When they brought the archbishop there, a devilish yelling went up, not like the usual shouts of men but worse than any human cries and beyond any imagining . . . they yelled in this way whenever they executed anybody or destroyed houses . . . Realising that his certain death was at hand . . . [the archbishop] knelt down and bent his neck for the blow. The axe struck his neck but not fatally . . . He had not yet taken his hand from the wound when the axe struck him a second time, cutting off the tops of his fingers and some of his arteries, and he fell to the ground. But he was not put to death until his neck and head had been pitifully mutilated by eight blows.

Thomas of Walsingham, The Great Chronicle
(trans. D. Preest)

THOMAS of Walsingham probably composed this passage in the 1380s or 1390s and certainly had access to those who had witnessed the events he describes. He is very hostile to the peasants – as all accounts are – and suggests that they got access to the Tower by royal permission. Other accounts, however, give the impression that, amidst wider confusion as the king left for his parley, the peasants simply forced their way in, marching as a body with banners. That would agree with the fact that no one was organised to resist them.

The chronicler Jean Froissart, from Hainault, likewise recounts that the peasants got access to a royal bedchamber. He describes it, however, as that of the Princess of Wales and adds that they tore her bed to pieces, which so terrified her that she fainted. Froissart also speaks of the demonic baying of the crowds; perhaps they called out in unfamiliar dialects.

Walsingham's account of the murder of Archbishop Sudbury reads in the main as a literary construct. In the full text he is represented as acting like Christ towards his tormentors. His capture in a chapel, quite possibly that of Saint John the Baptist in the White Tower, however, is otherwise corroborated. Similarly, the gruesome detail of being decapitated with eight strokes of a sword and losing his fingers in the process has the ring of an eyewitness account. The archbishop's head was subsequently set on London Bridge but – astonishingly – it survives at St Gregory's Church in his native Sudbury, Suffolk, a gruesome relic of the Peasants' Revolt.

Sudbury's fate almost certainly explains a curious episode that took place during the rule of his successor, Archbishop William Courtenay. In 1390 six tenants from the village of Wingham, Kent, were summoned to a tribunal at Saltwood Castle for mis-performing a customary duty to their lord, the archbishop. They had delivered straw to him 'not openly in carts for his glory, but closely in sacks upon their horses' backs for their own convenience'. They were sentenced to perform public penance one Sunday walking in procession 'with slow steps humbly and devoutly' in single file, wearing neither hoods nor shoes around the collegiate church of Wingham. On their backs, they carried open sacks displaying their contents of hay and straw. The first historian of Kent, William Lambarde, writing in 1570, viewed this episode as a tyranny: 'What was it . . . for this proud prelate thus to insult over simple men for so small a fault (or no fault at all).' Lambarde forgets, however, that the archbishop's predecessor had been murdered by the mob in 1381 and had special reason, therefore, to fear the omission of feudal duties. It was also probably to make an outward statement of his feudal claims that Archbishop Courtenay also splendidly modernised the gatehouse of Saltwood at about this time.

1386
SANDWICH
The Capture of a Timber Castle

On 14 August 1385 a small Portuguese force, with their English allies, won a resounding victory over the Castilians at the Battle of Aljubarrota, north of Lisbon. When the news of this encounter arrived in England the most powerful figure in Richard II's court, the king's uncle, John of Gaunt, decided to assert his claim by marriage to the Castilian throne. Gaunt's departure from England for over three years, on 9 July 1386, upset the political equilibrium of the realm. It also encouraged Charles VI of France, an ally of the Castilians, to build up his military strength and plan an invasion.

The king of France, who was preparing to invade England, at that time believed that the victory would not come from weapons alone, but that wooden walls [*muris ligneis*] were also necessary. So he gathered together carpenters from many places and told them to make a thick, dense wooden wall, 20 feet high, with towers capable of holding 10 men at every 12 feet along its length, the towers to be 10 feet higher than the wall beneath. He planned, so it is said, to erect the wall in the place where he was intending to land, so that it might keep off arrows and protect his own gunners [*gunnarios*], who would thus do terrible damage to our men. Also, when need arose, he could call his men back inside the protection of the wall, so that they could rest, when tired, and recover, when wounded. This wall, so it was said, was 3 miles long and was equipped with stout towers [*turribus firmis*] at frequent intervals, as I have said.

At the same time, our men out at sea encountered two French ships as they cut a furrow through the planes of the sea, making for Sluys. At once they joined battle, captured the ships and took them to Sandwich. They found on board part of the wall with its towers and they also captured the chief constructor of the whole wall [*magister totius fabricae*], an Englishman by birth who had been banished sometime previously. They also captured on board the master gunner. He, too, had previously been on the English side at Calais, when Sir Hugh Calveley had been captain there. And besides these finds, they also discovered various engines for throwing stones and demolishing walls, several guns, and a great quantity of gunpowder. The value of this gunpowder was higher than that of all the other spoils. So the part of the wall was put up at Sandwich, and a defence made by the enemy against us was put up by us against them.

Thomas of Walsingham, The Great Chronicle
(trans. D. Preest)

THE sheer scale of the timber fortification proposed here – three miles long, twenty feet high and with even taller towers every twelve feet – seems completely impossible. As a matter of fact, however, there is another contemporary description of the same structure in *Knighton's Chronicle* that makes it even larger: seven leagues or twenty-one miles long. Something on this scale would have absorbed stupendous quantities of wood and both sets of dimensions must be grossly exaggerated. That said, there seems no reason to doubt that Charles VI wanted a portable fortification to cover his landing – like William the Conqueror before him (see 1066 above) – or that it was a structure of exceptional size. In this latter regard, the identification of the master carpenter as a renegade Englishman is perhaps significant; the tradition of English carpentry, as reflected in such structures as the 1390s angel roof over Westminster Hall with its 69-foot (21.1-metre) span, was extraordinarily sophisticated in a European sense.

The other important detail of this description is the reference to guns and gunpowder. One of the first English drawings of such weapons appears in a book of advice written by a clerk named Walter of Milemete in 1327 for Edward III called *On the Nobility, Wisdom and Prudence of Kings* and they were possibly used in the field by English soldiers during the Crecy campaign of 1346. The first fortifications built to accommodate guns in England date to the late fourteenth century. These include town defences at Southampton, Canterbury and Norwich (where the city employed professional gunners from 1365) and such castles as Portchester, Hampshire and Cooling, Kent. A building account of 1381 for the latter makes the first English documentary reference to gun loops: the mason Thomas Crump made ten 'arketholes' – literally holes for hand-held guns called arquebuses that are described as '3 feet in length without cross slits' – and seven 'little doors' 2.5 feet square, presumably for larger guns.

The captured guns were evidently found together with heavy stone-throwing engines, presumably as part of a siege train. This is a reminder that guns only gradually displaced other weapons. They were relatively slow to fire and cumbersome, though evidently capable of inflicting terrible damage when massed together. It is noteworthy as well that they were in the care of a specialist and professional, a master gunner, another renegade Englishman. His former employment at Calais is significant because this border town, which remained an English colony in Northern France until the mid-sixteenth century, was consistently one of the most formidably fortified in Europe.

Finally, it is interesting to note the emphasis given in this account to the relative value of the captured gunpowder. Guns were hugely expensive weapons to make and the expertise necessary to operate them was difficult to secure. So too was the gunpowder they consumed complex and costly to manufacture.

1399
FLINT CASTLE
The Capture of Richard II

In the dying days of June 1399, Henry Bolingbroke, the dispossessed Duke of Lancaster, landed at Ravenspur on the Humber Estuary to reclaim his inheritance from Richard II. The king was in Ireland at the time and by the time he returned to Wales on 24 July or thereabouts, his authority had collapsed. Departing from his household late at night disguised as a Franciscan friar, he travelled restlessly to a series of the castles built by Edward I – Beaumaris, Caernarfon and Conwy – as if in search of security. A Frenchman in the party, Jean Creton, a valet de chambre of Charles VI, recorded that 'Reckoning nobles and other persons we were but sixteen in all' including a particular favourite of the king, the Earl of Salisbury. Also, that 'in his castles, to which he [Richard II] retired, there was no furniture, nor had he any thing to lie down upon but straw; really he lay in this manner for four or six nights, for in truth, not a farthing's worth of victuals or of any thing else was to be found in them'. The king finally came to Flint Castle (see 1277 above) and, already conscious that he had lost everything, awaited a meeting with the Duke of Lancaster, in the donjon *or keep. Much of Creton's account was written in verse but at this point he moved to prose so that he could more accurately narrate what happened.*

King Richard, who, early on the morning of the said Tuesday [22 August], arose, attended by sorrows, sadness, afflictions; mourning, weeping, and lamentations . . . having heard Mass, went up upon the walls of the castle, which are large and wide on the inside, beholding the Duke of Lancaster as he came along the sea-shore with all his host. It was marvellously great, and showed such joy and satisfaction that the sound and noises of their instruments, horns, business and trumpets, were heard even as far as the castle . . . they saw a great number of persons quit the host, pricking their horses hard towards the castle, to know what King Richard was doing. In this first company was the Archbishop of Canterbury, Sir Thomas Percy, and the Earl of Rutland . . . The archbishop entered first, and the others after him; they went up to the donjon. Then the king came down from the walls, to whom they made very great obeisance, kneeling on the ground. The king caused them to rise, and drew the archbishop aside; and they talked together a very long while. What they said I know not; but the Earl of Salisbury afterwards told me, that he had comforted the king in a very gentle manner, telling him not to be alarmed, and that no harm should happen to his person . . . They mounted their horses again, and returned to Duke Henry, who was drawing very nigh: for between the city of Chester and the castle, there are but ten little miles, which are equal to five French leagues, or thereabout. And there is neither hedge nor bush between them; nothing but the sea-shore, and on the other side lofty rocks and mountains . . . The king went up again upon the walls, and saw that the army was two bow-shots from the castle: then he, together with those who were with him, began anew great lamentation . . . The table being laid, the king sat down to dinner, and caused the Bishop of Carlisle, the Earl of Salisbury, and the two knights, Sir Stephen Scrope and Ferriby, to be seated, saying, thus, 'My good, true, and loyal friends, being in peril of death for maintaining loyalty, sit you down with me.' In the meantime a great number of knights, squires, and archers, quitted the host of Duke Henry and came to the said castle, desiring to behold their king; not for any good will that they bore him, but for the great thirst that they had to ruin him, and to put him to death . . . I do not think that I ever was so much afraid as I was at that time considering their great contempt . . . The king was a very long time at table; not for anything at all that he ate; but because he well knew that as soon as he had dined the duke would come for him, to carry him off, or put him to death . . . After this the duke entered the castle, armed at all points, except his bascinet [helmet] . . . Then they made the king, who had dined in the donjon, come down to meet Duke Henry, who, as soon as he perceived him at a distance, bowed very low to the ground; and as they approached each other he bowed a second time, with his cap in his hand; and then the king took off his bonnet, and spake first in this manner: 'Fair cousin of Lancaster, you be right welcome.' Then Duke Henry replied, bowing very low to the ground, 'My Lord, I am come sooner than you sent for me: the reason wherefore I will tell you. The common report of your people is such, that you have, for the space of twenty or two and twenty years, governed them very badly and very rigorously, and in so much that they are not well contented therewith. But if it please our Lord, I will help you to govern them better than they have been governed in time past.' King Richard then answered him, 'Fair cousin, since it pleaseth you, it pleaseth us well.' And be assured that these are the very words that they two spake together, without taking away or adding any thing: for I heard and understood them very well . . .

Thus, as you have heard, came Duke Henry to the castle and spake unto the king, to the Bishop of Carlisle, and the two knights, Sir Stephen Scrope, and Ferriby; howbeit unto the Earl of Salisbury he spake not at all, but sent word to him by a knight in this manner, 'Earl of Salisbury, be assured that no more than you deigned to speak to my lord the Duke of Lancaster, when he and you were in Paris at Christmas last past, will he speak unto you.' Then was the earl much abashed, and had great fear and dread at heart, for he saw plainly that the duke mortally hated him. The said Duke Henry called aloud with a stern and savage voice, 'Bring out the king's horses;' and then they brought him two little horses that were not worth forty franks; the king mounted one, and the Earl of Salisbury the other. Every one got on horseback, and we set out from the said castle of Flint, about two hours after mid-day.

Jean Creton, *The Deposition of Richard II* (trans. J. Webb)

RICHARD II's use of castles in this moment of crisis suggests that he regarded them as places of security and refuge. They proved to be neglected, however, and his cause, otherwise undermined by inconsistency and treachery, was doomed. This account vividly captures the realities of his capitulation: his view from the battlements (the walks of the keep are indeed unusually broad), his prolonged final meal in the main chamber of the keep and the threatening presence of onlookers. So too the exchange with the outwardly humble Duke of Lancaster and his deliberately humiliating departure on a small, cheap horse. A month later Richard II had been deposed and, towards the end of February 1400, he was murdered at Pontefract Castle, Yorkshire.

1401
CONWY CASTLE
Recapturing a Royal Castle

Conwy Castle, North Wales. Its rubble masonry exterior was originally rendered over and limewashed. In 1401 it was held by about forty men and had evidently been reprovisioned since Richard II's flight here two years previously, when the king had slept on straw and the building contained 'not a farthing's worth of victuals or of anything else'.

Within two years of Richard II's capture in Wales, Conwy Castle played a brief part in the opening phase of another political crisis. A territorial dispute between Lord Grey and a Welsh squire, Owain Glyn Dŵr, escalated into a full-scale rebellion against English rule. On 16 September 1400, Glyn Dŵr was acclaimed Prince of Wales and entered into conflict with the king's son, Henry of Monmouth (the future Henry V), who had been installed as Prince of Wales in October 1399. Glyn Dŵr and his followers could not compete with the resources available to the English Crown. As a result, they generally destroyed the castles they captured and resorted to guerrilla warfare (though they did enjoy some success in the field). Early in the decade-long rebellion two of Owain Glyn Dŵr's cousins, William and Rhys ap Tudor, tried to use Conwy Castle as a bargaining counter. It had evidently been reprovisioned since Richard II's visit in 1399. The rebels successfully tricked their way into the building while most of the garrison were at their devotions in the parish church on Good Friday, part of the solemn celebration of Easter.

On this same day, Good Friday [1 April], the brothers William ap Tudor and Rhys ap Tudor, who came from the island of Anglesey or Mon, since they failed to obtain the king's pardon for their part in the rising led by the aforesaid Owain, along with another 40 men entered Conwy Castle, which was most securely fortified with arms and provisions, and seized it as their stronghold, two of the watch having been killed after being tricked by one of the carpenters claiming that he was simply coming to do his usual work. Being immediately besieged by the Prince [Henry of Monmouth] and the people of the surrounding area, however, on May 28 following, having deceitfully bound from behind nine of their fellows whom the Prince particularly loathed, while they were sleeping following the night watch, they surrendered the castle on condition that their lives and the lives of others would be spared – a most shameful thing for them to have done, and an act of treachery against their fellows. They then promptly stood and watched while these nine, still bound, were handed over to the Prince, and firstly drawn, and then disembowelled, hanged, beheaded and quartered.

Adam of Usk, *Chronicle* (trans. C. Given-Wilson)

AS his name suggests, Adam, the author of this text, was from Usk, Monmouthshire, in the Welsh Marches. He was strongly sympathetic to Glyn Dŵr and was presumably promoted to the bishopric of Llandaff with his agreement in 1407. Confusingly, however, the appointment was made during the Great Schism of the Church by the antipope Benedict XII in Avignon – a rival to Innocent VII in Rome – and opposed by Henry IV. Adam's loyalties perhaps explain his strong disapproval of the dishonourable terms in which the castle was rendered up.

In this episode it was the strength of Conwy Castle that made it an effective place from which the Tudor brothers could initiate their negotiations. The final terms of the bargain, however, and the gruesome execution of nine of their companions, suggest that in the end it was they who needed to strike a deal. If so, they were lucky to escape with their lives. It's worth noting that Adam describes the siege as lasting for eight weeks but other sources make it longer.

A letter written by Henry IV to his son, Henry of Monmouth, tells the story of the siege from an English perspective and it's worth including it here. The original is written in French and is frustratingly undated. This makes it clear that the king already anticipated a negotiated conclusion with the terms set by the besieging force. It also gives an accurate impression of the numbers of the besieging force, a rare detail. The text begins with Henry IV reciting the contents of the last letter he received from his son and implies that there is presently a truce enforced:

> We have received your letter in answer; by the which, among other things, you have signified to us how that between our most dear and faithful cousin, Henry de Percy . . . and others of your council, on the matter touching Rhys and William ap Tudor, and other our rebels, their adherents, certain treaties had been settled; and how, and to what results the [rebels] . . . in the castle of Conwy, have finally arrived by their offer and supplication, (of which we have seen the copy,) and considering moreover, the good arrangement of men of arms and archers, and works [*des bastiles*], which you and our said cousin have made, for the siege of the said castle, giving us your advice that 120 armed men and 300 archers should remain employed upon the said siege, until the feast of St Michael [29 September], or the feast of All Saints [1 November] next coming, to the end that the said rebels might be punished according to their deserts, or that we should have at least some other treaty which should be agreeable to us and more honourable than was any one of the offers of our aforesaid rebels
>
> 1401, Henry IV, a letter to the Prince of
> Wales (trans. F. C. Hingeston)

It's an interesting comment on the resources demanded by the siege that the Tudor brothers led a force of about forty men, while Henry of

Monmouth was obliged to field a force of 420, more than ten times that number. The preponderance of archers illustrates the importance of the longbow and hints at the kinds of experience that the future king would take with him to the field of Agincourt more than ten years later.

The circumstances that prompted the Tudor brothers to seize Conwy are not now clear but it may be significant that both had been prominent in the service of Richard II and his father, the Black Prince. They were, in other words, natural opponents of the usurper Henry IV and their cause extended beyond Welsh identity alone. It's a further notable curiosity in this regard that another of their brothers also implicated in Glyn Dŵr's rebellion, Maredudd Tudor, was – through the marriage of his son, Owen, to Henry V's widow, Catherine of Valois – the great grandfather of the first Tudor king, Henry VII.

1403
ALNWICK AND WARKWORTH CASTLES
The Pretence of Loyalty

The great tower of Warkworth, Northumbria, was probably constructed to celebrate the ennoblement of Henry Percy in 1377. It ingeniously compresses a noble residence into a cruciform plan. It was probably from the comfort of its apartments that Henry IV penned his letter below in 1405.

In recognition of the huge landholdings and power he enjoyed in northern England, Henry Percy was created Earl of Northumberland by Richard II in 1377. The earl went on in 1399 to play a leading role in the deposition of the king who ennobled him and then, with his son Harry Hotspur, went on to quarrel with the king they had installed, Henry IV. Hotspur was killed

while in open rebellion at the Battle of Shrewsbury in 1403 and his father
was soon afterwards imprisoned at Pontefract. A group of royal officials
moved to seize his northern castles and held a council at Durham Priory on
25 September 1403 to determine a course of action. Despite being armed
with two written instruments of royal authority – an open or 'patent' letter
sealed with the great seal of the realm and a private letter sealed with the
king's personal or 'privy' seal – the Lords Furnival and Say were fobbed off by
the earl's dependants at the Percy castles of Alnwick and Warkworth. Here is
an excerpt from the official report written to Henry IV's council of what
happened:

And when at the castle of Alnwick the Lords Furnival and Say . . .
met beneath the gate William de Worthington constable of the
said castle, Master John de Wyndale, Clerk, William de Rondome,
John de Midilham, Thomas Clerk of said Alnwick, Richard
Bonde and a great number of others; and in the chapel of the said
castle the said Lord Say showed the letters patent of the king our
said most sovereign lord directing that he have surety and
possession of all the lordships, lands, tenancies and possessions
that were held by Henry, Earl of Northumberland . . .

The which said constable took the advice of the said John
de Wyndale and many others of those within the castle with
him and said that he had the safe keeping of the castle of the
said Earl of Northumberland by indenture and like the said
knights he had guard of the same and livery at the command of
the Earl of Northumberland and no other response would they
give me but that they were loyal to the king our said most
sovereign lord

THE impression is that the followers of the earl had rehearsed their
behaviour carefully. They received the king's officers in front of the
surviving gate at Alnwick Castle. Lord Say was then apparently invited
alone into the chapel, where he displayed the letters patent to the
assembled followers of the earl. The hall might have been a more obvious
chamber for such a gathering but the chapel was perhaps deemed more
suitable in the absence of the earl himself. Its stalls would also have
created a natural space for discussion and, additionally, this was the

province of John de Wyndale, elsewhere described as a chaplain. As literate and educated men, chaplains were often very closely associated with the head of the household and their private affairs. He was also subject to church law. The refusal on Wyndale's advice to submit the castle to the royal officers was followed by a profession of loyalty to the king's person. More considered insolence awaited at Warkworth:

> Within which castle was Sir Henry Percy [the son of the earl and not more than fourteen years old], who was ordered by the said Lord Say if he would at once leave and journey to the king our said most sovereign lord as he was ordered by the letters under privy seal addressed to him. The which [Sir Henry] said that he was always willing to do service to the king, our said most sovereign lord, when he was properly arrayed but he would not wish to determine a day (when he might do so) [*limiter le jour*]. And to fulfil this need the said Lord Furnival with the Lord Say called on the said Master John de Wyndale and the master of the wardrobe to get a bed appropriate to his estate, silver vessels, armour and horses, the which they would not do without instruction of the said Earl.
>
> October 1403, Thomas Neville, Lord
> Furnival despatch to Henry IV

In ordinary circumstances it would have been unimaginable to ignore a summons under the privy seal. Certainly, Sir Henry's specious assertion that he was inappropriately arrayed to travel to see the king would have struck a medieval audience as deliciously insulting; a claim to status and consideration from a boy in the face of a royal call to punishment.

A year after this astonishing performance the earl was restored to his property. He almost immediately signalled his discontent by joining the unsuccessful conspiracy in 1405 led by Archbishop Scrope of York to overthrow Henry IV. This time the king acted decisively and marched north at the head of an army. The earl fled. With a siege train to enforce his demands, the same castles surrendered rapidly to the king. From the comfort of Warkworth, Henry IV wrote a short note to the council to describe his success. Parts of the French text are lost:

know that the castle of Prudhoe, that was the possession of the Earl of Northumberland, has been rendered to us . . . [The captain of Warkworth refused to surrender the castle] . . . For a final response we swiftly sent our cannons to this castle. They served us so well that within seven shots the said captain and all the others of his company cried mercy and surrendered to our grace from the highest to the lowest and gave to us possession of the said castle on the first day of this month of July and within which I sent our men. And so were rendered to us all the castles of the said Earl except the castle of Alnwick, which we are confident that, by the grace of God, after such good and gracious exploits with the others, we will have our desire fully, and this quickly . . . I cannot write more at present. Given under our signet at the said castle of Warkworth the second day of July.

2 July 1405, a letter of Henry IV

The fall of the earl's castles in 1405 speaks of the importance of military force – and a siege train in particular – to back up royal authority. Without an army the royal officials who visited in 1403 were powerless to act; with one, the earl's followers were powerless to resist the king.

1 4 1 4
KENILWORTH CASTLE
A Retreat from Formality

Henry V succeeded to his father's throne in March 1413. From the first his focus was on English claims to territory in France; unfinished business from the Treaty of Brétigny negotiated by Edward III in 1360. He became increasingly frustrated with French responses to his demands but before he was irrevocably set on war he spent the six weeks of Lent 1414 – from 21 February to 6 April – at Kenilworth Castle. It was a place he had known from childhood and one he particularly favoured in later life. One of his chaplains, Thomas Elmham, later wrote a life of Henry V in metrical verse and – with the advantage of hindsight – drew an analogy between the thorny political and diplomatic issues he faced and an unusual project initiated by the king during his stay at Kenilworth. The excerpt comprises a prose introduction followed by part of a verse:

Chapter 11 – How his majesty the king kept Lent at Kenilworth Castle, and in the marsh, where foxes lurked among the brambles and thorns, built for his entertainment a green garden [*viridarium*]. It was as if he foresaw the tricks of the French against his kingdom and how he would manfully drive out these and other insidious enemies. On this site he constructed a delicious place which he caused to be called 'Pleasing Marsh' ['*Plesant Mareys*'] ... the course ground is sweetened with running water and the site is made nice. So the king considers how to overcome the difficulties confronting his own kingdom, the achievement of which will require correspondingly greater effort. He remembers the foxy tricks of the French both in deed and in writing and is mortified by the recollection

Thomas Elmham, *Memorials of Henry V*
(trans. M. W. Thompson)

WHAT this account does not mention, however, is the architectural focus of this project. Within this garden, and undoubtedly conceived with it, Henry V also began – by 1417 – a building described in accounts as the 'Pleasaunce'. The vestiges of this creation can still be traced in surviving earthworks. It stood at the north-west corner of the great artificial lake or mere at Kenilworth and resembled a small castle on a square plan with corner towers (the excavation of one revealed its internal dimensions as a mere ten foot square). Around the Pleasaunce was a double, water-filled moat and access to it from the mere by boat was provided by a short canal.

This was not a place of defence, however, but – as the name suggests – a stronghold against the cares of the world. Here the king could not only escape by barge from the castle itself, the demands of business and the formality of life with the great household, but also indulge in the delights of hunting. To accommodate him there was a self-contained timber-frame residence inside the enclosure. Two sixteenth-century surveys describe it as a two-storey structure 130 feet long and 36 feet wide comprising a hall, parlour, kitchen, pantry and buttery on the ground floor and a series of six chambers with unusually large windows raised over them. Presumably the windows offered good views over the park. The compact, regularised volume of the structure and its large windows suggest a building of superlative quality. That's a judgement confirmed by the fact that it was later transferred wholesale into the neighbouring castle by Henry VIII.

Park retreats of this kind, often with names suggestive of beauty or withdrawal, are a widespread phenomenon in England from the fourteenth century onwards. In the 1370s, for example, the Earl of Warwick erected 'Goodrest' in Wedgnock Park, one of the enclosed parks adjoining Warwick Castle, and in 1377–8 Henry V's grandfather, John of Gaunt, rebuilt 'Bird's Nest' near Leicester Castle. Henry VI's queen, Margaret of Anjou, likewise created her own *Placentia* or 'pleasant place' at Greenwich, above which was a tower with magnificent views across the Thames towards London on the site of what is now the Royal Observatory. The degree to which these luxurious buildings assumed the forms of castles is impossible to know, but the example of the Kenilworth Pleasaunce illustrates both the prestige of fortifications and a delight in their decorative use.

It's a curiosity that immediately after describing Henry V's work at Kenilworth, Thomas Elmham's metrical life refers to the insulting gift of gaming balls made by the Dauphin to Henry V that is famously supposed to have precipitated the Agincourt campaign of 1415. It's familiar today through Shakespeare's retelling in *Henry V*, act 1 scene 2. The real event on which this story is based almost certainly took place at Kenilworth Castle in 1414. Certainly, the fullest contemporary account of it was written by a canon of Kenilworth Priory, John Strecche:

> The French, in the blindness of harmful pride having no foresight, with words of gall answered foolishly to the ambassadors of the King of England, that because King Henry was young they would send him little balls to play with, and soft cushions to rest on, until what time he should grow to a man's strength. At which news the King was much troubled in spirit, yet with short, wise, and seemly words, he thus addressed those who stood about him: 'If God so wills and my life lasts, I will within a few months play such a game of ball in the Frenchmen's streets, that they shall lose their jest and gain but grief for their game. If they sleep too long upon their cushions in their chamber, perchance before they wish it I will rouse them from their slumbers by hammering on their doors at dawn.'
>
> John Strecche writings (trans. C. L. Kingsford)

Strecche does not speak of tennis balls, as in Shakespeare, or of French ambassadors. Rather a reported conversation relayed by English ambassadors returned from Paris. Presumably they had a formal audience with Henry V in the now-ruined interiors that were added to Kenilworth by John of Gaunt.

1439
TATTERSHALL CASTLE
Building in Brick

The keep or great tower of Tattershall, Lincolnshire, begun in 1439/40, elevated this castle in architectural terms to the level of the greatest and most ancient English castles. It made use of foreign expertise to produce bricks on an industrial scale but the technical details of the building suggest that its designer was English.

English ambitions in France during the early fifteenth century encouraged a period of intense cultural exchange with the Continent. One manifestation of this in architecture was the increased use of brick in grand English commissions of the period including castles. Bricks – essentially squared blocks of fired clay – had been continuously manufactured in England since the Roman period but for the most part as a cottage industry. In the early fifteenth century, however, specialist craftsmen from Northern France, modern-day Holland and the Baltic introduced to England the technology for firing the industrial quantities of regular bricks necessary for building at scale.

Tattershall, Lincolnshire, was the inherited seat of Ralph, Lord Cromwell, and the site of a substantial thirteenth-century castle. As a young man Lord Cromwell campaigned in France but the death of Henry V in 1422 and the accession of his one-year-old son, Henry VI, brought the focus of his activities – and that of many figures of his generation – back to England. In 1433 he was appointed to the lucrative office of Lord Treasurer, which he held for the next decade. Lord Cromwell not only reconstructed a major residence at Wingfield, Derbyshire, but concurrently transformed Tattershall. Work to the latter seems to have fallen into two phases, the first improvements and then, from 1439, plans to recast the building on a much grander scale with a great tower.

An incomplete series of building accounts drawn up by Thomas Crosby, 'supervisor of the works of Ralph, Lord Cromwell, at his castle of Tattershall', survive and there follow excerpts from two of them. The first lists the various uses of the stockpile of about 700,000 bricks, many of them made in kilns about four miles north of the castle at Edlington, during the year from April 1438 to May 1439.

From the foregoing bricks, it is estimated that there will be required for the masonwork of the moat lining [*le countre mure*] within the castle of Tattershall made by Matthew brickman and his mates as below: 182,000. On the new building of a large stable within the castle, at the west end of the Woolhouse, by Godfrey brickman and his mates, within the period of the account, as below: 236,000. On the foundations of a small house between the aforesaid stable and the Woolhouse, made by the said Godfrey brickman and his mates, as below: 46,000. Sold . . . from my lord's bricks in Edlington More: 1,700. On the mason work of my lord's mills at Tattershall: 25,000. Given from my lord's alms for the works of the fabric of the church of Edlington: 3,000. Used in various other works within the said castle, such as the repair of partitions in the chimneys and in the market house, delivered by the workmen day by day and not by the thousand, by estimate for the number of days work: 114,000. For the chimneys and windows of the said stable, of the works brick called hewn tile [*hewentile*]: 2,200. Total: 619,900 bricks.

There are leftover 137,600 bricks, whereas at the disposal of Baldwin Brickman there remain to be accounted for, at the kiln, out of the whole amount of bricks and accounted for there last year, 134,600; within the castle 3,000.

1438–9 building account (trans. W. D. Simpson)

THE account makes clear the diversity of building work within the castle, including lining the moat, the construction of 'a small house' and also agricultural buildings essential for the operation of the estate, such as the new stable and mills. It's implicit by the use of the term 'brickman' that the work of laying bricks is a specialism and Baldwin, who has responsibility for the kiln, is elsewhere referred to as 'the Dutchman'. Clearly his expertise was imported from the great brick-building region of the Baltic. The reference to 'hewn tile' is one of several technical distinctions inconsistently applied by the accountant – who seemingly had no building expertise – to different types of brick. This refers to bricks that were intended to be cut or moulded to form architectural details such as windows, doors or chimneys. Other denominations that occur in the account are 'large' and 'small' bricks as well as 'bricks called wall tile [*waltyle*]'. This extract also gives a sense of the numbers of bricks that building work might absorb, from the 3,000 offered as alms to Edlington Church to the 236,000 employed in a large stable building.

These numbers are important to bear in mind when reading the next account in the series from May 1439 to March 1440, where Crosby initially has 636,100 bricks in hand:

From which he reckons will have been used for the paving of the great stable and the building of the support there on two occasions both by days and also by thousands as vouched for by the carriers, 28,500. Also used in the new building of a wall of one house situated between the stable and the Milhouse, both as above and also by thousands as vouched for above in the present account, 48,600. And in diverse other works at the said castle, for example in renewing the walls, raising the two galleries and likewise walls of the castle at the end of the kitchen and its chimneys and elsewhere in many works carried out on a daily basis, as by estimate both in this way and also by the sworn testimony of the said carriers 2,095,900 bricks

1439–40 building account (trans. W. D. Simpson)

This enormous leap in the consumption of bricks – and the final figure given in the account for the year (which is not fully explained) is an astonishing 4,080,500 bricks – suggests a major new building initiative. To put that in context, the vast Battersea Power Station in London, begun in 1929, absorbed about 6 million bricks. Undoubtedly planned as part of the expansion of Tattershall Castle, but not actually mentioned until the next surviving account in the sequence from 1445 to 1446, is the great tower, or *le Dongeon*. This huge building evokes the great towers or keeps that had been a mark of the greatest castles in England since the eleventh century (see 1081 above). It was the architectural centrepiece not only of the castle but the whole lordly estate created by Lord Cromwell, replete with its agricultural buildings, a collegiate church, almshouse, school, market town, fishponds and parkland.

RICHMOND CASTLE
Castleguard

This fifteenth-century view of Richmond Castle, Yorkshire, is a rare example of a topographically accurate medieval view of an English building. It forms part of a manuscript that records the landholdings and duties of the Honour of Richmond, a huge estate granted to Alan Rufus, Count of Penthièvre in Brittany, by William the Conqueror sometime after 1071 (see 1086 above). Alan distributed the lands of the honour to his followers in return for both military and household service. The honour, with Richmond Castle as its focus, was an enormously valuable possession that descended intact into the late Middle Ages. This manuscript – of which there are several copies – was presumably compiled by one of its fifteenth-century owners in order to understand properly how the honour came into being and operated.

ILLUSTRATED here are the responsibilities of several major landholders in the honour to perform garrison duty, termed 'castle guard'. It's compiled for no clear reason with the names of figures alive in the 1190s. Perhaps that was the date of the earliest relevant record available to the clerk. According to this, particular individuals were responsible for defined sections of the defences (identified by their banners). The text beneath reads:

1 Place of Ranulph, son of Robert, in the castle of Richmond by the Chapel of St Nicholas

2 Place of the Constable in the enclosure of the tower

3 Place of Brian, son of Alan, in the great hall of Scolland

4 Place of Torphini, son of Robert Manfeld, between the kitchen and brewhouse

5 Place of Ranulph, son of Henry, to the western side of Scolland's Hall

6 Place of Conan, son of Helie, beside the enclosure of the tower to the eastern part outside the walls [i.e. the barbican]

7 Place of the Chamberlain to the east of Scolland's Hall beside the oven

8 Place of Thomas de Burgo to the west of the greater chapel of the canons within the walls.

By the early thirteenth century the practice of assigning castleguard in the manner shown here was widespread. It almost certainly explains the naming of individual towers in a circuit of walls after families or places, an association also sometimes underlined by the display of heraldry (as, for example, the family arms carved on the Plukenet Tower at Corfe, Dorset). It's not clear when this system first developed but it remained current at least into the fifteenth century. At the siege of Caister, Norfolk, in 1469, for example, a hurriedly assembled garrison of locals and servants was stiffened by a former soldier and four mercenaries. According to an inventory of the castle taken after the siege, at least two of these professionals occupied a tower that was named after them. The mercenaries, some of whom had served in Calais, were described by their employer, Sir John Paston, in a letter dated 9 November 1468, as 'proud men and cunning in the war and in feats of arms, and they can well shoot both guns and crossbows and amend and string them, and devise bulwarks and anything that should be strength to the place'. Clearly, their military expertise spanned the use and maintenance of weaponry as well as the construction of fortifications.

1462
ALNWICK, BAMBURGH AND DUNSTANBURGH CASTLES
A Northern Campaign

The bitterly contested Battle of Towton, fought on Palm Sunday (25 March) 1461 in blizzard conditions, was one of the most important encounters of the civil war known since the nineteenth century as the Wars of the Roses. It secured the throne for the Yorkist king, Edward IV (1461–70, 1471–83), and crippled the Lancastrian cause of his rival Henry VI without quite destroying it. Having escaped into Scotland, Henry VI's queen, Margaret of Anjou, was quick to strike back. She landed at Bamburgh, Northumberland, on 25 October 1462, in hopes of provoking a spontaneous general rising against Edward IV. This did not materialise but Bamburgh and nearby Dunstanburgh castles were rendered up to her by a Lancastrian sympathiser. Soon afterwards Alnwick also capitulated to the queen, allegedly for want of supplies. Edward IV marched north in November at the head of a large Yorkist army but fell ill at Durham. Command therefore passed to the so-called 'Kingmaker', Richard Neville, Earl of Warwick. One of those accompanying the force was John Paston, the seventeen-year-old son of a Norfolk lawyer and gentleman, who wrote to his older brother on 11 December from Newcastle.

The spelling in this letter is modernised but this is the first untranslated text in this book.

Right worshipful brother, I recommend me to you. Please you to know, that this day we had tidings here, that the Scots will come in to England within seven days after the writing of this letter, for to rescue these three castles, Alnwick, Dunstanburgh and Bamburgh, which castles were besieged, as of yesterday. And at the siege of Alnwick lies my lord of Kent and the Lord Scales; and at Dunstanburgh Castle lies the Earl of Worcester and Sir Ralph

Grey; and at the castle of Bamburgh lies the Lord Montague and Lord Ogyll, and other diverse lords and gentlemen that I know not; and there is [available] to them out of Newcastle ordinance enough, both for the sieges and for the field [i.e. battle], in case that there be any field taken, as I trust there shall none be not yet [*sic*], for the Scots keep no promises. My lord of Warwick lies at the castle of Warkworth, but three miles out of Alnwick, and he rides daily to all these castles for to oversee the sieges; and if they want vittles or any other thing, he is ready to purvey it for them to his power. The King commanded my lord of Norfolk for to conduct vittles and the ordinance out of Newcastle on to Warkworth Castle . . . and so we were with my lord of Warwick with the ordinance and vitals yesterday. The King lies at Durham, and my lord of Norfolk at Newcastle. We have people enough here. In case we abide here, I pray you purvey that I may have here more money by Christmas Eve at the furthest, for I may get leave for to send none of my waged men home again; no man can get no leave for to go home but if they steal away, and if they may be known, they should be sharply punished. Make as merry as you can, for there is no jeopardy toward not yet. And [if] there be any jeopardy, I shall soon send you word, by the grace of God. I know well you have more tidings than we have here, but these be true tidings.

Yelverton and Jeney are like for to be greatly punished for because they came not hither to the King. They are marked well enough, and so is John Bylyngforthe and Thomas Plater; wherefore I am right sorry. I pray you let them have warning thereof, that they may purvey their excuse in haste, so that the king may have knowledge why that they come not to him in their own persons; let them come or send excuse to me in writing, and I shall purvey that the King shall have knowledge of their excuse; for I am well acquainted with my Lord Hastings and my Lord Dacre, which be now greatest about the King's person . . .

I pray you let my mother have knowledge how that I, and my fellowship, and your servants are, at the writing of this letter, in good health, blessed be God . . . [John goes on to give numerous other greetings]

ALNWICK, BAMBURGH AND DUNSTANBURGH CASTLES

Written at Newcastle on Saturday next after the Conception of our Lady.

Your John Paston, the youngest

11 December 1462, John Paston letter

THE letter captures the excitement of a young man who finds himself in the centre of events and amidst a great concourse of people. John is clearly delighted to have been charged with the carriage of supplies to the Earl of Warwick the previous day and to relay his connection with those in the king's favour. His comments about the impossibility of getting leave and the punishment of those absent from the campaign underlines the degree to which it was important to Edward IV and his regime.

In the event, all three castles fell by Christmas. Three months later, however, they were yielded up again to a Lancastrian force. Margaret of Anjou pressed her advantage and marched with a force to besiege the Bishop of Durham's castle at Norham. A rapid campaign by the Earl of Warwick relieved Norham, but without a siege train his force was powerless to take the established Lancastrian castles. Indeed, Henry VI remained at Bamburgh and ruled what remained of his kingdom from his three Northumbrian bases for nearly a year. He even attempted, unsuccessfully, to capture Prudhoe Castle, Northumberland. For the first time since the Anglo-Saxon period, and enabled by castles, England had two concurrently regnant kings established within the borders of the kingdom.

1474
A LICENCE TO CRENELLATE
AND IMPARK
William, Lord Hastings

One of Edward IV's most trusted supporters, who shared in his many vicissitudes of fortune and served as both Lord Chamberlain and Lord Treasurer, was William, Lord Hastings. By a royal licence issued at Nottingham on 17 April 1474, he received permission to remodel no fewer than four manor houses across his estates as castles and enclose an astonishing 9,000 acres of parkland with reserved rights of hunting around them. The text reads:

Grant, of special grace, to William Hastings, knight, lord of Hastings, chamberlain, and his heirs, that they may build their manors of Ashby de la Zouch, Bagworth, Thornton and Kirby [Muxloe], co. Leicester, and their castle or manor of Slingsby, co. York, each severally, with stone and mortar, and enclose, wall, crenellate, and furnish the same with battlements and machicolations; and that they impark in Ashby de la Zouch three thousand acres of land and wood of their demesne, and in Bagworth and Thornton two thousand acres, and in Kirby two thousand acres, and in Slingsby two thousand acres, with the power to make deer-leaps in each of the said parks; and they shall have free warren in all their demesne lands and woods in the said counties and in the counties of Lincoln, Northampton, Warwick and Stafford; to hold all the foregoing to them and their heirs, so that no one shall enter the said lands, woods and parks to hunt without licence on pain of forfeiting £10 to the king; provided the said lands are not within the bounds of the king's forest.

17 April 1474, *Calendar of Charter Rolls*

FROM about 1200 the royal chancery (and its equivalents in the quasi-regal jurisdictions of Durham, Chester and the Duchy of Lancaster), amidst their other voluminous outpourings, began issuing licences permitting individuals to fortify or encastellate manors in their possessions with walls, towers and battlements. These licences – as in this case – often incorporated authorisation to enclose land for hunting. In the nineteenth century it was assumed that such licences represented an attempt by the king to regulate castle building in the realm and also precisely dated the buildings they referred to. They consequently became the focus of special study and were termed 'Licences to Crenellate', after the clause they usually incorporate authorising the crenellation – or erection of battlements – on buildings.

Depending on how you define them, about 550 licences of this kind have been identified between about 1194 – when one Richard Vernon was permitted to strengthen his house of Haddon, Derbyshire, with a wall twelve feet high (but, curiously, without battlements) – and 1589, when Sir Moile Finche was licensed to crenellate his mansion house at Eastwell, Kent. The vast majority were issued as 'patent' or public letters; that is to say they took the physical form of a charter with a royal seal attached on a thread of silk. This allowed them to be displayed and was in contrast to 'close' or private letters, where the seal fastened the folded document shut and had to be broken for the text to be read.

Rather than reflecting an attempt to regulate fortification, however, these licences were really passports to respectability, issued (and paid for) in response to a petition. Their value, in other words, was as evidence of social status; proof from the king that the petitioner was of the appropriate status to occupy a castle and hunt. As a consequence, most were supplied to members of the clergy, gentry and religious institutions rather than the high nobility (who usually built castles as they pleased). This licence, however, issued to Lord Hastings, is an exception to this rule and for a good reason: it's hard to parallel the scale or scope of the changes it authorises.

At one fell swoop it establishes the architectural and landed framework for a new lordship focused in Leicestershire irrespective of its historic castles (at least one of which, Belvoir, was actually ruined by Lord Hastings as an act of retribution). It also makes acknowledgement of the Hastings family links since the fourteenth century with Slingsby

Castle, otherwise a curious geographical outpost in this list. No wonder it was issued by 'special grace'.

Edward IV in fact chose to rule the kingdom through a small group of trusted individuals with enormous power in designated regions. In the 1460s, for example, William Herbert dominated Wales, and in the 1470s, Henry Percy, Earl of Northumberland, and his brother, Richard, Duke of Gloucester, controlled the north of England. All of these figures were castle builders. So too was Lord Hastings, who became virtual regent of the Midlands. His principal seat was evidently intended to be at Ashby de la Zouch. Despite the date of the licence, an account roll for the previous year – 1472–3 – reports 'diverse great works within the manor and the wages of carpenters, tillers, masons, plumbers and other artificers and their servants'. The intention seems to have been to create a castle on a square plan dominated in time-honoured fashion by a great tower.

In October 1480, while works were still under way at Ashby, Lord Hastings turned his attention to the rebuilding of Kirby Muxloe. A surviving series of weekly building accounts document the work to this spectacular brick castle encircled by a moat. No other record survives of major building at the other two sites in the licence, though 'Bagworth Castle' was repaired. It was noted in the 1540s by John Leland as 'the ruins of a manor place, like castle building'.

Lord Hastings was unusual among royal favourites for the respect in which he was widely held. That made him a serious obstacle to the ambitions of the royal uncle, Richard, Duke of Gloucester, the Protector and later Richard III, who summarily executed him at the Tower of London. Work to his incomplete castles ceased. With the death of Lord Hastings and the overthrow of Richard III in 1485, Edward IV's reorganisation of the Midlands went into partial reverse. The family rivalries it generated were still being played out in the Civil War of the 1640s.

1485
WARWICK CASTLE
Castles, Lineage and History

The Rous Roll offers an intoxicating mixture of history and legend. In this detail Richard III stands with Warwick Castle in his hand next to the child hero Eneas. An angel gives Eneas the miraculous shield emblazoned with a cross and serpent and he tramples on his vanquished opponent.

From the fourteenth century onwards there came into being an antiquarian tradition that sought to place castles and their development in a historical context. This scholarship was rooted in what we would understand as myth and legend but graduated seamlessly into documentary research and oral history. Its overwhelming obsession was tracing lineage. At Warwick, for example, the castle was connected with the exploits of a legendary paragon of chivalry, Guy of Warwick. One episode in his immensely popular story was given physical form in the fourteenth century: a chapel and effigy of him carved in the living rock were created at Guy's Cliffe, just outside the town, the place where he supposedly died. It attracted tourists of the stature of Henry V.

In the 1440s one John Rous, the son of a local gentry family, became the priest of Guy's Cliffe. Between 1477 and 1485 he compiled two illustrated rolls that told the history of Warwick and its earls, one in Latin and one in English. Each comprises a series of portraits of historical figures presented with a coat of arms and a short biographical text explaining their connection with Warwick. His story begins in legend and is partly rooted in objects held within the castle. Here is the tale of the boy hero Eneas and his cup – freely rendered from Rous's confusing text (clearly a compression of a long tale) – to give a flavour:

> Eneas. A king and queen's son, the eldest of his seven brothers and sisters, which others were at birth by enchantment shaped into swans with collars and chains of gold (a cup was half made of the chains and by a miraculous increase the half grew to the weight of the whole). When his mother was accused by the malice of her stepdame Lady Mattabryn, he – by God's provision, kept by a holy hermit at the day of her judgement, by warning of an angel – at his 7th year of age offered himself to fight for her. And the angel gave him a silver shield bearing the device of a cross with crosslets of gold. And in the battle time out of his cross sprang fire that burnt the eyes of his adversary and after a serpent that stung him to death. Of which Sir Eneas descended many great lords and ladies and especially the Earls of Warwick in whose treasury was kept the cup made of the chain aforesaid. I have drunk of the same [therefore] I dare the better write it.

ENEAS's cup – evidently a prized object in the castle treasury – made the distant past tangible. It had numerous parallels. By the fifteenth century, for example, Battle Abbey, East Sussex, built on the field of Hastings, owned six maple cups believed to have been owned by King Harold. And during the sixteenth century several north-western castles acquired 'lucks', such as the Luck of Muncaster Castle, Cumbria, cups that symbolise the fortunes of the owning family and can never be lost or broken. Rous, however, also sought out documentary evidence that a modern historian would use:

> William the Conqueror by inheritance Duke of Normandy and by conquest King of England . . . He rewarded his lords and gentlemen with marriage and livelihood in England according to their degree . . . Sir Harry Newburgh he made Earl of Newburgh in Normandy and Earl of Warwick in England and gave him the borough of Warwick freely and inseparably as heart and head of the earldom . . . the old privileges which, as by the Conqueror's free gift, the burgesses and inhabitants of the said burgh claim as for their free right unto this day; though they have no writing to show for them for they may not come to the treasury in the castle to seek it. And perhaps [*in hapis nev*] by oft despoiling of the said castle and treasury somewhere might be found some copy of the record of the said Earl Harry's creation with all possessions and freedoms rehearsed. The same king William enlarged the castle and diked the town and gated it and for the enlarging of the castle were pulled down among other things 26 houses that were tenants to the house of monks of Coventry as is written plainly in Domesday

In this passage Rous not only correctly dates the foundation of the castle to the Norman Conquest but refers to Domesday. He also illustrates how jealously guarded the muniment collection of the castle was. Elsewhere Rous commits to writing anecdotes that must be oral traditions derived from his privileged access to the castle and its household. One such, for example, relates to a game of chess during the civil war between Henry III and Simon de Montfort:

> William Mauduit [d. 1268] by title of his mother, Earl of Warwick . . . In his days was great war in the land. He held ever the king's part wherefore Sir Andrew Giffart by treason took the castle of Warwick and for that it should be no strength to the king he beat with his fellowship down the wall from tower to tower which unto Earl Thomas's days [d. 1369] after was hedged.

He took also with him the Earl and the Countess to Kenilworth Castle . . . At which time Dame Alice the Countess playing at chess in Kenilworth Castle with Sir Richard Mandeville knight took one pawn of his. And at the same moment he was challenged . . . at the castle gate. Then rises he and took that knight [at the gate] and brought him to the lady and with him [the prisoner] redeemed or ransom his pawn

It must also have been through conversation that Rous knew of intended work to the castle by Edward IV's brother, who was famously drowned in a butt of sweet wine imported from Greece, called malmsey, in February 1478:

George Duke of Clarence . . . a great alms giver and a great builder as shows at Tutbury, Warwick and other places. And there [at Warwick] in special ways he purposed to have done many things such as walling the town and making an outer ward to the castle, closing in the barn and the stable as the good noble Earl Sir Richard Beauchamp had purposed . . . Also this noble Duke would have made a set park of the Temple Fields against the castle for a Pleasance to be in the castle; and see the deer and the sport of them . . . but froward fortune maligned sore against him and laid all apart

John Rous, *The Rous Roll*

1 4 9 4
DURHAM CASTLE
A Prince Bishop's Palace

The vast hall at Durham Castle. Prior to Foxe's arrival there had been two halls opening to the left and right of the central doorway, each with its own episcopal throne. This unique arrangement expressed the dual secular and ecclesiastical authority of Durham's palatine bishops. Foxe partitioned up the hall to the left, hence the tiers of windows.

Some of the greatest castle builders and patrons of late fifteenth-century England were its bishops and archbishops. Throughout the Middle Ages this small circle of men exerted enormous influence over the secular and religious affairs of the realm and many sees possessed castles (see 1139 and 1375 above). During the Wars of the Roses with their abrupt political shifts, the bench of bishops became important for relative continuity through successive rival administrations. Indeed, in striking contrast to the experience of the nobility, not one of them was executed during the course of this dynastic conflict (though some were disgraced).

In 1494 the remarkable figure of Richard Foxe, one of Henry VII's most trusted servants, was appointed Bishop of Durham. Richard had been present at the Battle of Bosworth in 1485 and was an able diplomat and oversaw the logistics of the English invasion of France in 1492 (where he redesigned the water fortifications of Calais). As Bishop of Durham, Foxe was powerful and rich even by the standards of his peers, enjoying regal authority over what was effectively an independent principality or palatinate on England's northern border, as well as responsibility for its defence. Foxe remained Bishop of Durham for just seven years but in that time he transformed the castle. His achievements are briefly described in an anonymous obituary by a Durham monk:

Richard Foxe was consecrated Bishop of Durham in the year of our Lord 1494. He altered the hall in the castle of Durham, where there had before been two regal seats, one in the higher part of the hall, the other in the lower part of the hall. That in the upper part he left, but the place of the lower seat he enclosed with a buttery and pantry, and over this same work, he created balconies [*sedes*] for trumpeters or other musicians to play, in time of serving meals. And he made a counting house and an ample kitchen. And the household officials and the things pertaining to them, were accommodated with new chambers conveniently situated beside the western part of the hall and kitchen. He erected all in the most sumptuous manner.

He erected and began to build on the high tower of the same castle a hall and kitchen and no more; before he could complete the work he was translated to the Bishopric of Winchester. There was controversy between him and the Earl of Cumberland over the jurisdiction over Hartlepool. He founded a College at Oxford called Corpus Christi; to which he gave many possessions. Moreover he built a chapel of the most sumptuous construction at Winchester and there placed his most honourable tomb

attributed to William Chambre, *History of Durham*

THE great hall and 'high tower' on the motte of Durham Castle already had a long and complex history by the time that Bishop Foxe altered them. Both had most recently been recast more than a century earlier by Bishop Hatfield (d. 1381) and perhaps seemed old-fashioned by the 1490s. It is hard now to say much about Foxe's alterations to the tower because it has been altered so extensively since the sixteenth century. Its hall and kitchen must have been created within the stone shell of Hatfield's existing building, the lower half of which still remains on the castle motte. Presumably, Foxe intended to use the domestic apartments of the tower as a privy lodging, where he could escape from the regimen of life on the grand scale with his household in the castle bailey below. Henry VII was at this time constructing lodgings of this kind at Windsor Castle and lived within them to a degree that struck contemporaries – familiar with their kings living more publicly – as unusual.

The hall, kitchens and services Bishop Foxe created to serve his household, however, still survive virtually intact. This description of what he did only properly makes sense in the light of the unusual arrangements he inherited from Bishop Hatfield. It was Hatfield who had erected the two seats at either end of the hall interior. This unique arrangement aimed to express his dual role as both the secular and ecclesiastical ruler of the palatine of Durham. He had also extended the hall, making it the second biggest room of its kind in England (after the king's hall at Westminster). Foxe's changes to Hatfield's hall, in other words, conformed it to English norms with just one 'high' end to the room. Even in its shortened form, however, it was still a leviathan building and the trumpet lofts he added signalled the splendour and formality of eating here; trumpeting in meat dishes was a royal dignity.

When talking of these changes by Bishop Foxe, the seventeenth-century Oxford antiquarian Anthony à Wood additionally noted that 'on the wall, which parted the said Buttery from the Hall was a great Pelican set up, to show that it was done by him, because he [Foxe] gave the Pelican to his arms'. It's not clear what the authority for this statement is but Foxe certainly did adopt the emblem of a pelican feeding its young with blood pecked from its breast, the so-called 'pelican in its piety', an emblem of Christ's sacrifice for humanity. He also delighted, like many of his contemporaries, in decorating his buildings and possessions with his personal badge.

The kitchen and services added by Foxe were ranged around a timber-frame courtyard. These were not intended to be merely functional buildings but, like the food they produced, objects of opulence and wonder. Lord Darcy was shown them on a tour of the castle in the 1490s and was moved to write admiringly to Foxe: 'My lord, both I and my lady was in all your new works at Durham, and verily they are of the most goodly and best cast that I have seen after my poor mind, and in especial your kitchen passeth all other.' It's not hard to see today what moved him to wonder. The kitchen has huge brick chimneys with battlemented overmantels and the openings through which the food was passed into the courtyard – in fact a marshalling space where processions carrying food into the hall could be ordered – were carved with the words of a grace and the date 1499. It still operates.

As the obituary goes on to note, Foxe was translated to the see of Winchester, one of the richest ecclesiastical appointments in Christendom. He reputedly observed smugly of this appointment that 'Canterbury had a higher seat but Winchester was more succulent'.

1506
CAREW CASTLE
Garter Day with St David and St George

Carew Castle, Pembrokeshire, served as an appropriately martial setting for Sir Rhys ap Thomas's Garter Day celebrations. The grid windows to the right are late sixteenth-century additions to the building he knew. The castle was ruined in 1645 during the Civil War.

In 1505 Henry VII appointed Sir Rhys ap Thomas to the Order of the Garter. The Welshman had been a crucial figure in the Bosworth campaign of 1485, joining with Henry Tudor on his march to the battlefield where Richard III was killed. Sir Rhys subsequently played a leading role in the suppression of several rebellions against Henry VII. He also had numerous mistresses and many children. Unable to attend his inauguration at Windsor on the feast day of St George, the patron of the Order (and of England), he celebrated his new-found dignity a year later at his seat of Carew Castle, Pembrokeshire, on St George's Day, 23 April 1506.

A description of the celebrations, probably derived from a contemporary herald's account, was incorporated into a biography of Sir Rhys compiled in the 1620s by one of his descendants, Henry Rice. The event was a show of unity, drawing together families from across Wales with both Yorkist and Lancastrian sympathies. On the first day Sir Rhys chose five companies – five hundred men – of the 'tallest and ablest' from the assembled concourse. They performed manoeuvres on the second day and on the third, the feast of St George's Day, marched to the Bishop of St David's nearby palace at Lamphey. Here, in a staged entrance, Sir Rhys ostentatiously removed his armour and donned the robes of the Order of the Garter and processed to the chapel for Mass. This was celebrated in the notional presence of the king, who was provided with his own stall. Sir Rhys then returned to Carew with the Bishop, his company saluting the castle with a volley of shot. There he led a group of the most important guests into the building for a banquet past a painting of the patron saints of England and Wales:

St George and St David embracing one another, with this motto *nodo plusquam Gordiano* ['More than a Gordian knot']. In the first court, which was the *Platea* or common place wherein people did use to walk; two hundred tall men were arranged all in blue coats, who made them a lane into another lesser court, called the *pinacotheca*, in which the images, scutcheons, and coat armours, of certain of Sir Rhys's ancestors stood, and so they passed into the great hall, which hall was a goodly spacious room, richly hanged with cloth of arras and tapestry. At the upper end under a plain cloth of state of crimson velvet was provided a cross-table for the king: on each side, down the length of the hall, two other tables, the one for Sir Rhys alone, the other for the rest of the gentlemen. Here every man stood bare [headed], as in the king's presence. Within a while, after the trumpets sounded, and the herald called for the king's service; whereupon all the gentlemen went presently down to wait upon the sewer [who ordered the dishes on the table]. The sewer for the time, Sir Rhys appointed his son, Sir Griffith Rhys, who had been bred up at court, and therefore had some advantage of the rest in point of curiality and courtliness. Sir William Herbert, of Colebrook, the Carver, and Young Griffith, of Penrhyn, the *pocilator* or cupbearer.

When the king's meat was brought to the table, the bishop stood on the right side of the chair and Sir Rhys on the left, and all the while the meat was a laying down, the cornets, hautbois, and other wind instruments were not silent. After the table was served and all set, the bishop made his humble obeisance to the king's chair, and then descended to say grace, which done, he returned again to his former station. Much pleasant discourse passed between them for a time, which ever and anon was seasoned with diversity of music. When they saw their time, the table was voided and the meat removed to the side board for the waiters. Then the king's chair was turned and so every man [was] at liberty to put on his hat. The king's service being finished, Sir Rhys went to his own table, taking only the bishop along with him, whom he placed at the upper end at a mess all alone, and himself at some distance sat him down at another. All the gentlemen there present were pleased; for Sir Rhys's more honour, to stand by and give him the looking on, until his first course was served . . . The fare they had, you will easily believe was good, being provided as for the king. Such cheer as they had, was attended with much pleasant discourse, diverse passages of mirth, free from all offence, passed from one to the other. The king, queen, and prince's health were often drunk among them and the bards, prydydds accompanied by the harp sang many a song in commemoration of the virtues and famous achievements of those gentlemen's ancestors there present

Henry Rice, *A Life of Sir Rhys ap Thomas*

RATHER than a drunken revel of popular fiction, a late medieval celebration was opulent, theatrical and regimented. Its visual gestures were obvious and given emphasis by the quantity of people involved. A case in point was the painting of two saints, their embrace more inextricable than the Gordian Knot (an intractable bond that Alexander the Great cut open with his sword). Also, the two hundred men in blue coats – the colour of the Order of the Garter – lining the route to the feast.

The crucial point of emphasis here was Sir Rhys's personal connection with the king, hence the service of a meal to an empty chair. This was very complex in point of etiquette, which explains the noted advantage of Sir Griffith Rhys acting as sewer after spending time at court. It's likely that the Latin names given to the different parts of the castle were dreamt up to lend a further veneer of sophistication to the occasion.

Whatever the case, the castle offered an appropriately martial backdrop to what Sir Rhys also evidently intended to be a celebration of his ancestry and military prowess. In the former regard, the decoration of the inner court (or *pinacotheca*) with an armorial history of his forebears is significant. So too the distinctively Welsh touch of the songs of the bards.

The banquet took most of the day but afterwards formal challenges were issued for the jousting the next day. Sir Rhys presided over the occasion as a judge in gilt armour and ingeniously managed to declare everyone a winner, an important thing if the party was to break up cheerfully. The next day, to the same end and by prior arrangement, he declared his son the loser of another encounter. There followed some hunting, the performance of a comedy and a sermon. As the gentlemen departed Sir Rhys distributed blue ribbands as tokens of the occasion, just as Edward III did after his Round Table (see 1344 above).

Carew Castle is today a ruin but a great bed doubtless made for it by Sir Rhys survives at St Fagans outside Cardiff. It is appropriately carved with scenes of battle as well as the emblem of the Order of the Garter.

1520
DOVER CASTLE
A Diplomatic Encounter

A detail of a sixteenth-century painting of the Field of Cloth of Gold showing Henry VIII's palace with its sculpted figures hurling stones from the turrets, an idea first encountered in English architecture in the thirteenth century. The building was a temporary structure erected for the event.

While Henry VIII and his courtiers built and occupied buildings designed and furnished in the most up-to-date fashion, ancient castles remained important residences and might even continue to serve as Tudor palaces. In 1518, after complex negotiations, Cardinal Wolsey secured a universal peace treaty between all the major powers of Europe. It was a considerable diplomatic achievement (though, perhaps inevitably, it secured nothing of the kind). Bound up with the negotiations was an agreement that Henry VIII would meet the French king, Francis I, the following year. That event was postponed, however, to accommodate the election of the new Holy

Roman Emperor in 1519. Francis I entered the polls and so too, incredibly, did Henry VIII. Both lost, however, to the Hapsburg contender Charles V, who now additionally suggested a 'passing visit' to England on his journey from Spain to the Low Countries. To accommodate this Henry VIII delayed his departure to meet Francis I and, after remaining windbound in Corunna for an entire month, Charles V finally arrived off Dover on 26 May. An anonymous herald describes his reception and accommodation in Dover Castle on the first night of his four-day stay in England:

The Emperor landed at Dover in whose company was the Queen of Aragon with diverse and many noble estates which were received at the seaside by the Lord Cardinal with diverse of the Lords and gentles; which emperor so accompanied at 10 of the clock at night by torchlight was brought to the castle of Dover where he rested that night. And there Sir Edward Ponynge at that time Lord Warden of the Cinque Ports brought the keys of the castle onto the Emperor who made answer like an honourable prince saying that he would none receive for he knew well that he was out of danger and in as great safeguard as though he were in his own realm or dominion. The same night about two of the clock after midnight the King's Highness came to Dover by torchlight and as soon as the Emperor heard of his coming he rose and met with the King at the stairhead whereas either of them embraced the other in arms full lovingly so that it was right honourable to see the meeting of these two excellent princes and there they talked familiarly a long time together and always the King our master had the Emperor on his right hand.

An anonymous herald's account

THE meetings of kings and emperors was a rarity not least because the attendant risks were so great. Quite apart from the dangers of treachery – hence the offer made to the emperor of the key to the castle and his friendly rejection of it – there was the more straightforward problem that monarchs used to having their own way in everything might not enjoy the company of an equal. Maintaining in public the good temper of two individuals intensely jealous of their honour and sensitive to the niceties of protocol was no small challenge either. The hurried arrival of Henry VIII by torchlight speaks of an urgent desire to welcome and please his guest; as does the emperor's reciprocal gesture of rising and dressing at 2 a.m. to meet his host.

Their place of meeting at the 'stairhead' can be precisely located on the landing at the entrance to the great tower or keep of the castle, built in the 1180s. This landing was just outside the royal lodging itself, implying that the castle had become the emperor's and that he had courteously stepped outside it to greet his guest. In a carefully managed return, however, Henry VIII stood as host with the emperor on his right. The next morning Henry and Charles set off with all their attendants to Canterbury, where they were entertained in the Archbishop of Canterbury's palace. After a visit to the shrine of Thomas Becket they rested and then went to Mass. Dinner that night was served to the accompaniment of music sounded by the emperor's trumpeters and the next day his household served a feast that continued into the early hours. The following day the party rode back towards Dover and divided, with the emperor departing via Sandwich. Henry VIII returned to Dover Castle, where he stayed for three days before setting sail for Calais. For him, there followed one of the most famous diplomatic encounters of his reign.

To the roar of gunfire in the late afternoon of 7 June 1520, the Feast of Corpus Christi, Henry VIII rode through the gates of Guînes in the Pas-de-Calais with a great retinue of 3,500 men on foot and horseback. He was travelling to meet Francis I, King of France, who set out from nearby Ardres to arrive with a similarly brave – some said braver – show at exactly the same moment. The two monarchs met midway on what was then English soil, riding forward to embrace each other on horseback. Their meeting was the opening episode in an exactingly choreographed eighteen-day encounter amid tents and temporary buildings familiarly known as the Field of Cloth of Gold. The centrepiece of the English camp – famously recorded in an anonymous painting – was a temporary palace in the form of a castle with towers, battlemented walls and the figures of defenders hurling stones. It was architectural theatre but it spoke eloquently of the most admired quality in international relations then and now: might. Castle architecture celebrated this quality better than any other.

A century later the keep at Dover was again renovated and pressed into service as the point of reception for another royal visit, the arrival of Charles I's bride Henrietta Maria. Its cosmetic modernisation did not impress her chamberlain, who derisively described the building as 'made *à l'antique*. A little tablet was erected in the building, now lost, that commemorated the occasion with a couplet: 'All places of this Castle, only this / Where Charles and Mary, shar'd a Royal kiss.' This twelfth-century building could still serve as a royal palace five centuries after its first construction.

1 5 2 1
THORNBURY CASTLE
A Ducal Seat

Thornbury Castle, Gloucestershire, in 1822 by J. C. Buckler, showing the 'stately lodging' with its magnificent compass windows and ornamental chimneys that in 1521 overlooked a formal garden enclosed by battlemented walls and two-storey timber galleries. The galleries led to the adjacent 'chapel and parish church'. The north side of the inner court is just visible to the right.

On 16 April 1521, the Duke of Buckingham was arrested on board his barge on the River Thames. A descendant of Edward III, he had a claim to the throne to rival that of Henry VIII. That fact, combined with his haughty and reckless behaviour, made him many enemies and an easy target for court intrigue. He was arraigned for treason before his peers in Westminster Hall and executed a month and a day after his arrest. European observers were aghast at his treatment but it was grist for the mill in Tudor England. The king's officers were quick to survey his immense estates and their report provides a snapshot of his multiple residences including a clutch of castles. The chief of these – and the place he had been summoned from prior to his arrest – was at Thornbury, Gloucestershire. In 1521 the castle was in the process of splendid reconstruction around two square wards or courts. The survey additionally takes the reader into the gardens, enclosed by walls and galleries, and then to the orchard and parkland beyond:

The manor or castle there standeth on the north side of the parish church having an inner ward and an outer ward four square. The coming and outing into the said inner ward is on the west side. The south side is fully finished with curious works and stately lodging. The said west side and north side be but builded to one chamber height. All these works being of fair ashlar [cut stone] and so covered with a false roof of elm and the same covered with light slate.

The east side containing the hall and other houses of office is all of the old building and of an homely fashion.

The outer ward was intended to have been large with many lodgings; whereof the foundation on the north and west side is taken and brought up nigh to laying on a floor. The windows, jambs, cevones [?] with other like things are throughout of free [cut] stone; and the residue of rough stone cast with lime and sand.

On the south side of the said inner ward is a proper garden and about the same a goodly gallery conveying above and beneath from the principal lodging both to the chapel and parish church. The outer part of the said gallery being of stone embattled and the inner part of timber covered with slate.

On the east side of the said castle or manor is a goodly garden to walk in closed with high walls embattled. The conveyance thither is by the gallery above and beneath and by other privy ways.

Besides the same privy garden is a large and goodly orchard full of young grafts well laden with fruit, many roses and other pleasures. And in the same orchard are many goodly alleys to walk in openly. And roundabout the same orchard is conveyed on a good height; others goodly alleys with resting [*roosting*] places covered thoroughly with white thorn and hazel. And without the same on the outer part the said orchard is enclosed with sawn pale and without that ditches and quickset hedge.

From out of the said orchard are diverse posterns [gates] in sundry places at pleasure to go and enter into a goodly park newly made called the New Park having in the same no great plenty of wood but many hedgerows of thorne and great elms. The same park contains nigh on 4 miles about and in the same be 700 deer or more.

The late Duke of Buckingham hath enclosed in the said park diverse men's lands as well of free hold as copy hold and no recompense as yet is made for the same . . . wherin of necessity some redress must be [made].

1521, an anonymous survey

THE account goes on to describe two other older parks adjoining the castle, Marlwood with three hundred deer, and Eastwood with at least five hundred fallow deer and fifty red deer.

Thornbury Castle was never completed but its ruins survived to be restored and that makes it easy to understand what the surveyor saw in 1521. The incomplete outer ward remains. So too the lodging range with its 'curious works', by which the surveyor clearly meant its elaborate projecting windows and richly carved brick chimney stacks. One of these chimneys is dated 1516 and carved with tiny arrow loops and battlements, like a miniature castle. The surveyor notes that the 'stately lodging' is built of cut stone, a very expensive finish relative to the rubble masonry with cut stone detailing of the outer ward. It was all better, however, than the merely 'homely' quality of the earlier manor buildings that would no doubt have been swept away had the work continued.

The lodgings overlooked a 'privy garden', which still preserves its enclosing and battlemented wall of stone. Built against this wall were the two-storey galleries that gave access to the gardens and also to the chapel and parish church (which was also superbly rebuilt in this period). Excavation of the lower gallery walks has revealed floor tiles decorated with the Stafford family emblem of a knot. This device was also created in the garden itself as a planted pattern. Opening from this relatively small and formally designed garden was an orchard with walks, alleys and bowers; even the surveyor, weighing everything up with an eye to its value, sounds impressed. And from this opens up the first of three parks. It's so new that the stands of trees have yet to mature. That the duke has enclosed land without recompensing existing owners is a reminder of how intrusive parks were and the degree to which the powerful could act with impunity when it came to developing their houses and associated amenities. It's frustrating that the surveyor takes us around the castle without going into it but the contents of the building were not his responsibility.

1522 AND 1536
FARLEIGH HUNGERFORD CASTLE
Murder and Poison

Castles continued throughout the Tudor period to figure as a backdrop to the domestic lives of noble families. Their role was not always a happy one. Farleigh Hungerford Castle, for example, was the setting of extreme domestic cruelty over three sequential generations. On Monday 25 August 1522 two yeomen, William Mathewe and William Inges, late of Heytesbury, were brought to court at Ilchester, Somerset, and charged with a brutal murder four years previously on 26 July 1518. The timing of the trial, which explicitly implicated Lady Agnes Hungerford – the chatelaine of the castle – as having directed their crime, was no coincidence. She had just been widowed and presumably, therefore, her husband, Edward, Lord Hungerford, had both known about it and protected those responsible. The court roll states that the two yeomen:

with force and arms made an assault upon John Cotell, at Farley, in the county of Somerset, by the procurement and abetting of Agnes Hungerford . . . And a certain linen scarf called a *kerchier* which the aforesaid William, and William, then and there held in their hands, put round the neck of the aforesaid John Cotell . . . and there feloniously did throttle, suffocate, and strangle [him] . . . And afterwards the aforesaid William, and William, the body of the aforesaid John Cotell did then and there put into a certain fire in the furnace of the kitchen in the Castle of Farley aforesaid, and the body of the same John in the fire aforesaid in the Castle of Farley aforesaid in the county of Somerset aforesaid did burn and consume . . . The jurors being sworn found each of the prisoners to be guilty of the crimes with which they were charged.

27 November 1522, Coram Rege Roll

THE base of the oven in which the murderers disposed of the body still survives in the ruins of the castle. So too does a tower that was perhaps the setting for another act of domestic cruelty exacted by Edward's son and heir, Walter, on his third wife, Elizabeth. She was the daughter of John, Lord Hussey of Sleaford, who recommended his future son-in-law to the service of Henry VIII's secretary Thomas Cromwell. The connection served both men well but the marriage was a disaster. In 1536 Elizabeth wrote to Cromwell in piteous terms stating that she was a prisoner in a tower at Farleigh Hungerford Castle. The letter goes on to explain that Lord Hungerford had tried to divorce Elizabeth on false grounds. Also, that an instruction by Cromwell that he should pay his wife's maintenance had encouraged his chaplain, John Lee, to try and poison her:

> And so am I, your most woefullest and poorest beads woman, left in worse case that ever I was, as a prisoner alone, and continually locked in one of my lord's towers of his castle in Hungerford, as I have been these three or four years past, without comfort of any creature, and under the custody of my lord's chaplain, Sir John Lee, which hath once or twice heretofore poisoned me . . . I have oft feared, and yet do every day more than other, to taste either of the meat or drink . . . wherefore many and sundry times I have been and yet am fain to drink water, or else I should die for lack of sustenance, and had, long ere this time, had not poor women of the country, of their charity, knowing my lord's demeanour always to his wives, brought me to my great window in the night such meat and drink as they had, and gave me for the love of God, for money have I none wherewith to pay them, nor yet have had of my lord these four years four groats.
>
> And thus, my singular good lord, I am like to perish I fear me very soon, unless your good lordship, moved with pity and compassion, will command my said lord Hungerford, now being in London as I believe, to bring me before your lordship . . . and to the intent that I may, upon causes reasonable, be divorced from my said lord, or else require him to suffer me to come out of prison. And then will I come up on foot with some poor body unto your lordship, for the security of my life, if it may please you

to condescend thereunto, as I shall most humbly beseech your good lordship, for surely I will not longer continue this wretched life with him; I had rather destroy myself, or beg my living from door to door. And therefore, on the reverence of Jesus Christ, let not his fair, crafty, and subtle tongue longer defraud your good lordship in this matter. But require his lordship to send for me, and safely to be brought before your lordship, without further delay; or else to command some other man at your lordship's pleasure to fetch me from him. And in so doing I shall be most bound to pray, as I do evermore, to God for the preservation of your honourable estate long to endure.

By your most bounden beadswoman

Undated letter of about 1536 from Elizabeth, Lady
Hungerford to Thomas Cromwell

Elizabeth's description of herself as a beadswoman – a woman who prays on behalf of another – underlines her abject dependence on Cromwell, though it's not clear if the letter had any effect. She did outlive her husband, however; Lord Hungerford was executed on Tower Hill on 28 July 1540, for treason and a variety of charges including sodomy. He died on the same day as his patron, Cromwell. Elizabeth went on to marry again, this time to the Catholic gentleman Robert Throckmorton of Coughton, Warwickshire, who was knighted in 1553, the year before her death. Lord Hungerford's son and heir was married twice and, in re-enactment of his father's behaviour, divorced and abandoned his second wife, for which he was in turn imprisoned.

1539
DEAL CASTLE
Resisting Invasion

This drawing of a 'Castle in the Downes' is a presentation design resembling Deal Castle, Kent, one element of the fortifications built by Henry VIII to command the anchorage beneath the Downs during the political crisis and invasion scare of 1539. The design was almost certainly drawn up by royal craftsmen active at Hampton Court Palace, which helps explain its resemblance to the battlemented banqueting houses erected in the pleasure grounds there. Common to both are centralised and lobed plans, which were evidently admired as perfect architectural forms. Henry VIII's fourth wife, Anne of Cleves, was feasted in the incomplete shell of Deal Castle when she first landed on English soil in December 1539; presumably she was meant to admire the conceptual complexity of the building.

FEW English medieval architectural drawings or 'plats' survive. This example, however, gives some idea of the conventions used in the most sophisticated. The bird's-eye view simultaneously indicates elevation and plan. Excitingly depicted with roaring guns (but without gunners), it's also an image calculated to catch the eye of Henry VIII. The castle comprises a central tower encircled by lobed earthworks. Its lowest level is countersunk in the depth of the moat. Entrance to the building is via the bridge in the foreground and the interior of the lobe is walled off for security.

Viewed in the context of artillery fortifications elsewhere in Europe, where the value of angle bastions that created forts on star-shaped plans was understood, the design looks deeply eccentric.

The invasion scare of 1539 prompted the wholesale survey of royal castles across the realm. It also resulted in the construction of seventy-three new fortifications right around the coast of England and Wales as well as in Jersey and the Channel Islands. By 1547 they had absorbed the stupendous sum of £376,500, the vast majority of it derived from the suppression of the monasteries. Henry VIII's vanished palace at Nonsuch, Surrey, the prodigy building of his reign, cost a mere £25,000.

1540
BELVOIR CASTLE
A Castle Restored

Sir Thomas Manners, Lord Roos, won himself a place in the intimate circle of the young Henry VIII by his skill at jousting. As a reward, in 1525 he was created Earl of Rutland, a title that virtually demanded that he restore the ruinous family castle of Belvoir, Leicestershire, beside his titular county. Henry VIII's chief mason, carpenter and plumber were accordingly dispatched to Belvoir in 1528. A decade later the earl was a major beneficiary of the suppression of the monasteries, securing the property of several in 1539 including neighbouring Belvoir Priory and Croxton Abbey. These both stood close to the area recently affected by the Pilgrimage of Grace, a popular uprising catalysed by Henry VIII's closure of monasteries. The earl, therefore, made a concerted attempt to transform the now-empty monasteries, with a particular focus on sweeping away their churches. Surviving accounts from 1540–3, some bound in pages cut from monastic manuscripts, record the expansion of Belvoir Castle with a grand new gallery and works to the great hall, in part using materials from Croxton Abbey (which he also adapted for use as a lodge to the castle). In 1540 there are entries for:

Item paid to . . . John Hall for four days casting down stone at the abbey church for the new cause in the castle ward.

Item paid to Samson Ausebroke for his board wages working at Thurgarton upon the gallery made to stand between my Lord's lodging and the nursery in Belvoir Castle, from June 6 to July 3, at 16 pence the week.

Item paid to Richard Williamson, junior, for 4 weeks board wages working upon the ceiling of the hall in the castle, at 16 pence the week.

AUSEBROKE, one of two carpenters of this name in the accounts, was evidently framing timbers for the new gallery remotely, a common medieval practice. Thurgarton is about fifteen miles from Belvoir across the River Trent in Nottinghamshire.

The destruction of Croxton Abbey continued into 1541, presumably to supply the castle with materials, and the new gallery at Belvoir was finished with a costly bay window of cut stone. So too was the hall roof with a louvre over the central hearth. This must have been a showpiece and its well-paid creator was brought in specially from Enfield, Essex:

Item, May 21, to Adam Walson for two dozen ties [of trettes] for scaffolds at Croxton, when he took down the window above the high altar and other stone 12 pence.

Item paid, July 6, to Thomas Myner for plucking down of the steeple at Croxton, by great [altogether] 40 shillings 4 pence.

Item paid, June 4, to John Smyth, of Cawton, freemason, for two weeks work in hewing of the free stone for the bay window in the new gallery, at three shillings four pence the week.

Item paid, October 1, to William Chapman, of Enfield, carpenter, for 16 days work about the louver for the hall at eight pence the day, and for his son for like work.

Item paid, the last day of July, to [eighteen] diverse workmen in casting [earth] down the hill beside the causeway [cawsey] before the porter's ward, and the hill of the backside of the great tower.

This last earth-moving operation comprised sixty-two days of labour and may have related to terracing in the garden, which was now furnished with another borrowed building of timber, a banqueting house:

Paid, August 27, to Sampson Ausebroke for his board wages and the charges off his horse at Nottingham by the space of four days in taking down the banqueting house there, and one day in providing of carriages to bring home the same timber . . . Harry Ausebroke for working at Nottingham Castle in taking down the banqueting house by the space of three days and for working in the chambers over the wardrobe at Belvoir by the space of 2 days . . . Robert Forster the like.

Item paid to Edmond Wilkinson for two days at Belvoir and two days at Croxton in taking up paving stone for the entry going into the hall at Belvoir.

In this way the ruin of other buildings augmented Belvoir. The accounts are otherwise full of curious detail. Here are clutch of reward payments that give a glimpse of life in the castle in 1541:

Item, January 23, to the keeper servant that keeps two of the Queen's Graces bears which was baited at the castle of Belvoir 20 pence.

Item to the children of Newarke which played at Belvoir the Twelfth Day [Twelfth Night] in reward then 5 shillings.

Item to the players of Nottingham here the Twelfth Day in reward, 3 shillings 4 pence.

Item, March 6, to Mr. Markham barber for hair cutting [*nottyng*] my Lord Talbot, Lord Roos and the rest of my Lord's children, Browne, Pollard and Strelley, against my Lord his coming from the court 2 shillings.

Item given in reward . . . to a servant of Sir William Bassett's which was a baker for his service done at the bakehouse for the trial of his cunning 20 pence.

Smartening up the family in anticipation of the earl's return suggests he was a formidable father. More certainly, the family loved delicacies and the baking competition is entirely in character and a reminder of the splendour of the late medieval table.

1545
WRESSLE CASTLE
A Study in Paradise

A view of the late fourteenth-century castle at Wressle, Yorkshire. The Paradise was in the top of the tower to the right. Sadly, nothing survives of its furnishings. The exterior of the building is austerely detailed to give an outward impression of strength. This treatment was appropriate to a castle and set off the opulence of the interiors to advantage.

One remarkable source of information about castles in the mid-sixteenth century derives from the topographical notes in Latin and English of John Leland, a self-styled 'antiquarius' (or antiquarian), a title borrowed from Continental humanist usage. He toured the threatened monastic libraries of England during the 1530s in pursuit of manuscripts and became interested in the topography of England. He claimed that there were no 'castles, principal manor places, monasteries and colleges, but I have seen them and noted in so doing a whole world of things very memorable'. Leland went mad around 1547.

One of his most enthusiastic castle descriptions relates to Wressle,
Yorkshire, built in the late fourteenth century. Leland was clearly surprised
that something so old could be so fine. As with most Tudor observers, the
merely venerable held no charms for him. He describes a building of two
courts – the outer or 'base court', with its service buildings, was largely of
timber frame but the inner was of stone with corner towers and a gatehouse.
Parts of the latter still survive in ruins. As a bibliophile, he was particularly
struck by a study in one of the towers called Paradise. His description suggests
a series of eight book cupboards, each surmounted by a reading desk or lectern
that could be pulled down breast high on channels to rest books at a
convenient height for reading:

Most part of the base court of the castle of Wressle is all of timber.
The castle itself is moated about on three-parts. The fourth part is
dry where the entry is into the castle. The castle is all of very fair
and great squared stone both within and without. Whereof (as
some hold opinion) much was brought out of France. In the castle
be only five towers, one at each corner almost of like bigness. The
gatehouse is the fifth, having five lodgings in height, three of
the other towers have four heights in lodgings: the fourth contains
the buttery, pantry, pastry lardery and kitchen. The hall and the
great chambers be fair, and so is the chapel and the closets.

To conclude, the house is one of the most proper beyond
Trent and seemeth as newly made: yet it was made by a younger
brother of the Percys, Earl of Worcester, that was in high favour
with Richard II . . .

The base court is of newer building . . . One thing I liked
exceedingly in one of the towers, was a study called Paradise,
where was a closet in the middle of eight squares latticed about:
and at the top of every square was a desk ledged to set books on
coffers within them and these seemed as joined hard to the top of
the closet and yet by pulling one or all would come down, breast
high in rebates, and serve for desks to lay books on.

The gardrobe in the castle was exceedingly fair. And so were
the gardens within the moat, and the orchards without. And in
the orchards were mounts of topiary work [*opera topiario*] writhen
[twisting] about with degrees like turnings of cockleshells, to

come to the top without pain. The River Derwent runneth almost hard by the castle and about a mile lower goes into Ouse. This river at great rains rages and overflows much of the ground there about being low meadows. There is a park hard by the castle.

John Leland, *Itinerary*

THE final description of the gardens and park as an integral part of the whole is strongly evocative of the description of Thornbury (see 1521 above). The existence of topiary is a particular curiosity and the failure of Leland's English and his careful description of the corkscrew cut hints at its oddity. Surely this must be some of the earliest seen in Britain.

Leland evidently relied on the servants of the castle to tell him about the history of the building. Indeed, this is what he always did. It's a reminder that in the sixteenth century there were no other obvious sources of information about buildings or places beyond what locals told you. Then, as now, such sources of information could be wildly inaccurate. That's the case here: the castle is in fact built of local limestone.

A few years prior to Leland's visit, in August 1537, an official, Robert Southwell, wrote a letter to Thomas Cromwell, the king's secretary, from Wressle. He was reporting on a complete survey of the estates of the late Earl of Northumberland. The earl had used the castle as his principal seat. He died after a long, painful illness in his mid-thirties. Estranged from his wife and without children, he bequeathed nearly all his estates to the king.

Southwell reported that he had never seen a finer inheritance more blemished by the folly of its owner and the dishonesty of his servants but marvelled at its overall magnificence. 'The honours and castles [of the late earl]', he concluded, 'purport such a majesty in themselves . . . as they are in manner as mirrors or glasses for the inhabitants 20 miles compass every way from them to look in and to direct themselves by.' There could be no clearer indication of the admiration these great buildings both ancient and modern commanded, nor of their continued dominance in the English landscape.

1553
FRAMLINGHAM CASTLE
Securing the Succession

Mary retired to the safety of the twelfth-century walls of Framlingham, Suffolk, as she prepared to assert her claim to the crown in 1553. Set on each of the towers that encircle the castle is a richly decorated late medieval brick chimney, an outward expression of the comforts within this fortification.

The death of Edward VI at Greenwich on 6 July 1553 set in train an internal crisis over the succession to the throne. The Duke of Northumberland, who controlled the government, famously undertook a self-interested attempt to install the sixteen-year-old Lady Jane Grey (Northumberland's daughter-in-law) as queen instead of Henry VIII's daughter, Mary Tudor. Mary was not prepared to be denied her inheritance. She slipped away to Kenninghall, Suffolk, where her cause began to attract wide support. When Northumberland marched from London to capture her she moved for security to Framlingham Castle. This narrative of these dramatic events was written in Latin by a Suffolk gentleman, Robert Wingfield of Brantham, an eyewitness and fervent supporter of Mary.

Now that men from all ranks of life were joining her every day, the queen's forces were wonderfully strengthened and augmented, and on the sovereign's instructions her personal council discussed how they could best move their headquarters; for with consummate judgement the queen recognised that her house was utterly inadequate to withstand an enemy attack or fitly to accommodate her much increased forces and household. Therefore after suitable consideration they very wisely chose Framlingham, the strongest castle in Suffolk, and the ancient capital seat of the famous Dukes of Norfolk, where they might await further reinforcement and, if necessity demanded, fight a determined enemy with steadfastness and courage for the right to the throne . . .

She hurried on to reach Framlingham Castle about 8 o'clock in the evening, where as many as possible of the local gentry and justices, together with a crowd of country folk, awaited her highness's arrival in the deerpark lying below the castle.

IN occupying Framlingham, Mary was using the castle as a military base from which she could either defend herself or launch an attack on her enemies. While she waited there the ranks of her supporters were swelled by a continuous stream of arrivals. Many of her followers had no military experience and were rapidly trained up by her commanders. She agreed to inspect a review of her troops beneath the walls of the castle on 20 July and showed as much delight in the martial display as her father might have done:

When the battle-line seemed fully drawn up, sacred Mary rode out from Framlingham Castle about 4 o'clock (the day was a Thursday), to muster and inspect this most splendid and loyal army. While her Majesty was approaching, the white horse which she was riding became rather more frisky at the unaccustomed sight of such an army drawn up in formation than her womanly hesitancy was prepared to risk, so she ordered her foot soldiers, active and dutiful men, to lift up their hands to help their sovereign . . .

Her Majesty, now on foot, went round both divisions of the army speaking to them with exceptional kindness and with an approach so wonderfully relaxed as can scarcely be described, in consideration of their esteem for their sovereign, that she completely won everyone's affections. After this inspection of the divisions, scarcely had the queen remounted her horse when a large detachment of cavalry suddenly streamed forth and beat and trod the ground with such a thunderous noise and spread so widely through the field that it seemed like one enemy in pursuit of another.

The queen was much delighted with this show and spent three hours there before returning to the castle. On her return she was greeted with most welcome news, scarcely to be hoped for, that Northumberland had abandoned hope of success because of the continual desertions of his supporters, and on 19 July had likewise taken flight from Bury in the middle of the night

Robert Wingfield, The Life of Mary Queen of England (trans. D. MacCulloch)

Northumberland was soon arrested and the queen made a triumphal progress to London, staying en route in Robert Wingfield's house in Ipswich. It's noteworthy that Mary's coup mounted from East Anglia is the only example of a successful uprising against the authority of central government in the Tudor period. Mary also became the first regnant queen of England. Both achievements, fundamentally, reflected Mary's popularly perceived legitimacy as Henry VIII's heir.

1554
COOLING CASTLE
The Spanish Marriage

Mary's determination to marry Philip II of Spain proved enormously unpopular and in 1554 provoked a circle of former soldiers to plan rebellions in different parts of the country. All the uprisings were unsuccessful except that organised in Kent by Thomas Wyatt. Having planned his rebellion at Allington Castle, Wyatt raised his standard in neighbouring Maidstone on 25 January. The rebel forces in Kent failed to meet but at Rochester a government force led by the Duke of Norfolk defected to Wyatt. His enlarged force then marched on to deal with Lord Cobham at his castle at Cooling, where the local levies had been gathered. Cooling fell around nightfall to the rebels and Lord Cobham penned this hurried – and in the original largely unpunctuated – note to explain his failure:

To the Queen's most excellent majesty – haste, haste, post haste, with all diligence possible, for thy life, for thy life

It may please your most excellent Majesty to be advertised that this day at 9 o'clock Wyatt with his whole force of 2000 men and above removed from Rochester and approached to my castle, assaulting the same in most forcible manner they could; but I declaring my true subjection towards your highness and calling them traitors made to them defiance resisting their force and defending my castle with such power as I had until 5 o'clock at after noon having no other munitions or weapons but four or five handguns four pikes and the rest blackbills (the fault whereof I may well ascribe unto your grace's officers of the bulwarks and ships making earnest request, as well to my Lord of Norfolk as to them, for the same howbeit I could never get none). The rebels perceiving that I was bent to resist them – having two g[reat] pieces of ordinance [guns] that the Duke of Norfolk left among them at his retiring – laid battery to the gate of the castle, and also did fire the same. And [they also] laid four other pieces to another side of the castle, which did so sore batter the castle and the gates that without that they could never have prevailed. At which assault four or five of my men were slain and diverse hurt, which did so discourage the commons that I had therein assembled for the service of your highness, that they began to mutiny and whisper to one another. And I there standing in defence at the gates, with my sons against them, in doubtful assault until my gates with the drawbridges were so battered and fired down but they were ready to invade me. I perceiving behind me both my men to shrink from [me] and my shot to be wasted was then compelled to yield; where if power had served to my true heart and service towards your highness I would have died in your grace's quarrel. If your grace therefore will assemble such force in convenient time as were able to encounter with so few in number – being not above 2000 men and yet not 500 of them able and good armed men, but rascals and rake-hells as live by spoil – I doubt not but your grace shall have the victory of them so [provided] that they be guided and manhandled by such an approved captain as can discreetly lead them. They [the rebels] enforced me to promise them, upon mine honour, to be with them tomorrow at Gravesend. Yet notwithstanding I will remain faithful in heart towards your highness advertising [relaying to] your grace from time to time of their proceedings. And for the better trial of my good service towards your highness to be done unfeignedly, yea, and more effectually than I have written, it may please your grace to send someone whom your grace shall appoint to view my house, whereby your grace shall understand that I have – as well in this as in all other your grace's former commandments – shewed myself a true and ready servitor towards your highness. Although I understand I have been otherwise reported to your highness, wherein my doings and the country shall utter and witness the truth as my conscience hath inwardly meant good faith towards your grace, which I shall so continually bear while life doth last. Thus making my continual prayer for the preservation of your highness with strength and fortune to subdue your enemies I most humbly take my leave of your grace from Cooling Castle in haste the 30 January 1553 [1554]

Your grace's most humble and true subject and servant to the end

Letter to Queen Mary

COOLING Castle was constructed in the 1380s by John, 3rd Lord Cobham. It stands on a low, marshy site and in 1554 comprised two rectangular baileys walled in stone and with drum-shaped angle towers. The water-filled moats around would have provided it with its defensive strength and explain why Wyatt focused his energies on the gate, which was relatively accessible. This building still survives and it doesn't look particularly defensible. Rather, it bears a remarkable fourteenth-century brass inscription in the form of a sealed charter bearing the rhyme: 'Know those that are and who shall be, that I am made in help of the country; in knowledge of which thing, this is charter and witnessing.'

In his letter Lord Cobham emphasises that the castle only fell because of Wyatt's artillery (which he notes had been captured from the Duke of Norfolk). Clearly he thought the damage done to the building would be sufficient to persuade an impartial observer of the intensity of the fighting, hence his request for an official to visit and bear witness to his account. Assuming he was telling the truth about the numbers of weapons he possessed, it's hard to imagine how Lord Cobham made any effective resistance at all. Again, it's made clear that this lack was not the result of carelessness but reflected his earlier attempts to satisfy the queen's officers and the Duke of Norfolk's needs.

Wyatt marched on from Cooling to London, where he found the gates of London Bridge held against him. Crossing the Thames at Kingston he marched towards the City from the west. He eventually surrendered on Fleet Street and was later tried and executed. Mary's councillors were eager to discover what part Mary's half-sister and future queen, Elizabeth, had played in the rising. It seems clear that she did communicate with Wyatt but was careful enough to avoid being implicated. Particularly suspicious was her attempt shortly before the rising to travel to Donnington Castle, Berkshire. As Mary had shown at Framlingham the previous year, castles were convenient and secure rallying points. Within a few weeks, on 18 March, Princess Elizabeth was imprisoned in the Tower. But she survived.

1559
TOWER OF LONDON
The Knights of the Bath

It seems too good to be true that the Knights of the Bath could really have anything to do with washing, but such is the case. By long tradition the coronation began with a royal procession through the City of London from the Tower to Westminster Abbey. From at least the late fourteenth century it was the custom for the king to appoint a group of knights for the occasion. They prepared themselves for their initiation in the White Tower, the eponymous and dominating keep of this royal castle, with a banquet, a bath and haircut, oaths and a vigil. The ceremony was described as long established in 1485 and is first documented in 1399, for the coronation of Henry IV. Elements of it, however, may be drawn from much earlier ceremonies of initiations to knighthood.

This account of what happened, reproduced here from a transcription, was originally compiled by Anthony Anthony, a gunner at the Tower of London and an officer involved in the Ordnance, the body responsible for weapons and military supplies based there. He was also the creator of a remarkable illustrated roll of Henry VIII's warships known as the Anthony Roll. His rugged text is broken into segments, like a recipe, with the first ingredient being eleven knights. It is very specific in some details, as for example the 'ceiled' or covered beds (in the manner of a four-poster bed) having silk curtains and say and linen covers. The chapel mentioned was presumably that of St Peter ad Vincula in the shadow of the White Tower:

The order of the making of Knights of the Bath for the coronation of Queen Elizabeth the 13th of January [1559]

Item eleven knights as follows

Item the said knights having a banquet in the said White Tower before their entering to the bath.

The said knights entered into a hall in the said White Tower and then and there was prepared eleven ceiled beds which beds closed with curtains of silk and gold before every ceiled bed a bath covered with red say and white linen cloth and upon every bath the [coat-of-]arms of every knight.

Item every of the said knights sitting before their baths there being barbers ready to wash and trim them to have shaven the knights' beards the Queen's Majesty pardoned for their beards. And so being washed and trimmed entered into their baths naked and the musicians played upon their instruments.

Item immediately the Lord Arundell being Lord Steward of England, the Lord William Howard being Lord Chamberlain . . . went with the Herald at Arms to every knight and gave them their oaths and so kisses the book. And that done the Lords departed and the knights went out of their baths and went to bed and every knight was brought a bowl with hypocras [spiced wine].

Item at three of the clock in the morning the said Knights of the Bath rose out of their beds and were clothed in long side gowns of russet cloth with hoods over their heads . . . and the musicians playing and so conducted with torch staves to the church in the Tower. And the knights sitting in the choir. And then and there the parson of the said church kneeling said the procession in English . . .

Item one of the Queen's chaplains said Mass and at the consecration he heaved not up the host. And when Mass was done all the said knights every of them a perch [taper] of wax in their hands with half a groat [tuppence] and so offered the said perch kneeling upon their knees and kiss the patten and so returned to their places. And immediately the musicians played and there the knights were served with bread, suckets, comfits and hypocras and that done were conducted to the White Tower and there the knights dancing and leaping and after that went to bed.

Memorandum the 15th of January and in 1558 [1559] being upon a Saturday the Queen's Majesty was honourably conducted with all the nobles and peers of the realm spiritual and temporal from the Tower of London through the City of London to her majesty's Palace of Westminster. And at her majesty's going out of the Tower of London there was a great shot of guns and chambers to the number of 900 shot.

Notes made by Anthony Anthony

THIS ceremony outlined in this text differs in a number of respects from earlier treatise descriptions. In some points the difference merely reflects changing fashions, as, for example, the queen forgiving the knights their fashionable beards; in years gone by these would have been shaved off. So too would the beds have been without curtains, knightly simplicity being a quality appropriate to the solemn religious themes of the occasion.

More significant are the clear simplifications and shortening of the vigil, which has to do with the change from Catholic usage under Elizabeth's predecessor and half-sister, Mary I. The use of the word 'Mass' and the ceremony of kissing the 'patten' (presumably a pax) – literally a board with an image of the Crucifixion, that was passed from one knight to another and kissed as a symbol of union and peace – look back to Catholic practice. The noted use of English rather than Latin, however, underlines the new queen's Protestant sympathies. So too does the explicit note that during the Mass the host was not 'heaved up' for the congregation to see. This implicitly denied the Catholic belief that the consecration was the moment at which the host actually becomes the body of Christ.

At the next coronation in 1603 preparations for the ceremony of the Order of the Bath offer a few further details that flesh out Anthony's account. They reveal, for example, that the room used for the beds was on the second floor of the Tower and that it was known as 'Casar's Hall' [sic]. The White Tower was then widely believed to have been built by Julius Caesar (see 1598 below) and the intention may have been to link the order to the deep past. Remarkably, the fixings for the ceilings or canopies over the beds have been tentatively identified in this room. An outbreak of plague, however, caused the coronation procession to be cancelled and the ceremony was transferred to St James's Palace. The coronation procession has never started from the Tower since. In 1725 the Order of the Bath was refounded as an order of chivalry with its seat in the former Lady Chapel at Westminster Abbey, where its knights still have their stalls.

1562
PONTEFRACT CASTLE
Royal Heritage

This drawing of Pontefract Castle was prepared as part of a survey of the Duchy of Lancaster commissioned from Sir Ambrose Cave in 1562. The Duchy was the single greatest medieval patrimony in the kingdom with its roots reaching back into the thirteenth century. Following the usurpation of Henry IV in 1399 it became a possession of the Crown, which it still remains. It's a mark of the particular care taken by Sir Ambrose that he illustrated his survey with a series of drawings of the Duchy castles. These were prepared to help inform decisions taken about the future of the buildings by a group of the most senior officials and the queen herself sitting remotely in southern England. In every case the decision was to preserve the building, in the case of Pontefract because it was 'an honorable castle to be maintained and kept for the goodliness of the house and for the defense of the country'.

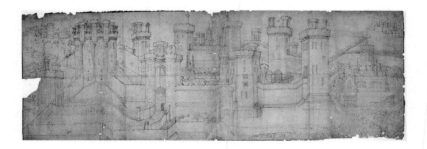

PONTEFRACT was perhaps the greatest castle in the possession of the Duchy and one that commanded admiration until its destruction in 1649 following the Civil War. Its most distinctive feature was the great tower shown to the left of the drawing. The whole upper section of this structure was added at the command of John of Gaunt in 1374. He ordered that it be made taller than any other tower in the castle and heightened using stone cut from the castle ditch. The inner ward of the castle is shown encircled by high walls and six massive stone towers. The only structures visible within it are a chapel with its richly ornamented porch (the chapel was later rebuilt by Elizabeth I on a different site) and, beyond it, the louvre and chimneys of the kitchen. Just left of centre is the main gate enclosed within a fortified apron or barbican. Access to this was at right-angles to the main gate through the tower to the extreme left of the view.

When this survey was made, Pontefract remained in use as an occasional residence of its constable, the Earl of Shrewsbury, and was considered large enough to accommodate the queen, should she travel to the North (but she never did). In the 1640s the castle played an important role in the fighting in Yorkshire. When it finally fell, the Grand Jury of Yorkshire petitioned Parliament that 'those walls which have harboured so much tyranny and oppression, may not stand, but be levelled with the ground, that this nest and cage of all villainy may be destroyed, that those unclean birds which have now left it, may never roost themselves again there'. Parliament obliged, as the modern visitor can still appreciate.

1575
KENILWORTH CASTLE
A Royal Visit

Elizabeth I travelled every summer on progress and was lavishly entertained wherever she went. She visited Kenilworth Castle on four occasions but her final, nineteen-day, visit there, between 9 and 27 July, was outstanding both for its length – this was the longest such stay she ever made – and the opulence of the entertainment she met with. It seems to have been a last attempt by the owner of the castle, Robert Dudley, Earl of Leicester, to try and persuade the queen to marry him. There are two full accounts of the stay and these extracts interleave them. The first comes from George Gascoigne, a player and writer otherwise employed by the Earl of Leicester, who here recounts the first two stages of the theatrical welcome the queen received as she first arrived at Kenilworth: a prophecy delivered by a sibyl (a man dressed as a prophetess) followed by a trumpet fanfare seemingly played by giants – the real players were hidden – that carried her back to the golden age of King Arthur.

Her Majesty came thither (as I remember) on Saturday, being the 9th of July last past: on which day there met her on the way, somewhat near the castle Sybilla, who prophesied unto her Highness the prosperous reign that she should continue, according to the happy beginning of the same . . . Her Majesty passing onto the first gate, there stood, in the leads [roof] and battlements thereof, six trumpeters hugely advanced [proportioned], much exceeding the common stature of men in this age, who had likewise huge and monstrous trumpets counterfeited, wherein they seem to sound: and behind them were placed certain trumpeters, who sounded indeed at her majesty's entry. And by this dumb show it was meant, that in the days and reign of King Arthur, men were of that stature; so that the castle of Kenilworth should seem to be kept by Arthur's heirs and their servants. And when her Majesty entered the gate there stood Hercules for porter, who seemed to be amazed at such a presence . . . overcome by view of the rare beauty and princely countenance of her Majesty, [he] yielded himself and his charge [the castle], presenting the keys unto her Majesty

George Gascoigne, *A Brief Rehearsal*

WE now take up the narrative of the welcome as it is related in the second source, a long letter attributed to Robert Langham (or Laneham), the keeper of the council chamber door. He has a slightly different version of events from Gascoigne. According to him, the gigantic porter emerges grumbling at the noise from his lodge. Catching sight of the queen, however, he is amazed and:

yields up his club, his keys, his office and all and on his knees humbly prays pardon of his ignorance and impatience, which her Highness graciously granting, he caused his trumpeters, that stood upon the wall of the gate there, to sound up a tune of welcome: which, beside the noble noise, was so much more than pleasant to behold, because these trumpeters, being six in number, were every one an 8 foot high, in due proportion of person beside, all in long garments of silk suitable, each with his silvery trumpet of a 5 foot long . . . this music maintained from them very delectably, while her Highness [passed] all along this Tiltyard road onto the inner gate next [to] the base court of the castle: where the Lady of the Lake (famous in *King Arthur's* book) with two nymphs waiting upon her, arrayed all in silks, attending her Highness coming: from the midst of the pool, where upon a movable island, bright blazing with torches, she floated to land, met her Majesty with a well penned meter [verse] and matter after this sort: viz first of the anciency of the castle, who had been owners of the same even till this day, most always in the hands of the earls of Leicester; how she had kept this lake since King Arthur's days; and now understanding of her Highness's hither coming, thought it both office and duty, in humble wise, to discover her and her estate; offering up the same lake and her power therein, with promise of repair unto the court.

It pleased her Highness to thank this lady, and add withall, 'We had thought indeed the lake had been ours, and do you call it yours now? Well, we will herein commune more with you hereafter.'

Robert Langham, *A Letter*

This final pleasantry – at which surely the Lady of the Lake blanched in embarrassment and everyone else laughed sycophantically – played on the idea that as queen, Elizabeth I already possessed the castle and its lake, and had no need, therefore, to be offered it by another. The text of the Lady of the Lake's poem is given by Gascoigne and it attributes the creation of the castle to the fictional Kenelm, king of Mercia.

The queen's ensuing stay was accompanied by every kind of entertainment, from bear-baiting and hunting to fireworks and a rustic party or brideale. Another supposedly historical interlude was a mock battle between the Danes and the English fought under the command of Captain Cox, a mason from Coventry well versed in chivalric literature. There was a cavalry engagement on hobby horses followed by an infantry battle. The Danes won but were carried off as prisoners by English women. This apparently hilarious scene was enacted beneath the queen's window for her amusement but, according to Langham, 'her Highness beholding in the chamber delectable dancing' failed to notice it and the whole thing had to be repeated the next day. The episode echoes the performance by Bottom and his fellows in Shakespeare's *A Midsummer Night's Dream*. There were besides many more theatrical interludes, some of them with pointed themes. Not all of them came off, including a small ship battle on the mere around the castle of the Lady of the Lake (in fact a heron house) and a play written by Gascoigne entitled *Ahtebasile* or *Zabeta* (thinly veiled plays on the name Elizabeth).

If it was Dudley's intention to win the hand of Elizabeth I by his entertainment at Kenilworth, the ploy failed. The visit, anyway, certainly followed one affair, by which Dudley had a son in 1574, and was followed in 1578 by his second marriage, much to the queen's anger, to Lettice née Knollys. Elizabeth was, nevertheless, deeply affected by the earl's death in 1588 and famously preserved his last letter to her. It should be added that the Kenilworth entertainment of 1575 became publicly celebrated following the publication of Walter Scott's novel

Kenilworth (1821), which for dramatic reasons linked the queen's visit to the death of Dudley's first wife, Amy Robsart. There were contemporary suspicions that Dudley attempted to murder his wife in order to make a marriage to Elizabeth I possible, but Amy's death in 1560 – ostensibly from falling down a staircase – could equally have been accidental.

1588
THE HOUSE OF WOLLATON
A Biblical Device

The south front of Wollaton, Nottinghamshire, completed by 1588 for Francis Willoughby. He was a highly educated and complex character, who quarrelled with his family and was ruined by the expense of his new seat. The house is laid out on a symmetrical plan with an almost identical facade on each of its four sides. With its corner turrets and huge central tower the whole composition bears an unmistakable resemblance to a towered castle with a central keep. The hilltop setting of the building adds to the impression, though it originally stood within an encircling grid of formal gardens. It was designed by Robert Smythson, who is described on his tomb in the neighbouring parish church as 'gent. architector and survayor unto the most worthie house of Wollaton'. Smythson's claim to be a gentleman and his use of the Roman-inspired title of architect underline respectively his social status and interest in Classical architecture.

AT Wollaton Smythson shoe-horns the asymmetrical plan of a great medieval house into a regular composition decorated with Classical motifs such as pilasters or half-columns integral to the walls. At the heart of the building is the great hall, its windows visible just above the level of the encircling two-storey ranges. Built on top of this is a prospect chamber with magnificent views over the surrounding parkland. The small turrets attached to it are evocative of those found on medieval castle keeps such as the White Tower at London. The window tracery of the hall and prospect chamber is medieval in inspiration and in striking contrast to the more fashionable grids of windows in the lower parts of the elevation.

The sources for the design of Wollaton are many and varied, a reflection of Willoughby's intellectual interests. There survives a building plan amongst his papers, for example, derived from a 1560 design by the French architect Jacques Androuet du Cerceau that bears close resemblance to Wollaton less its central tower. No less important as an inspiration may have been King Solomon's Temple in Jerusalem, as reconstructed from a description by the Jewish historian of the first century AD, Josephus. The Elizabethans delighted in the idea of symbols or emblems that conveyed hidden meaning or significance – what they termed 'devices' – and a biblical source for the building would have been particularly satisfying. Not exclusive of this, the form of the building might also allude to the opening of Psalm 18, rendered in the Bishop's Bible (1568) as 'God is my stony rock and my fortress, and my deliverer: my Lord, my castle in whom I will trust, my buckler, the horn of my salvation, and my refuge'.

The castle-like forms of Wollaton are to be encountered widely in major Elizabethan buildings, including the turreted Hardwick Hall, Derbyshire, begun 1590, or the main front of Burghley, Lincolnshire, designed 1575, with its great gatehouse, turrets and towers. Such residences have been dubbed by twentieth-century architectural historians as 'prodigy buildings', as indeed they are. Beside great medieval castles such as Kenilworth, Pontefract or Windsor, however, they are also relatively small.

1598
TOWER OF LONDON
A Foreign Tourist

When Paul Hentzner, a lawyer born in Silesia, landed at Rye in August 1598 he officially stated that his business was 'none but to see England'. His visit was part of a wider tour or Itinerary across Germany, France and Italy that he wrote up in Latin and published in Nuremberg in 1617. He gives a full description of London and its sights including the Tower, which was already becoming established as a tourist attraction. Visits could be arranged or paid for and enabled the curious foreigner to see the stores of the royal Wardrobe, which had been held here for security since the Middle Ages. These included clothes and arras (or tapestry), as well as weapons and armour.

On the way out, Hentzner was also shown the royal bestiary. Again, this had been housed in the Tower since the thirteenth century and moved by Edward III into the barbican (how Hentzner missed it on the way in is hard to explain; perhaps he came in via a postern or river gate). He also mentions the scaffold for political executions on Tower Hill. The Tower's reputation as a place of aristocratic imprisonment and, for the unfortunate, a prison of no return, was already well established:

The castle [*arx*], or Tower of London, called Bringwin and Tourgwin, in Welsh, from its whiteness, is encompassed by a very deep and broad ditch, as well as a double wall very high. In the middle of the whole is that very ancient and very strong tower, enclosed with four others, which in the opinion of some, was built by Julius Caesar. Upon entering the castle [*arcem*], we were obliged to quit our swords at the gate, and deliver them to the guard. When we were introduced, we were shown about 100 pieces of arras belonging to the crown, made of gold, silver, and silk; several saddles covered with velvet of different colours; an immense quantity of bed furniture, such as canopies, and the like, some of them most richly ornamented with pearl; some royal dresses, so extremely magnificent, as to raise any one's admiration of the sums they must have cost.

We were next led into the armoury, in which are these particularities: spears, out of which you may shoot; shields, that will give fire four times; a great many rich halberds, commonly called partisans, with which the guard defend the royal person in battle; some lances, covered with red and green velvet, and the body armour of Henry VIII; many, and very beautiful arms, as well for men as for horses in horse fights; the lance of Charles Brandon Duke of Suffolk, three spans thick; two pieces of cannon, the one fires three, the other seven balls at a time; two others made of wood, which the English had at the siege of Boulogne, in France, and by this stratagem, without which they could not have succeeded, they struck terror into the inhabitants, as at the appearance of artillery, and the town surrendered upon articles; 19 cannon of a thicker make than ordinary, and in a room apart, 36 of a smaller; other cannon for chain shot; and balls proper to bring down masts of ships. Crossbows, bows and arrows, of which to this day the English make great use in their exercises. But who can relate all that is to be seen here? Eight or nine men, employed by the year, are scarce sufficient to keep all the arms bright.

The mint for coining money is in the Tower.

. . . On coming out of the castle, we were led to a small house close by, where are kept a variety of creatures, viz three lionesses, one lion of great size, called Edward VI from his having been born in that reign; a tiger, lynx; a wolf, excessively old; this is a very scarce animal in England, so that their sheep and cattle stray about in great numbers, free from any danger, there without anybody to keep them; there is besides, a porcupine, and an eagle. All these creatures are kept in a remote place, fitted up for the purpose with wooden lattices, at the Queen's expense.

Near to this castle, is a large open space, on the highest part of it is erected a wooden scaffold, for the execution of noble criminals; upon which they say, three princes of England, the last of their families, have been beheaded for high treason. On the bank of the Thames close by, are a great many cannon, such chiefly as are used at sea.

P. Hentzner, *A Journey into England* (trans. R. Bentley)

HENTZNER repeats the widely held belief that the White Tower was a Roman building. Why he gives its names in Welsh is an open question but he may have supposed this to be its original name. The Tower had housed the royal menagerie since at least 1235, when Henry III received the gift of three leopards or lions from the Holy Roman Emperor. To these the King of Norway added a polar bear in 1252 (it was allowed to fish in the Thames) and the King of France an African elephant in 1255 (it lived for only two years). The menagerie survived many vagaries of fortune until 1826, when the Duke of Wellington transferred most of the animals to Regent's Park. The practice of keeping animals in castles as objects of display had parallels across Europe. At Český Krumlov Castle in the Czech Republic, for example, the Rosenbergs claimed descent from the Orsini of Rome and adopted the *ursina* or small bear as their heraldic beast. In the late sixteenth century they also put bears in the moat and, astonishingly, they remain there as a popular visitor attraction.

Hentzner's visit almost exactly coincided with the first detailed drawn survey of the Tower by Haiward and Gascoyne of 1597, now known only through an eighteenth-century copy. It makes it possible to visualise what he saw in great detail. This translation of his *Itinerary* has a fascinating association, having been published by Horace Walpole at his house, Strawberry Hill, in 1757. Walpole, a fellow of the Society of Antiquaries, was fascinated by medieval architecture and we will encounter him again as the writer of one of the first Gothic novels, *The Castle of Otranto* (see 1764 below).

BERKELEY CASTLE
A Tale of a Toad

When the steward of the Berkeley estate in Gloucestershire, John Smyth, set about compiling a history of the family in the early seventeenth century (see 1342 above), he gave over a considerable amount of space to describing what was known about the murder of Edward II at their family seat of Berkeley Castle on 21 September 1327. The murder was a claim to popular fame, so it was a matter of prestige that it should have occurred within the castle walls. That said, as a faithful retainer, Smyth was also keen to exonerate the family of all direct responsibility for the affair. He explains, therefore, that the king was 'courteously received' as a prisoner at the castle on 5 April but that soon afterwards the then owner, Thomas, Lord Berkeley, was:

commanded by letters to use no familiarity with Edward the late king, but to deliver over the government of his castle . . . which with heavy cheer . . . perceiving what violence was intended, he doth. And forthwith departed from his castle to other [of] his dwelling places. When, soon after, the late king was shut up in a close chamber, where with the stench of dead carcasses laid in a cellar under him, he was miserably tormented many days together, and well nigh suffocated therewith . . . But that not sufficing to hasten his death, which was desired and covertly commanded . . . Sir John Maltravers and Sir Thomas de Gurnay and their accomplices, rushed in the night time into his chamber, and with great and heavy featherbeds smothered him, thrusting an hollow instrument like the end of a trumpet or glisterpipe into his fundament, and through it a red hot iron up into his bowels, whereby he ended his life, with a lamentable loud cry heard by many both of the town and castle

John Smyth, *The Lives of the Berkeleys*

WHATEVER the truth of this account – and the barbaric means of murder could as easily be an invention as true; we will never know – the event came to be celebrated in the castle itself by a natural prodigy, of which John Smyth also gives these details:

> In this castle and in this place called the keep it was where king Edward II in the dungeon chamber there was so barbarously murdered . . . Out of which dungeon, in the likeness of a deep broad well going steeply down in the midst of the dungeon chamber in the said Keep, was (as a tradition tells) drawn forth a toad in the time of king Henry VII, of an incredible bigness, which in the deep dry dust in the bottom thereof had doubtless lived there divers hundreds of years; whose portraiture in just dimension, as it was then to me affirmed by divers aged persons, I saw about 48 years ago drawn in colours upon the door of the great hall, and of the outer side of the stone porch leading into that hall, since by pargetors or pointers of that wall washed out or out-worn with time; which in breadth was more than a foot, near 16 inches, and in length more: Of which monstrous and outgrown beast the inhabitants of this town and in the neighbouring villages round about fable many strange and incredible wonders, making the greatness of this toad more than would fill a peck, yea, I have heard some who looked to have belief say from the report of their fathers and grandfathers that it would have filled a bushell or strike, and to have been many years fed with flesh and garbage from the butchers; but this is all the truth I know, or dare believe.
>
> John Smyth, *A description of the Hundred of Berkeley*

IT'S hard to think of a creature more perfectly calculated to evoke revulsion in the seventeenth century than a gigantic, wart-covered and clammy toad, particularly given that these animals were widely supposed at the time to be poisonous. By implication this specimen was found in the space beneath Edward II's cell, where Smyth thought that the rotten carcasses were laid to kill the king by their stench. Might its great age allow for a direct connection with the murder itself? Perhaps the toad heard Edward II's dying scream? That it was fed with butcher's offal merely adds to its other repellent qualities. Rather like an angler describing to advantage the fish that got away, Smyth gives the toad's lengths and breadth but leaves the reader to imagine its gargantuan bulk. After all, a peck, a bushell and a strike – respectively 16, 64 or 128 dry pints – make the difference between a prodigy and a terrifying monster.

The placement of two images of the toad at the main entrance to the great hall – one in the porch and one on the door itself – could not have been more prominent. Castle halls were commonly used to display heirlooms illustrative of the building's legendary history (see 1290 above). Indeed, no visitor could have entered Berkeley without seeing the painting and its disappearance may indicate that it came to be regarded as ridiculous. Certainly, Smyth continues after the latter passage to narrate a colourful tale about a witch of Berkeley in the time of Edward the Confessor (d. 1066). Her daemon or familiar, in the form of a chough, warned her by its singing of her death. To try and escape being carried off to hell she persuaded her children to bind her body fast in an animal skin and place it in a stone coffin sealed with cement and chains. Her ploy failed: demons broke open the coffin and her body was summoned away on a great black steed. It was less the truth of such stories that mattered to Smyth, perhaps, than the fact that they made the history of the place and its eponymous family memorable.

1622
NAWORTH CASTLE
Cannibalising a Castle

A view of Naworth Castle, Cumbria, which was restored from decay in the early seventeenth century and the interiors fitted out with a splendid collection of late medieval furnishings and paintings stripped from Kirkoswald Castle, about fifteen miles away. By the nineteenth century the castle had become a prized architectural heirloom of the Earls of Carlisle, with their modern seat at Castle Howard, Yorkshire.

A survey of Naworth Castle, Cumberland, in 1588–9 described the building as 'of good strength and built four square with a gatehouse'. The surveyor goes on to add, however, that 'one of the squares thereof hath never been finished further than the walls thereof, of two or three stories high', and adds that the whole was 'in very great decay'. Some of this damage may have resulted from the fact that the castle had been the focus of a rebellion a few years previously, in 1570, and defied a royal army. By 1602 Naworth had come into the possession of the antiquary and Catholic, William, Lord Howard, who began to restore it. His household accounts record that his workmen were stripping materials from another major castle in the county at Kirkoswald to repair Naworth. In 1622, for example, there are payments 'for taking down the roof of the chapel at Kirkoswald' and '. . . putting up the roof of the chapel [in Naworth]'. This roof was not a utilitarian structure but one splendidly painted with an ancestry of Christ and signed by its creator, 'Lucas Egliment, painter 1512'. Much else passed between the two buildings and in about 1675, Edmund Sandford reminisced that:

> This great castle of Kirkoswald was once the fairest fabric that ever eyes looked upon. The hall I have seen one hundred yards long; and the great portrait of King Brut lying in the end of the roof of this hall. And all his succeeding successors, kings of Great Britain, portrayed to the waist, their visage, hats, feathers, garbs and habits, in the roof of this hall. Now [the roof is] translated to Naworth Castle, where they are placed in the roof of the hall, and at the head thereof
>
> Edmund Sandford, *A Cursory Relation*

IN his description of the length of the hall at Kirkoswald, Sandford has clearly exaggerated but the details of his description are otherwise corroborated by antiquarian description and early nineteenth-century drawings. The hall roof, comprising well over sixty panels, was almost certainly inspired by the imagery of Richmond Palace, Surrey, created by Henry VII following a great fire in 1497. By a strange irony, Lord Howard was also a friend of the antiquary, herald and headmaster, William Camden, who did so much to debunk the long-established legend it celebrated: that King Brut was the founder of Britain.

Tragically, in 1844, a fire destroyed both the hall and the chapel ceilings at Naworth. There were preserved from the flames, however, several sculptures including the massive, sixteenth-century heraldic supporters representing a bull, gryphon, ram and dolphin known as the Dacre Beasts (carved from an ancient oak and now at the Victoria and

Albert Museum) and the interior of one tower. Within the latter there remains a large altarpiece dated 1514 and bearing the arms of Lord Dacre, a commander at the English victory over the Scots at Flodden the previous year. The provenance of all these survivals is uncertain but they were certainly brought here by Lord Howard. The sculpture probably comes from Kirkoswald but the altarpiece may come from Lanercost Priory, close to Naworth.

Because castles were architectural expressions of ancestry, this kind of recycling of fixtures was particularly appropriate. It also illustrates the admiration in which medieval objects might be held. And in this case the interest in the past went much further. The proximity of Naworth to Hadrian's Wall meant that there were many Roman antiquities to collect as well. In 1671 Sir Daniel Fleming, another visitor, described the castle as housing 'a good library of manuscripts and . . . in the garden walls are fixed several stones with Roman inscriptions'.

1634
LUDLOW CASTLE
An Exhortation to Virtue

A view of Ludlow Castle, Shropshire, seat of the Council of the Marches, above the River Teme. The castle remained a focus of social life into the eighteenth century and a ball was last held here in 1719. Six years later Daniel Defoe described it as a ruin. The dense surrounding woodland is a picturesque product of twentieth-century neglect. The clearance of castle earthworks over centuries can create unique ecosystems.

On 29 September 1634, John Egerton, Earl of Bridgewater, arrived at Ludlow Castle to take up office and his seat as the president of the Council of the Marches. To celebrate the occasion a masque or entertainment with scenery, music and dancing was performed. Masques were staged events and their texts, laced with Classical references, seem slightly stilted to a modern reader. What made them fun – fancy-dress parties with spoken lines, if you will – however, was that the audience knew the performers and took part. In this case the verse text was written by poet John Milton at the invitation of Henry Lawes, the music master of the earl and countess's numerous daughters.

For the occasion Lawes himself took the role of the presiding 'attendant spirit' and the Bridgewaters' three youngest children acted the parts of a virtuous maiden and her two brothers. The maiden gets lost in a forest and is abducted and imprisoned by the magician Comus. She is freed by her brothers with the help of a nymph from the River Severn. This river, of course, demarcated the English border with Wales and one of its tributaries, the Teme, flows beneath the walls of Ludlow. The final episode that follows the rescue brings the action to Ludlow with a change of scene, 'presenting Ludlow Town, and the President's Castle', and the moral of the story home. The attendant spirit presents the three actors to their parents with a song:

Noble Lord and Lady bright,
I have brought ye new delight.
Here behold so goodly grown
Three fair branches of your own.
Heaven hath timely tried their youth,
Their faith, their patience, and their truth,
And sent them here through hard assays
With a crown of deathless praise,
To triumph in victorious dance
O'er sensual folly and intemperance.

The spirit's final song of farewell then concludes:

Mortals, that would follow me,
Love Virtue; she alone is free.
She can teach ye how to climb
Higher than the sphery chime;
Or, if Virtue feeble were,
Heaven itself would stoop to her.

IN effect, the conclusion of the masque drew an analogy between the story and real life. It dignified the child actors, or 'three fair branches', implying that they had – both in fiction and in fact – been tried and proved. The word chosen – 'assays' – felicitously referred specifically to the testing of precious metals. No less important to the earl, about to take up responsibility for the administration of justice as president of the Council of the Marches, the plot was an admonition to virtuous behaviour. It also warned that those too weak to support themselves would find divine protection. As is conventional in masques, the whole plot had starkly differentiated voices of good and evil, which made its message even clearer.

The text of the masque was first published in London three years later by Lawes as *A Mask Presented at Ludlow Castle 1634 on Michaelmas Night*, but later became known by the name of the magician – *Comus*. It was almost certainly performed in the thirteenth-century great hall of the castle, the conventional space for public entertainments (though plays were sometimes performed more privately in the great chamber of a house). The night-time celebration of the masque perhaps enabled the more effective use of dramatic lighting.

The set depicting Ludlow and its castle in the final scene does not survive but it sounds like a topographic view, a pertinent treatment given the role of the nymph from the River Severn in the action. This masque, in other words, celebrated just government, associated it with the family exercising royal authority and located it in the castle that served as their official seat.

1635
WINCHESTER CASTLE
The Ceremony of the Court of Eyre

When Lieutenant Hammond, a traveller interested in architecture and history, passed through Winchester in late August 1635, he admired the castle in his journal. His visit coincided with a court of eyre, an itinerant court that exercised jurisdiction over areas of land designated as royal forest, and he attended its proceedings over two days. It sat in the great hall of the castle, by long English tradition the conventional setting for the exercise of justice. The eyre had been a cornerstone of the medieval legal system but had become an anachronism nearly two centuries earlier in the fourteenth century. What Hammond actually witnessed, therefore, was the revival of this medieval court – and the forest laws it policed – by Charles I as a means of raising money without recourse to Parliament.

In his account, Hammond first describes the elevated inner bailey of the castle – with its four towers and thirteenth-century apartments recently modernised by the Earl of Portland – before descending to the hall in the yard beneath it. His prose is very arch, as for example his comparison of the hall and round table (see 1290 above); or the 'tears' of St Bartholomew, which, by way of reference to Winchester's bishop-saint, Swithun, can be understood to mean that it poured with rain as the dignitaries arrived.

I found at the west end of it [Winchester], upon a high mounted hill, a strong and spacious castle, which is very ancient, yet not much racinated; for of late years it has been much repaired, and beautified, by the late Lord Treasurer of England [Richard Weston, Earl of Portland].

This castle is built four square, with four great towers at the corners, two of them are round and two square. The hall, kitchen, guard chamber, privy chamber, the king's bedchamber, and many other fair chambers for the noble officers, and court train, all made very complete and handsome at the earl's great cost. So many stairs, or ascents, as are up to the hall, from the first entrance of the ascending bridge; so many are there down again under the castle into deep vaults and cellars, where the keepers may securely quarter themselves, if any occasion be.

From hence I marched down again to see what manner of hall and [round] table that brave and warlike worthy the British prince [Arthur] kept above 1000 years since, which are both fit for so royal a prince. What the one [the hall] exceeded in longitude, the other [the table] did in rotundity. For I found the hall 50 paces long and very broad, with two rows of goodly marble pillars. For the other, his 'Table' as they call it, with his whole jury of courageous warlike knights [painted] round about it, showed no end of his bounty.

And now I am here (although it be a little digressing and retarding of my journey, yet) I could not part from the stately Hall until I had both seen and heard the noble proceedings of so high and honourable a court as did then sit there . . .

On Monday morning his lordship [the Earl of Holland, Chief Justice in Eyre in all the royal forests south of Trent] came from Sir William Udall's house accompanied with the Earl of Southampton (who was deeply interested in this great business) with diverse knights and gentlemen of the shire, and the high sheriff thereof, and his attendants, making it all about 200 horse, and 10 coaches. The mayor [of Winchester] with his brethren in scarlet, received his lordship at the Eastgate on the same morning it being Saint Bartholomew's Day [24 August]. The saint, (though not their own St Swithun) entertaining him with weeping tears, which soundly washed the scarlet weeds [robes] of their grave worships. Then after a small time of repose at Captain Tucker's house, not far from that gate, where his lordship lay, by the said two judges in their scarlet, Mr Mayor, and his aldermen in theirs; Mr High Sheriff, with all his retinue in their colours; some 12 of the king's guard with their royal badges; the king's trumpeters and the high sheriff's, was he guarded and attended in this majestic manner to the great hall, where they sat in royal state, most of the knights, esquires and chief gentlemen of the country bearing offices in [the] New Forest, Wulmer Forest, and Chale Forest, attending at this great and high court.

Here was exceeding great crowding of people, to see and hear, so that there was but a little room for strangers, as I was; yet obtained I that favour from one of the guard, as to get a convenient one, not only to see the great state of the court, and the order of their sitting therein, but also to hear the honourable proceeding thereof, the which in brief, as well as my memory gave me assistance, by way of parenthesis take thus:

First an 'oyez' [call of 'hear ye'], was made, and silence commanded until the commission and letters patent were read . . .

[There follows a long list of different episodes in the ceremonial, involving the officers of the forest presenting themselves and yielding up their symbols of office – including rods, hunting horns and marking axes – on bended knee, with the exception of the Earl of Southampton]

All of which business took up Monday and Tuesday forenoon and some part of the afternoon, before the Earl of Holland had time to make a pithy and short preparatory to the charge that was to be delivered by the Lord Chief Justice Finch; in which his lordship intimated that since his Majesty had honoured and in trusted him with this great service, his great and special care should not be wanting therein, to do his Majesty all due and right for service, and the subject no wrong; and how glad he was to see so full an appearance of such a noble gentleman, which did evidently manifest their love and obedience to their sovereign, which he heartily thanked them for . . .

[There then followed a long lecture by Justice Finch on the Common Law, which he claimed as the earliest 'national law in the world', with passing reference to the Romans, the Danes, King Canute, William the Conqueror, Richard I, Henry III, Magna Carta etc.]

By this time his lordship (as he had good cause) was wearied and I (as I had just reason) with crowding and thrusting, was

213

quite overtired; and his lordship ending there makes my work here and close with my long parenthesis

Lieutenant Hammond, *A Relation of a Short Survey of the Western Counties*

CHARLES I's revival of medieval practices such as the eyre was deeply unpopular and helped precipitate civil war in the 1640s. The ensuing hostilities involved and destroyed many castles across Britain and Ireland. There are many eyewitness accounts of the fighting, but here it's necessary to choose just one narrative of a siege to illustrate the fate of these buildings.

1645
SCARBOROUGH CASTLE
The Fall of the Keep

Intense artillery bombardment in 1645 caused the partial collapse of the twelfth-century keep at Scarborough, Yorkshire. The castle and harbour allowed the Royalist garrison to interrupt coastal traffic and helped starve London of Newcastle coal. Following the 1745 Jacobite Rising a barracks was erected in the castle. It was finally blown to pieces by German battleships in 1914.

In September 1642, during the first hostilities of the Civil War, a local gentleman, Sir Hugh Cholmley, received a commission from Parliament to raise a regiment and garrison Scarborough Castle. Soon afterwards, however, Sir Hugh changed sides along with his force of about six hundred infantry, a hundred cavalry and a hundred mounted foot soldiers. While he rode to York to pledge allegiance to the king, his cousin with a party of forty sailors briefly

215

recaptured the castle for Parliament. Happily for Sir Hugh, he persuaded his relative to give it back. At grass-roots level, the early loyalties of the Civil War had more to do with local and familial relations than high political ideals.

Scarborough provided a harbour to the king's forces in Yorkshire and allowed for the interruption of the coal trade from Newcastle, on which London depended for fuel. Following the Royalist defeat at Marston Moor in 1644, therefore, Parliament closed in on Scarborough. Early in 1645 Sir John Meldrum invested Scarborough and after three weeks, on 18 February, the garrison fell back from the fortifications of the town into the castle. A short lull in the fighting followed, during which time Sir John Meldrum tried to negotiate a surrender. Forty or so members of the garrison ran away and then the siege, recounted here by Sir Hugh in his memoirs, began in earnest with the Parliamentary force moving its guns:

near to the sea cliff for more advantage to batter [the castle], Meldrum there in person giving direction about them, his hat blows off his head, and he catching to save that, the wind being very great blows his cloak over his face, and he falls over the cliff amongst the rocks and stones at least steeple height. It was a miracle his brains were not beaten out and all his bones broken, but it seemed the wind together with the cloak did in some sort bear him up, and lessen the fall. Yet he is taken up for dead, lies three days speechless, his head open and the bruised blood taken out, though a man above three score year old, recovered this so perfectly that within six weeks he is on foot again, and begins to batter the castle . . . so furiously that in three days the great tower split in two, and that side which was battered falls to the ground, the other standing firm being supported by an arch of stone that went through the midst. There were near 20 persons upon the top of the tower when it cleft, yet all got into the standing part, except two of Captain Richard Legard's servants which were in the turret where their master lodged . . .

The fall of the tower was a very terrible spectacle, and more sudden than expected, at which the enemy gave a great shout and the besieged nothing dismayed betook them to their arms, expecting an assault, by omission of which the enemy lost a fair opportunity, the falling part of the tower having obstructed the passage to the gatehouse so that the guard there for the present could have no release from their friends. This fall of the tower put the enemy into such heart and confidence, so that the next day, about 6 o'clock in the evening, Meldrum writes to the governor that he intended that night to be master of the castle and all the works, that if the governor would render, he should have good conditions, but if he would not, and that any of his soldiers lost a drop of blood in the entrance, there should not a person within the castle have quarter.

It happened the governor at the present was very busy in the ordering some affairs of the garrison, and so returned the drummer with this message, the next morning he would return him his answer in writing. But Meldrum had made preparation for an assault, and his heart and haughty spirit could admit no delay, so that about 9 o'clock that night the enemy began to assault the gatehouse, and having taken a work close without the gate, endeavoured to mount the walls, but so sharply repulsed they were forced to retire leaving diverse dead bodies in the work, and having of their party slain and wounded above 200 in that encounter. The stones of the fallen tower were thrown freely amongst them and did the greatest execution.

The fall of the tower had dislodged the governor, his lady, and most of the gentleman and officers of quality, who were forced to betake themselves to poor cabins reared against the walls and banks in the castle yard, which though it was a spacious place containing 12 acres of ground, yet it was much annoyed and disquieted from the ships, which was continually playing with their ordinance into it.

Sir Hugh Cholmley, Memoirs and Memorials

IN testimony to these events the broken remains of the twelfth-century keep still dominate Scarborough. Clearly visible within them, moreover, are the springs of the internal arch mentioned in Sir Hugh's account. Soon after these events Meldrum was shot in the stomach and died. Then the besieging force changed its tactics and began to starve the castle out. The garrison ran out of gunpowder, money – silver tableware cut up and stamped with its bullion value sufficed – and finally food.

When further reduced by scurvy, and with just twenty-five soldiers fit for duty, Sir Hugh surrendered on 25 July 1645. Civil War sieges often hinged on the presence or absence of heavy cannon. Without a decisive advantage it was common for the two sides to sit things out. Some medieval castle buildings, however, such as the fifteenth-century Yellow Tower of Gwent at Raglan, Monmouth, proved remarkably resistant even to heavy bombardment.

1648–9
KENILWORTH CASTLE
Vanishing Monuments

These three views of Kenilworth Castle, Warwickshire, engraved by the Bohemian-born artist Wenceslaus Hollar, were published by the scholar, herald and antiquarian Sir William Dugdale in his voluminous The Antiquities of Warwickshire *(1656). They underline the sheer scale of this great residence and its setting, which had developed by stages since the early twelfth century around the focal point of its keep, here called Caesar's Tower. Hollar probably based the views on a prospect of the castle made by Dugdale, according to his journal, on 6 September 1649. What's certain, however, is that by the time they appeared in print the castle was in ruins.*

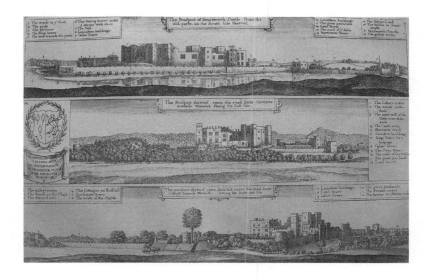

THE CASTLE

Two months before Dugdale's visit, the castle commander was informed:

> To avoid charge in keeping a garrison in Kenilworth Castle, or danger if it should be surprised and kept by an enemy, it is to be made untenable, and we desire you to see that it be made so. The great tower called Caesar's Tower, we desire taken down, and also the outward wall; what remains of the house being only for habitation, will not be tenable by an enemy, in regard of the greatness of the windows and its other natural weakness. Let the place be put into a posture not dangerous to the country, and no unnecessary spoil made of the house, as it relates to habitation, which might prejudice the present possessor, or the value of the sale by the state.
>
> 24 July 1649, Order in Council

THE ensuing damage, or 'slighting', was devastating, with parts of the structure blown up and materials ruthlessly stripped out. At the conclusion of the work all the principal buildings were ruinous. Nor was Kenilworth alone in this misfortune; across the kingdom, in the name of peace, castles were similarly overthrown or partially blown up. Few owners were in a position to complain but the Earl of Huntingdon, for example, made his feelings about the treatment of Ashby de la Zouch known:

> By Order of Parliament bearing the date 1648 Ashby house the only convenient mansion of the said earl of Huntingdon (and standing monument of his worthy ancestors) was to be slighted. To which order the said earl consented and submitted: And out of his tender affection to the country's quiet and benefit (which he foresaw providing for) did not so much interrupt the authorities that commanded it as to plead for his own private convenience . . . Hoping always the intent of the order had been such as the letter thereof held forth, the slighting and only making untenable of the said house: and not the demolishers men willing to understand (for their easy dispatches) the razing and utter ruin, not only of the piles themselves but of the very ruins of them: so the unexpected detriment of the materials and untollerable loss of the said earl unless the Parliament will afford

him such a compensation as their justice hath before allowed others (not so deeply grieved) and their honour will not (he trusteth) suffer them to deny unto him.

[endorsed] The state of the Rt Hon Ferdinando
Earl of Huntingdon's case about the reparation
for demolishing Ashby Towers

The fate of Kenilworth and Ashby is a reminder of how fundamentally the architectural landscape of England was changed by the Civil War. Like England's monasteries a century before, most were ruined without record. That makes the Kenilworth views exceptional. But for the brief overthrow of the established political order following the execution of Charles I in 1649, many more medieval castles would probably have remained in use to the present.

1649
SKIPTON, APPLEBY, BROUGH AND BROUGHAM CASTLES
A Patrimony Restored

Skipton Castle, Yorkshire, as rebuilt by Lady Anne Clifford after the demolition of the defences by order of Parliament in 1649. Lady Anne also worked on the church, visible to the left, with its set of family tombs. The character of her architectural patronage is typical of English noblewomen from the fifteenth century onwards.

Lady Anne Clifford was born to greatness in 1590, the daughter of Margaret Russell and George Clifford, 3rd Earl of Cumberland. The death of her brother a year later left her as the infant heiress to a huge patrimony organised around a group of castles in Cumberland, Westmorland and Yorkshire. In 1605, however, by the terms of his will, her father disinherited her in favour of his brother. Anne and her mother launched a long-running legal challenge to this settlement and in 1609 the former married Richard Sackville, 3rd Earl of Dorset, a favourite of the Prince of Wales, perhaps with the hope that he could help her case. Despite this, in 1617, James I irrevocably determined the succession in favour of George Cumberland's will. What kept Anne's hopes alive for her Clifford inheritance, however, was that in the absence of further heirs the property might revert to her. Having been widowed in 1624 she married again to the Earl of Pembroke, who helped her uphold her claim. It finally came to fruition with the death of the 5th Earl of Cumberland without heirs in the midst of the Civil War in 1643.

Anne remained in London until the fighting began to subside and, on 11 July 1649, set out to claim her patrimony. Her own account of this process is recorded in a voluminous series of autobiographical manuscripts. She emerges as a woman of almost obsessively regular habits, intensely aware of her ancestry as well as the anniversaries of important dates in her own life. To her the coincidences of dates revealed the inscrutable workings of divine providence. Having left London in July 1649, a city to which she would never return, she travelled north:

And so by easy journeys in that road, I came to Skipton the eighteenth day of that month into my castle there, it being the first time of my coming into it after the pulling down of most of the old castle, which was done some six months before by order of Parliament because it had been a garrison in the late Civil War. And I was never till now in any part of that castle since I was nine or ten weeks old.

About the twenty-eight of that month I went unto that old decayed tower at Barden, it being the first time that I was ever in that tower. And then I continued to lie in Skipton castle till the seventh of the month following, which was August. And 7th of that month of August I removed from Skipton Castle to Appleby Castle and lay by the way at Kirby Lonsdale.

So the eight day of that August in 1649 I came into Appleby Castle the most ancient seat of my inheritance and lay in my own chamber there where I used formerly to lie with my dear mother and there I continued to lie till about the 13th of February following, this 8th of August being the first time that I came into the said Appleby Castle ever since I went out of it with my dear mother the 8th day of October in 1607 . . . and the 18th day of this August I went through Whinfell and into Brougham Castle for a while, in which castle and park I had not been since the 9th of December in 1616 (when I was Countess of Dorset) till this day. And the 15th day of this August I went into my decayed castles of Brough and Pendragon and into Wharton Hall, where I had not been since August or September, 1607 till then. Proverbs 20:24. [Man's goings are of the LORD; how can a man then understand his own way?]

Lady Anne Clifford, The Life of Me

FOR Anne these castles constituted a physical manifestation of her patrimonial claims and she immediately set to work repairing them in hierarchical order of importance, starting with Skipton and Appleby. She then also began reorganising the tombs in the principal churches associated with these buildings as dynastic mausolea for her family and also establishing charitable foundations. Concurrent with these activities was the preparation of a definitive family history, the *Great Books of Record*.

It would be possible to characterise Lady Anne as an eccentric architectural patron, restoring castles while a new social and architectural order was taking root in Commonwealth England. And it's true that her position was bizarre: she was a figure of declared Royalist sympathy who by virtue of her sex and marriage to the Parliamentarian Earl of Pembroke was able to reclaim her inheritance and restore her ancestral castles. That said, she spent an estimated £40,000 on building, which puts her in the first division of architectural patrons amongst her contemporaries. Added to which, the nature of her patronage – beautifying castles and developing both family mausolea and charitable institutions in their shadow – was actually very conventional for a member of the nobility. It's also paralleled by some other aristocratic survivors in the 1650s, such as Lady Hungerford.

These patterns of patronage are undoubtedly medieval and in Lady Anne's case they consciously revived lapsed family associations; two of the castles she restored, Brough and Pendragon, had been ruins for more than a century when she came to them. They also evoked for her a yet deeper history. Appleby, Brougham and Brough had keeps that were known to Lady Anne respectively as Caesar's Tower, the Pagan Tower and the Roman Tower. Her claim to these buildings was by right of birth but they in turn had a claim to the landscape itself and the very roots of British history.

1665
ROCHESTER CASTLE
Exploring a Ruin

The Medway Raid, a British fiasco and Dutch triumph, depicted by Willem Schellinks within a decade of the event. The ruins of Rochester Castle are a major landmark in this view, much more prominent than the cathedral spire to the far right. They are shown as Pepys would have seen them commanding the end of the great medieval bridge.

Until people began to appreciate castle ruins from an antiquarian or aesthetic perspective, they really were just abandoned sites, often stripped of valuable materials, buried in rubble and overgrown. Where appropriate the land covered by the ruins might be leased out for agriculture or industry. That said, the sheer scale of some ruins naturally attracted interested travellers. The keep at Rochester, for example, is a case in point. Commanding the Medway crossing it was among the tallest secular buildings of pre-industrial

England. The last documented repairs to it took place in the late fourteenth century and the building may have fallen into disrepair soon afterwards. What is certain, however, is that the roof and internal floors had disappeared prior to the Civil War: in August 1635 Lieutenant Hammond observed that 'a man may adventure an ascent of 140 stairs up to the top thereof, without any great danger'. It was a casual visit repeated thirty years later by the diarist Samuel Pepys as he waited for his dinner to be prepared at a nearby inn on 2 October 1665.

Thence to Rochester; walked to the Crown, and while dinner was getting ready, I did there walk to visit the old castle ruins, which hath been a noble place; and there going up I did upon the stairs overtake three pretty maids or women and took them up with me, and did *besarlas muchas vezes et tocar leur mains* [kissed them many times and touched their hands] and necks, to my great pleasure: but Lord, to see what a dreadful thing it is to look down precipices, for it did frighten me mightily, and hinder me from much pleasure which I would have made to myself in the company of these three if it had not been for that. The place hath been very noble, and great in former ages.

PEPYS was moved by the ancient nobility of the ruined keep but on this occasion the distraction provided by the 'three pretty maids' seems to have overwhelmed any interest he might have had in the building (not that his diary otherwise suggests that he was particularly curious about the past). That his amorous adventure – rendered in a characteristic mixture of French and Spanish – was interrupted by vertigo rather than the presence of other people suggests that they had the place to themselves. Evidently, there was nothing at all to tell him what he was looking at or explain its history.

Two years later, in June 1667, the keep presided impotently over the fiasco of the Dutch destruction of the English fleet in the Medway Raid. The great tower figures prominently in a painting (later engraved) of this triumph produced in Holland by Schellinks. In the immediate aftermath of this humiliating disaster Pepys, who worked for the Navy Board, returned to Rochester. He found the town full of soldiers and went out to view the results of the attack, marvelling at all the Dutch had achieved and the abject failure of the response. Having satisfied his curiosity, he returned to town and, hoping for a quick getaway the next morning, had a bed prepared at another local inn. While the bed frame 'was being corded', or prepared, he and his fellow, Creed, again had time on their hands:

> Here in the streets, I did hear the Scotch march beat by the drums before the soldiers, which is very odd. Thence to the castle, and viewed it with Creed, and had good satisfaction from him that showed it us touching the history of it. Then into the fields, a fine walk

It should be explained that the English March was a specific and authorised drumbeat, so hearing another measure in an English town was like hearing someone else's national anthem being played. Clearly, when the two men came to the castle they chanced upon someone who could tell them about its history (or what passed for it). Information of this kind was, of course, extremely difficult to come by and even access to a good seventeenth-century library would have helped Pepys very little in this regard. Castle ruins represented the past but they were not very articulate testimony to it beyond being massive and imposing. Occupied castles, by contrast, had families to keep their history in currency.

1667
CAPHEATON
Replacing Castles

Capheaton, Northumberland, painted by the Dutch artist Peter Hartover in the 1670s. The view was probably fixed in panelling or an overmantle, evidence of a growing taste for topographical views of country houses. Capheaton cannibalised the fabric of an earlier castle and illustrates the Restoration aesthetic for new houses. The 'redoubt' created for the stair is unfortunately invisible to the rear.

While some castles were restored and others slid into irreversible ruin after the Civil War, a third group of buildings was simply replaced. The Restoration of Charles II in 1660 that followed Oliver Cromwell's Commonwealth undoubtedly created a sense of a new beginning. To those who had been in exile, ancient family residences in poor repair held little appeal. In such cases, new houses were often created from the cannibalised remains of old ones. Such occurred at Capheaton, Northumberland, the home since the thirteenth century of the Swinburne family (and still so today). They had remained Catholic, which left them exposed to the predations both of Scottish troops and Parliament during the Civil War. To complicate matters further, the head of the family was murdered in 1643, leaving his third wife either pregnant or just delivered of a baby boy, John. According to family tradition, the infant was spirited away to a monastery in France and, unaware of his parentage, was later identified by his description of the family tabby cat and a silver punch bowl. In 1660 he was confirmed in his estates and, on 26 September, elevated to a baronetcy. Perhaps Capheaton Castle was badly damaged because as early as 1653 his guardians set aside timber for the infant John 'to build his house at Capheaton'. It was not until 9 December 1667, however, that the plans for the new building were finalised and the following contract — shorn of repetitions and some legalese — drawn up with the mason Robert Trollopp to build a square house of three floors with a pitched or 'Italian' roof:

Robert Trollopp shall ... sufficiently, substantially and workmanlike in every respect and purpose make, frame, erect and build near unto the ground or place where an old building or castle is now standing at Capheaton aforesaid one new house which shall be and contain in length 28 yards and in breadth 20 yards from outside to outside. That there shall be a cellar underneath the whole front of the said new house, which shall have an ascent of 2 foot high up to the first floor. That the height from the top of the first floor to the underside of the second floor shall be 13 foot and the height from the top of the second floor to the underside of the garret or third floor shall be 13 foot also. That there shall be 18 rooms in the said new house: on every of the said three floors six rooms (besides closets and passages) with a chimney conveniently made and placed in every of the said 18 rooms. That all the front of the said new house shall be of hewn stone or ashlar work with rustic pilasters from the ground table to the eaves [*muddyllyons*] and shall have a balcony built over the hall door ten foot square supported by two pillars ... That the back of the said house shall be built and walled with the best wall stones and have a redoubt [*reddoot*] in it to break 10 foot out of the range for the enlarging the great stairs. That the said new house shall have handsome stone windows and all the chimneys in the said house shall be hewn . . .

In consideration whereof Sir John Swinborne doth promise . . . [to pay] . . . the said Robert Trollopp the sum of £500 of lawful money of England . . . £30 thereof in hand upon the sealing and delivery of these presents. £50 thereof upon the laying of the foundation of the said house . . . £50 when the first floor [is] laid . . . £50 when it is [at window] transom height of the first floor . . . £50 when the second floor is laid . . . £50 when it is transom height above the second floor . . . £50 when it is fit and ready for the roof . . . £50 when the roof is on . . . £50 when it is all slated and the chimney is all topped . . . £50 when all the lead work and plumbers work is done and the windows glazed and the other £20 when the said house is done and finished as is aforesaid . . . And shall also grant unto the said Robert Trollopp to have use and employ [of] all the materials as stone, timber, iron, lead and glass that shall be or may be found, had or gotten in or about the said old castle at Capheaton aforesaid. And further shall promise and get for the said Robert Trollopp, quarried rent free for the working and getting of stones and slates for the building and finishing of the said new house; he, the said Robert Trollopp or his workmen digging for and getting the said stones and employing the stones gotten in and about the said old castle in the building and finishing of the said new house. And shall fit and furnish the said Robert Trollopp and his workmen with all such timber as shall be used and employed about the building and finishing of the said new house more than the timber gotten in and about the said old castle. And shall likewise find and provide all lime and sand for the whole work. And shall cause to be laid and placed all the said materials . . . near to the place where the said house shall be built . . . [and] free liberty of ingress and regress too and fro, in, on or about the lands and grounds there the said house be built until the same be done and finished.

9 December 1667, indenture

THIS contract offers a fascinating insight into the process of constructing a house in the late seventeenth century. In some details it bears close comparison to medieval building contracts (see 1348 above). Trollopp undertook to complete the contract by 11 November 1669, and receipts for several of the payments by instalment are noted on the indenture itself, making it possible to trace the progress of the work. The text must have been drawn up with reference to a plan or model that no longer survives. The need for clarity about the provision of materials makes clear the degree to which the new building was born from the castle that pre-existed it. Nothing is known, however, about the form of the castle itself.

Robert Trollopp, who certainly designed the new house, made his career in the north of England. He is first documented at York in 1647 and was invited to Newcastle in 1655 to build a new Guildhall and Exchange. This he did at a cost of £2,000 to a design agreed in a pasteboard model and, 'according to the best authors now in English', evidence of the published sources from which he drew architectural inspiration. With his son, Henry, he established a regional practice that included several houses and work on a fort at Lindisfarne in 1675, evidence, perhaps, of experience as a military engineer in the Civil War. If so, that might explain his surprising description of the staircase turret of the house as a 'redoubt'.

Not everyone chose to cannibalise castle ruins. At Brampton Bryan, Herefordshire, a new house developed beside the devastated remains of the medieval castle besieged in 1643 and heroically defended by Brilliana, Lady Harley. Preserving its remains may have been an act of family piety.

1670
WINDSOR CASTLE
Armour as Architecture

The guard chamber at Hampton Court, Surrey, preserves the much-restored remains of its architectural decoration created in the seventeenth century using weapons. Such displays, which are also found in carved form on funerary monuments, reflect the continued fascination with the trappings of war as decoration.

Windsor Castle survived the Civil War and Commonwealth by a whisker. The clergy of St George's Chapel were thrown out but the castle itself was one of eight royal residences reserved to the state in 1649. Then, in 1652 it was condemned to demolition by Parliament for cash. In the event, however, only the Great Park was sold up and the castle buildings remained in use, for the main part as a prison.

Passing through Windsor with his wife by carriage on 8 June 1654, the diarist John Evelyn visited the castle at the nadir of its fortunes. He found the tomb of 'our blessed martyr King Charles' and admired the prospect from the Round Tower on the motte. The castle as a whole he judged to be 'large in circumference, but the rooms melancholy and of ancient magnificence'. Following the Restoration, Prince Rupert, a nephew of Charles I and veteran commander of the Civil War, was installed as constable and restored his apartments in the Round Tower on the motte in a startling new martial idiom. As Evelyn noted in his diary on 29 August 1670:

Note, that Windsor was now going to be repaired, being exceedingly ragged and ruinous: Prince Rupert constable had begun to trim up the keep or high round tower, and handsomely adorned his hall, with a furniture of arms, which was very singular; by so disposing the pikes, muskets, pistols, bandoliers, holsters, drums, back [plates], breast [plates] and headpieces as was very extraordinary: and thus those huge steep stairs ascending to it, had the walls invested with this martial furniture, all new and bright, and set with such study, as to represent pilasters, cornices, architraves, friezes, by so disposing the bandoliers, holsters, and drums, so as to represent festoons, and that without any confusion, trophy like. From the hall, we went into his bedchamber and ample rooms which were hung with tapestry, curious and effeminate pictures, so extremely different from the other, which presented nothing but war and horror, as was very surprising and divertissant. The king passed most of his time in hunting the stag and walking the park, which he was now also planting with walks of trees et cetera.

John Evelyn, diary

THE display that Evelyn admired extended up the long covered staircase that rises up the motte at Windsor and formed the ascent to Prince Rupert's apartment in the Round Tower. As his response makes clear, it struck him as a novel decorative treatment not only because it was curious to see armaments turned to art but also because it spoke of 'war and horror'. The explicit connection he makes is with the display of arms in 'trophies', or Roman triumphal processions. In these regards the display reflected the prince's experience as a soldier and also the martial character of his office as constable resident within the keep of a great castle. Evelyn also enjoyed the aesthetic contrast between the warlike approach and the inner luxury of the apartment itself, a contrast long explored in castle architecture (see 1360 above and more generally in *Sir Gawain and the Green Knight*). This display of armour was subsequently extended into the guard chamber, or first interior, of the royal apartment. It was here that guards filtered visitors, only allowing the most favoured access to the person of the prince and the rooms beyond.

One of the figures undoubtedly involved in mounting the weapons for Prince Rupert was the royal gunsmith, John Harris of neighbouring Eton. When Charles II subsequently restored his own apartments at Windsor (see 1683 below), Harris also helped decorate the king's guard chamber – occupied by the Yeomen of the Guard – within them. For a short period thereafter, elaborate hangs of weapons became specifically associated with guard chambers: Harris did the same for James II in his guard chamber at Whitehall and then for William III at Hampton Court. Only the last of these now survives, though in much adapted form. Harris's most extravagant creation, however, was the Small Armoury at the Tower of London commissioned in 1696. This was by now a well-established visitor attraction (see 1598 above) and Harris's extraordinary creations included an 'organ' ten ranges high with pipes made of blunderbusses and two thousand pairs of pistols. Such displays underline the degree to which the trappings of war continued to fascinate the Stuart court.

1 6 7 8
DOUBTING CASTLE
The Capture and Escape of Christian and Hopeful

Doubting Castle as depicted in the first edition of *The Pilgrim's Progress*. The Giant Despair is represented as Hercules with his club and the skin of the Nemean lion. The tiny faces of his prisoners peer pathetically from behind their dungeon grill.

The Pilgrim's Progress (1678) by the nonconformist John Bunyan is one of the most influential devotional works in the English language. It's a ruggedly told but compelling allegory of two souls – Christian and Hopeful – in pursuit of salvation. At every stage in their journey they encounter people and places whose significance, like those of the souls themselves, is underlined by their names.

Such is the case here with Doubting Castle, a stronghold commanded by the Giant Despair; his name illustrates the final fate of those that give way to doubt. In the first edition of The Pilgrim's Progress, *this narrative was illustrated with a crude woodcut of a giant, dressed like the hero Hercules with a club and lion's cloak, standing in the archway of a battlemented building. Beside him, two tiny faces peer out from a black dungeon through an iron grating. It's interesting to note that at the time he wrote this, Bunyan was himself imprisoned in Bedford, where he languished for over a decade. We take up the story as Christian and Hopeful lie down to rest for the night.*

Now there was not far from the place where they lay, a castle, called Doubting Castle, the owner wherof was Giant Despair, and it was in his grounds they now were sleeping; wherefore he getting up in the morning early, and walking up and down in his fields, caught Christian and Hopeful asleep in his grounds. Then with a grim and surly voice he bid them awake, and asked them whence they were? And what they did in his grounds? They told him, they were Pilgrims, and that they had lost their way. Then said the Giant, you have this night trespassed on me ... The Giant therefore drove them before him, and put them into his castle, into a very dark dungeon, nasty and stinking to the spirit of these two men: Here then they lay, from Wednesday morning till Saturday night, without one bit of bread, or drop of drink, or any light, or any to ask how they did ... good Christian, as one half amazed, brake out in this passionate speech, What a fool, quoth he, am I thus to lie in a stinking dungeon, when I may as well walk at liberty? I have a key in my bosom, called Promise, that will, I am persuaded, open any lock in Doubting Castle. Then said Hopeful, that's good news; good brother pluck it out of thy bosom and try: then Christian pulled it out of his bosom, and began to try at the dungeon door, whose bolt (as he turned the key in) gave back, and the door flew open with ease, and Christian and Hopeful both came out. Then he went to the outward door that leads into the castle yard, and with his key opened the door also. After he went to the iron gate, for that must be opened too, but that lock went damnable hard, yet the key did open it; then they thrust open the gate to make their escape with speed, but that gate, as it opened, made such a creaking, that it waked Giant Despair, who hastily rising to pursue his prisoners, felt his limbs to fail, so that he could by no means go after them. Then they went on, and came to the King's highway again, and so were safe, because they were out of his jurisdiction.

John Bunyan, *The Pilgrim's Progress*

BUNYAN had served in the New Model Army during the Civil War of the 1640s, an experience that perhaps helps explain why the pilgrims struggle and battle at every stage of their journey. In this combination of devotional and warlike themes his writing forms a fascinating parallel to those of St Aelred (see *c.* 1150 above). So too does the description of the castle as having many layers of doors, though in this case the endeavour is to escape them.

Doubting Castle fits into a long tradition stretching back into the Middle Ages that characterises castles as sinister buildings; places of torture and imprisonment (see 1241 above). It also projects forwards, as we shall see, into the 'Gothic' novel, not to mention into the modern use of these buildings as prisons (see 2012 below). There is another side to these buildings – of luxury and high living – but that experience of them has always been limited to the tiny minority who have been privileged to occupy or own them.

WINDSOR CASTLE
A Baroque Stronghold and Palace

In 1660 Charles II restored both the Order of the Garter and its associated College of St George in Windsor Castle. He also reclaimed the Great Park and appointed his cousin constable with lodgings in the Round Tower (see 1670 above). Nevertheless, in the early part of his reign, during the height of his popularity, he spent very little time at the castle. That changed suddenly after it became publicly known in 1673 that his brother and heir, the future James II, had converted to Catholicism. Public opinion in London began to turn against the king and it was abruptly announced in 1674 not only that the king would celebrate Easter at Windsor but that the court would remain there over the summer. The castle was undoubtedly seen as offering a degree of security and protection against popular violence.

To make it suitable for occupation, work began to re-cast Edward III's buildings in the Upper Ward. The project was overseen by the architect Hugh May and eventually absorbed more than £100,000, a stupendous sum. Work on the apartments of the king and queen was completed by 1678 with huge illusionistic paintings on allegorical themes by the artist Antonio Verrio, who was born at Lecce in the heel of Italy. In 1678, fuelled by the malicious inventions of Titus Oates, there followed another wave of anti-Catholic hysteria. As the future of the Stuart monarchy hung in the balance, the king put in motion Verrio's redecoration of the two principal public interiors in the castle, St George's Hall and the Chapel Royal. On 16 June 1683, the diarist and courtier, John Evelyn, came to admire them. He besides extolled the decorative woodcarving by Grinling Gibbons, a craftsman he had discovered and introduced to the king, the landscaping round the building and an engine that pumped water into the castle:

That which now at Windsor was new and surprising to me since I was last there was that incomparable fresco painting in Saint George's Hall, representing the legend of St George, and triumph of the Black Prince, and his reception by Edward III; the vault or roof not totally finished. Then the chapel of the Resurrection, where the figure of the Ascension is, in my opinion, comparable to any paintings of the most famous Roman masters. The Last Supper also over the altar (I liked exceedingly the contrivance of the unseen organs behind the altar) nor less the stupendous, and beyond all description, the incomparable carving of our Gibbons, who is (without controversy) the greatest master, both for invention, and rareness of work, that the world ever had in any age, nor doubt I at all that he will prove as great a master in the statuary art. Verrio the painter's invention is likewise admirable, his ordnance full and flowing, antique and heroical, his figures move. And if the walls hold (which is the only doubt, by reason of the salts, which in time, and in this moist climate prejudices) the work will preserve his name to ages. There was now the terraces almost brought round the old castle. The grafts made clean, even, and curiously turfed. Also the avenues to the New Park, and other walks planted with elms and limes, and a pretty canal, and receptacle for fowl. Nor less observable and famous is the exulting of so huge a quantity of excellent water, to the enormous height of the castle, for the use of the whole house, by extraordinary invention and force of Sir Samuel Moreland.

John Evelyn, diary

VERRIO's decoration as described by Evelyn emphasised not only the majesty of the king but also his divinely derived authority. The hall and chapel were aligned end to end and formed part of a single range within the castle. In the course of the remodelling of this range Hugh May moved the dividing wall between the two rooms to enlarge the chapel and shorten the hall. Both spaces had a focal point at one end – respectively an altar in the chapel and a throne in the hall – and windows on one side only. Verrio used the long blank wall opposite in each room as a huge canvas. In St George's Hall he used this to create the illusion of a parallel hall in which a triumph was being celebrated by life-sized figures.

The scene was presided over by the enthroned figure of Edward III. His son, the Black Prince, was shown in the centre of the wall leading two captive kings, David II of Scotland and John the Good of France. Both kings had really been brought to Windsor as captives, though at different times. All this imagery related to the Order of the Garter, which was founded by Edward III (see 1344 above). St George, the martial patron of the order, as well as of England, was depicted above the throne and the emblem of the Garter appeared round each of the circular clerestory windows that lit the room. Events celebrated in this throne-room were implicitly refracted through the lens of history.

In the centre of the ceiling was an image of Charles II in the heavens with the crown suspended above his head. This formed a counterpart image to that in the centre of the chapel ceiling, which showed Christ ascending into glory. On the main wall of the chapel, meanwhile, was another image of Christ healing the sick in the Temple at Jerusalem. Since the Middle Ages it had been believed that anointed kings had the miraculous power to cure scrofula by touch, for which reason the disease was called the King's Evil. Charles II revived the practice of 'touching for the King's Evil' in a relatively modest way during his exile. This chapel now became the setting for this ritual and in 1682 alone he touched nine thousand sufferers. At the end of his reign it was estimated that he had touched 92,107 people with the complaint.

Evelyn was fully aware that these interiors and their art needed to stand international comparison. Grinling Gibbons is one of the few English sculptors whose name and naturalistic sculpture has remained popularly familiar to the present, justifying Evelyn's extravagant praise. His 'statuary art' refers to the artist's desire to work in the more prestigious material of marble, particularly for funerary monuments (in which Gibbons did enjoy some success). The formal planning of the castle surrounds has been subsequently overlaid and the special mention of the water system is a reminder that such an astonishing convenience was quite as notable in the seventeenth century as the building and its decoration.

Both hall and chapel interiors were destroyed in 1828 during George IV's extravagant remodelling of Windsor Castle.

WARWICK CASTLE

All Mere Fiction

A view of Warwick Castle in 1748 by Canaletto. The apartments that Celia Fiennes admired occupy the massive range overlooking the river. The motte with its 'vast prospect' and approached up a spiral path is visible to the left.

In 1697, at the age of thirty-five, a gentlewoman living in London called Celia Fiennes began a journey that would take her to Yorkshire and the Peak District. It was one of numerous trips she undertook on horseback across the kingdom, initially for the good of her health and for recreation. She stayed at inns or in country houses where she had some family connection. Such travels were becoming fashionable – although a single woman on the road with a servant would have been unusual – and she wrote up an account of them. She regularly visited houses but was little interested in antiquities, art or nature, which makes her observations all the more unusual and interesting.

Instead her comments are often practical and show an interest in domestic
arrangements. Here is her impression of Warwick Castle:

Warwick Castle is a stately building; it's now the Lord Brooke's
house. You enter through two large courts into a noble hall
wainscoted, with in it is a large parlour all wainscoted with cedar,
which is full of fine pictures of the family and beyond that is a
drawing room and bed chamber with good tapestry hangings; they
are old but so good work and so beautiful the colours still, you
would admire it, and the work so curious all of silk that the very
postures and faces look extreme lively and natural, and the groves,
streams and rivers look's very well on it. There was good velvet
chairs in the rooms and good pictures. Within the bed chamber is
closets, out of one you look to the river even at the end window,
there is so great a level you may see near 20 mile. Stowe-on-the-
Wold you see which is as far, it's all full of enclosures and woods
most of the country. All these rooms are very lofty and large and
larger than most houses I have seen, the gardens fine and many
without each other, with good gravel and grass walks, squares of
dwarf trees of all sorts and steps to descend from one walk to
another, the whole of which I saw at one view on the top of the
mount [the motte], together with the whole town and a vast
prospect all about, the mount being very high and the ascent is
round and secured by cut hedges on the side of the path. At the
entrance of the first court the porter diverts you with a history of
Guy, Earl of Warwick, there is his walking staff nine foot long and
the staff of a giant which he killed that's twelve foot long; his sword,
helmet and shield and breast and back all of a prodigious size, as is
his wife's iron slippers and also his horse's armour and the pottage-
pot for his supper – it was a yard over the top; there is also the
bones of several beasts he kill'd, the rib of the dun-cow as big as half
a great cartwheel: two miles from the town is his cave dug out by
his own hands just the dimension of his body as the common
people say, there is also his will cut out on stone, but the letters are
much defaced; these are the stories and mere fiction, for the true
history of Guy was that he was but a little man in stature though
great in mind and valour, which tradition describes to posterity by

being a giant. Such will the account be of our hero King William
III though little in stature yet great in achievements and valour.

Celia Fiennes, *Through England on a Side-Saddle*

TO Celia Fiennes the form of Warwick Castle was clearly not very
interesting and even her description of it being arranged around two
courts suggests a misremembering of what she saw. Certainly, it's difficult
to reconcile with the fabric of the building as it then existed, unless she
regarded the stable yard as a court. Passing into the house she notes
the quality of the pictures and some chairs but she chiefly marvels at
the tapestries, which to her eye are old but beautiful. It's likely that
needlework was at least a childhood pastime so the admiration of the
fabrics would have come easily to her. Some of her passing observations,
however, also merit consideration. She comments, for example, that one
room is panelled in cedar. With the growing reach of British trade in the
late seventeenth century, exotic woods were increasingly being used in
domestic interiors. Celia otherwise uses the word cedar to describe these
exotic woods generically. Some gave the interior a strong and distinctive
smell, which may additionally account for their appearing noteworthy.
She was also struck by the size of the rooms, a reminder of the changes
in the scale of grand domestic living in England since the late sixteenth
century.

The views from the castle and its formal gardens were much more
interesting to her than the architecture. By this date the castle motte had
been converted into a mount, or viewing hill, from which she could
enjoy all the garden compartments. The reuse of mottes as vantage-
points within gardens is documented in several major castles such as
Belvoir and Durham from the mid-sixteenth century onwards. The
possessions of Guy of Warwick still survive at the castle as curiosities, as
does the chapel at Guy's Cliffe with its remarkable rock-cut effigy (see
1485 above). Her final comparison of William III and Guy is very
unexpected and hints at a new spirit of Protestant patriotism.

1715
BLENHEIM CASTLE
A Grateful Nation's Gift

*This engraving shows the newly completed garden facade of 'Blenheim Castle'
as it appears in* Vitruvius Britannicus *(1715), a collection of architectural
designs compiled by Colen Campbell. Below is the elevation as it appears today.*

As the title implies, *Vitruvius Britannicus* is a patriotic work and in his
preface Campbell regrets that 'so many of the British quality have so
mean an opinion of what is performed in our own country; tho', perhaps,
in most we equal, and in some things we surpass, our neighbours'. With
this volume in hand, he goes on to explain, it will be possible to assess

Britain's buildings justly. The particular contrast he draws is with recent Italian architects who have corrupted the 'Antique simplicity' of their forebears – notably the work of the sixteenth-century Vicentine architect Andrea Palladio – 'with capricious ornaments, which must at last end in Gothic'. Campbell, in other words, sought in this volume to demonstrate how British architects had developed a Classical tradition of architecture that had inherited the mantle of Palladio and also, by extension, that of Ancient Rome. Such ideas had a particular resonance given the nation's growing power, wealth and global trade networks.

One figure at the heart of Britain's new-found confidence was the soldier John Churchill, Duke of Marlborough, whose military success culminated in his victory over the French at the Battle of Blenheim in 1704. He was loaded with honours by a grateful nation, including the manor of Woodstock, part of a 22,000-acre estate in Oxfordshire. Significantly, this was the birthplace of one England's great medieval chivalric figures, the Black Prince, son of Edward III and the victor of another celebrated victory, Poitiers. Money was also provided to build a great house here named after Blenheim and the duke himself chose the architect, a former soldier and playwright, Sir John Vanbrugh.

As Campbell explains of this illustration in his book: 'The Manner is Grand, the Parts Noble, and the Air Majestick of this Palace, adapted to the Martial Genius of the Patron . . .' There are trophies of arms and flaming grenades on the parapet of the main block and between them the figure of Marlborough on horseback trampling his enemies. The symmetrical facade terminates in towers that are made to appear rugged by the articulation of each course of masonry and at basement level the round openings ornamented with lions' heads resemble cannon embrasures. Vanbrugh's use of windows with semicircular heads is highly unusual in a domestic context and probably derives from the remodelled Windsor (see 1683 above). No wonder Blenheim was entitled a castle in the accompanying text. What's perhaps confusing to a modern audience, however, is that this is not a castle in a medieval idiom at all. Campbell disdained the Gothic (though he did include the remarkable, castle-like frontage of Hampton Court, Herefordshire, of about 1710 in his publication); instead, this is a Classical castle suitable for the leading general of Britain in its character as a second Rome.

In assuming this character Blenheim was not an isolated undertaking for Vanbrugh. Famously, for example, he attempted something similar at Castle Howard, Yorkshire, which his associate Hawksmoor described in a letter of 1734 as 'the seat of one of the chief nobles of Britain, it is both a castle and palace conjoined'. Posterity has tended to admire the palatial character of both buildings but their quality as castles was important as well.

Indeed, to some patrons of the period the idea of the castle was so important that they consciously celebrated it. Again, those with military experience loom large. One such, for example, Sir John Germaine, commissioned William Talman – an architect best known for his Baroque remodelling of Chatsworth – to enlarge the ancient house he had acquired by marriage at Drayton, Northamptonshire, with a duplicate medieval tower (the work was contracted for in August 1702). No less remarkable are the elaborate designs for castles drawn up on paper by John, 2nd Duke of Montagu, clear evidence of his informed antiquarian interest in these buildings. He campaigned with his father-in-law, the Duke of Marlborough, and in about 1714 began to recast his seat at Beaulieu, Hampshire, a former Cistercian monastery, as a castle.

1726
NEWARK CASTLE
The Jaws of Time

A view of Newark Castle, Nottinghamshire, drawn and engraved by Samuel Buck. It is part of a set of engravings advertised for subscription as 'Proposals for the publication of . . . twenty-four views of castles . . . in the counties of Lincoln and Nottingham, November 1, 1726'. In this printed advertisement Buck promised to 'rescue the mangled remains' of 'these aged & venerable edifices from the inexorable jaws of time'.

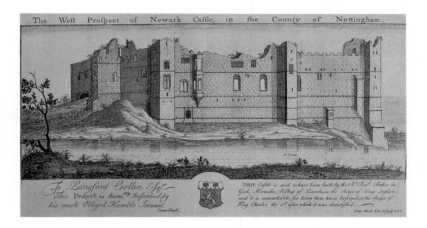

EACH print is entitled across the top. In the lower frame is a dedication, usually to the owner or subscriber. In this case it's Langford Collin esquire, burgess of neighbouring Nottingham and a figure with antiquarian interests. To the lower right is a very compressed history of the site, which correctly identifies Alexander, Bishop of Lincoln, and a nephew of Roger, Bishop of Salisbury (see 1139 above), as a major figure in the development of the castle. The reference to the Civil War may explain the dedication of the plate. Collin was a great grandson of a gunner, Laurence Collin, who had formed part of the garrison at Nottingham during the Civil War and subsequently settled there (with the backing of Oliver Cromwell). He may have been involved, therefore, in the fighting at Newark. In acknowledgement of the defining importance of the River Trent as a boundary between northern and southern England, there is a small annotation of its name in the engraving itself.

Samuel Buck became involved in recording antiquities in his native Yorkshire from 1719 (Collin was resident for a period in York at about this time, so this is probably where the two men met). Soon afterwards he was introduced to the newly founded Society of Antiquaries and its first secretary, William Stukeley, an outstanding early scholar of Stonehenge. The society's fellowship of influential and wealthy antiquaries encouraged him first to engrave a group of his Yorkshire drawings, which were published in 1726. His subsequent call for subscriptions towards drawings in Lincolnshire and Nottinghamshire marked the start of a hugely ambitious new initiative: engravings of antiquities across the whole of England and Wales. He began to work with his brother, Nathaniel. They travelled and sketched over the summer and engraved in the winter. By 1753 they had created 423 engravings of castles, abbeys and ruins besides eighty-one prospects of towns and cities. These were published in London each year as seventeen sets of – usually – twenty-four engravings by county and priced at the considerable sum of two guineas.

The engravings compiled by the Bucks constitute the first national survey of historic monuments and are immensely valuable as such. Judged against the illustrations being published in journals with antiquarian interests, such as the *Gentleman's Magazine*, the Bucks' work is of high quality. Compared to almost all other topographic art of the period, however, they are naive. That's true whether they are set beside the occasional work of other artists (see 1730 below) or the engraved survey of great aristocratic seats, *Britannia Illustrata*, by the Dutch artists Jan Kip and Leonard Knyff, from 1708 (comprising aerial views, of which there was already a long tradition, see 1539 above). Also the painted views that were becoming a popular feature of the decoration of the halls of country houses. The relative quality of the engravings is a reminder that these views were not really conceived as being of value for aesthetic reasons. Rather they were specialist records of a select group of monuments intended for a small interest group.

1730
STAINBOROUGH AND WENTWORTH CASTLES
The Monument to Ancestry

This engraving by Thomas Badeslade dated 1730 comes from the fourth volume of Vitruvius Britannicus *(see 1715 above), published in 1739. It shows an aerial view of the great Baroque house known from 1731 as Wentworth Castle, Yorkshire, created for the nominal Tory, soldier and diplomat Thomas Wentworth.*

THE name Wentworth Castle referred to a dynastic feud over the inheritance of Charles I's favourite, the Earl of Strafford, executed in 1641. Strafford's title became extinct following the death of his son without children in 1695. Thomas, a great nephew, clearly expected to inherit Strafford's patrimony and his seat of Wentworth Woodhouse, Yorkshire. Instead, it passed by the terms of a will to another member of the family who – to add insult to injury – was a Whig in his politics. In 1708, therefore, the aggrieved Thomas bought the neighbouring estate of Stainborough and renamed it Strafford Hall. He did so with the explicit purpose of reviving the extinct earldom of Strafford in his favour

249

and eclipsing his rival. When he won his suit for the earldom the house became Wentworth Castle – one up on Wentworth Woodhouse – and he completed what became known as Stainborough Castle at the top right of this view.

The surrounds of Wentworth Castle were redesigned from about 1711 by the garden designer George London, who created much of what is visible here including the octagonal pool with cascade in the foreground. Notice the huge screen of iron in the foreground, which opened out the views towards and from the castle. Intervisibility was central to the Baroque aesthetic. To the left is a formal garden centred on a single statue and a parterre. Beyond is a monumental hedged garden undoubtedly inspired by – and built in competition with – the contemporary gardens at Castle Howard, Yorkshire. From this a wooded walk led uphill to Stainborough Castle, the name literally translating as 'stone burgh'. The implied previous existence of a 'burgh' or fortification here must explain why the eighteenth-century castle building bears an inscription, 'Rebuilt 1730'. The castle is encircled by a wall with four towers named after Thomas's children.

The two castles depicted here underlined Thomas's status as Earl of Strafford in different ways. One showed him as a modern nobleman of taste and power, the other as a figure dignified by history. This idea of familial history being expressed by the juxtaposition of buildings in this way has a history in England stretching back at least to the sixteenth century. The carefully preserved vestiges of the thirteenth-century abbey church facade at Newstead, Nottinghamshire, for example, speak of the monastic origins of the house, and in 1590 Bess of Hardwick famously and pointedly erected the New Hall at Hardwick immediately beside its predecessor, the now-ruined Old Hall.

The astonishing bloodless war of architecture and landscaping begun by Thomas, Earl of Strafford was arguably lost in the end to Wentworth Woodhouse which, as a tool of electoral politics, grew to become – with Stowe, Buckingham – one of the largest neo-Classical houses in Britain. Stainborough Castle, however, and much of its surrounding landscape, has recently been restored yet again.

1745
CARLISLE CASTLE
A Jacobite Defence

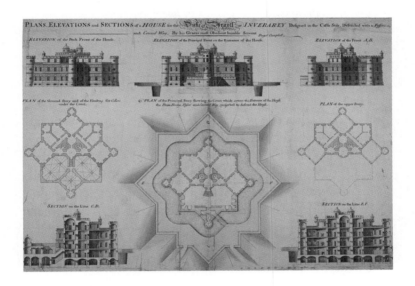

A design for Inverary Castle, Argyll, seat of the Duke of Argyll, by the military engineer Dugal Campbell and probably drawn up in 1744, just before the Jacobite rising. Its centralised, star-shaped plan is clearly derived from artillery forts and the entrance is fortified. The new castle actually took a different form but incorporates the fosse or ditch that constitutes the main protection of this extraordinary house.

The arrival of Prince Charles Edward Stuart, familiarly known as Bonnie Prince Charlie, on the west coast of Scotland on 23 July 1745, and the Jacobite rising in support of his claim to the throne, unexpectedly forced Carlisle Castle back into military service. As his rebel army, composed largely of Highlanders, marched south into England, frantic preparations were made to repair the long-neglected defences of the town and to provision the castle. Despite these efforts the city resisted the Jacobites for just four days and the castle surrendered at 10 a.m. on Friday, 15 November. The prince continued south, leaving a garrison behind. A month later, having travelled as far as Derby, he retreated back through Carlisle with the Duke of Cumberland, the youngest son of George II, leading a Hanoverian force close on his heels. The prince, contrary to all advice, insisted on leaving a garrison to hold the city. A series of letters written to a prebend of the cathedral, Dr John Waugh, who was safely retired in York at the time, describe the siege of the town and castle that ensued. All but the last were written by Joseph Nicolson, a gentleman and steward of the Bishop of Carlisle, who later became a considerable antiquary:

Honoured Sir,

As I told you in my last, the main body of highlanders continued their march into Scotland, and got safe over [the River] Esk, except about six or seven that perished there; but left a garrison of about 300 or 400 men at Carlisle, who yet hold out the town in defiance of the Duke and his brave army, who yesterday surrounded the town [21 December]. The rebels have fired a great many cannon since yesterday about noon, when they began that dreadful work. The Duke, it's said, is extremely exasperated, has sent for some of Wade's artillery (for he has none along with him), and some 18 lb [cannon] from Whitehaven, which are expected to be up tomorrow, and many feel the whole town will be laid in ashes . . .

December 22, 1745, 8 at night – I hear the Duke expresses prodigious wrath at giving up Carlisle to the rebels.

THE business of getting artillery to Carlisle took several days. Perhaps Christmas slowed things down. In the meantime, work began to the siege works with trenches and battery positions, the last protected by fascines, wicker drums filled with earth. The first guns arrived on 27 December and that evening Nicolson wrote again:

The Duke's army has now (this evening only) with the help of the bishop's coach horses, and the whole countryside besides, got six cannon ready for the batteries, and hope to begin to play tomorrow morning, many hands being at work night and day in making trenches, fascines et cetera. God send a happy and ready aid; for otherwise it is to be feared that many of the inhabitants will be starved as well as ruined.

This eager support from the countryside reflected both local fear of the Highland army and also concern for the town's population, which was caught in the fighting. The first guns that arrived were capable of firing cannon balls weighing 18 lbs.

Poor miserable Carlisle continues in the same situation I wrote in my last . . . only the Duke's people got one battery of six 18-pounders, completed on Primrose Bank . . . on Friday night [27th], and played upon the castle most furiously on Saturday [28th]; and, as it's said, dismounted seven of the rebels' cannon, and made some small breaches in the walls. Yesterday [29th] there was a sort of cessation occasioned, as I hear, by our want of ball [ammunition]; but last night they got a very ample supply with two more 18-pounders and four 24[-pounder]s, and will renew the attack this day [30th] with the utmost vigour . . . the officers say that they hope to be in the town tomorrow night; but I am greatly afraid the work will not be so soon done.

Joseph Nicolson to Dr John Waugh, correspondence

In fact the 24-pound guns never opened fire: Another correspondent wrote to Dr Waugh the next day, New Year's Eve:

I have an account this day from my brother Carleton, dated at his highness' [the duke's] headquarters at Blackhill, yesterday [30th], 12 o'clock, that the rebels hung out the white flag on Sunday night, that a colonel went from his highness to know their terms, who had returned and gone again to the city and, said 'no quarter' . . . He tells me the rebels fired several times on Sunday [29th] with powder only, and is pretty certain they have no ball, but plenty of grape shot. They have given for answer they are willing to submit to the laws, and that our troops are at liberty to enter the town at pleasure; how it will terminate we shall soon hear . . .

W. Hutchinson to Dr John Waugh, correspondence

The garrison surrendered to the king's pleasure and were briefly imprisoned in the cathedral before being taken south for trial (given the gentry support for the Jacobites in the north, the government suspended local justice to avoid lenient sentencing). Bonnie Prince Charlie's army, meanwhile, continued north to Glasgow and then besieged Stirling Castle for a period. After a half-victory over Hanoverian forces at Falkirk the '45 Rebellion began to fall apart and the Battle of Culloden, on 16 April 1746, brought it to a horrendous close. The government reprisals afterwards were famously brutal and earned the duke his reputation as 'Butcher' Cumberland. The Jacobite governor of Carlisle, Francis Townley, a Lancashire gentleman who fought with a French commission (and was arguably, therefore, a prisoner of war), was hung, drawn and quartered with several fellow officers. The spectacle diminished the enthusiasm even of London juries to return guilty verdicts of Jacobites.

For a period Carlisle Castle became a Jacobite prison. Such was the pressure on space that numbers were thinned by execution, with men drawing lots for immediate hanging or future transportation. Meanwhile, its fortifications were updated and the building provided with new barracks. It was one of several castles updated for military use in this way immediately after 1745. Carlisle Castle remained the headquarters of the Border Regiment until 1962.

1764
THE CASTLE OF OTRANTO
The Gothic Novel

The Marquis of Vincenza's daughter, Isabella, has just been saved from an unhappy marriage by an astounding accident. Just before the wedding ceremony in the chapel of the Castle of Otranto her husband-to-be was crushed by the miraculous descent from the heavens of a gigantic helmet replete with a vast black plume. The father of the groom, Manfred, described as a prince, fears in his son's death the fulfilment of a prophecy that promises to end his male line. To avert this he calls Isabella to his chamber and states his intention to divorce his blameless wife, Hippolita, and marry her instead. Isabella is horrified and races from the room. Manfred, meanwhile, is distracted from coercing her into agreement by the appearance of the sighing ghost of his grandfather, which descends from a nearby portrait. We follow Isabella:

The lady, whose resolution had given way to terror the moment she had quitted Manfred, continued her flight to the bottom of the principal staircase. There she stopped, not knowing whither to direct her steps, nor how to escape from the impetuosity of the Prince. The gates of the castle, she knew, were locked, and guards placed in the court. Should she, as her heart prompted her, go and prepare Hippolita for the cruel destiny that awaited her, she did not doubt but Manfred would seek her there, and that his violence would incite him to double the injury he meditated, without leaving room for them to avoid the impetuosity of his passions. Delay might give him time to reflect on the horrid measures he had conceived, or produce some circumstance in her favour, if she could – for that night, at least – avoid his odious purpose. Yet where conceal herself? How avoid the pursuit he would infallibly make throughout the castle?

As these thoughts passed rapidly through her mind, she recollected a subterraneous passage which led from the vaults of the castle to the church of St. Nicholas. Could she reach the altar before she was overtaken, she knew even Manfred's violence would not dare to profane the sacredness of the place; and she determined, if no other means of deliverance offered, to shut herself up for ever among the holy virgins whose convent was contiguous to the cathedral. In this resolution, she seized a lamp that burned at the foot of the staircase, and hurried towards the secret passage.

The lower part of the castle was hollowed into several intricate cloisters; and it was not easy for one under so much anxiety to find the door that opened into the cavern. An awful silence reigned throughout those subterraneous regions, except now and then some blasts of wind that shook the doors she had passed, and which, grating on the rusty hinges, were re-echoed through that long labyrinth of darkness. Every murmur struck her with new terror; yet more she dreaded to hear the wrathful voice of Manfred urging his domestics to pursue her.

Horace Walpole, The Castle of Otranto, Chapter 1

ACCORDING to its author, Horace Walpole, *The Castle of Otranto* was born of a half-remembered dream. Waking one morning, 'all I could recover was, that I had thought myself in an ancient castle (a very natural dream for a head like mine, filled with Gothic story), and that on the uppermost banister of a great staircase I saw a gigantic hand in armour. In the evening I sat down and began to write, without knowing in the least what I intended to say or relate.' It took him two months to complete and is full of strange twists, supernatural incidents and suspense. The novel was a huge success and reads today like an engaging cross between a Jacobean play and a Gilbert and Sullivan operetta.

The origins of the novel would not have been apparent to its first readers. As first printed, *The Castle of Otranto* purported simply to be a translation by one William Marshal Gent. of a book published in Naples in 1529 that had been 'found in the library of an ancient Catholic family in the north of England'. The preface goes on with antiquarian exactitude to date the events of the story between 1095 and 1243 and archly concludes:

'Though the machinery is invention, and the names of the actors imaginary, I cannot but believe that the groundwork of the story is founded on truth. The scene is undoubtedly laid in some real castle. The author seems frequently, without design, to describe particular parts. "The chamber," says he, "on the right hand;" "the door on the left hand;" "the distance from the chapel to Conrad's apartment:" these and other passages are strong presumptions that the author had some certain building in his eye.'

Such verisimilitude of detail is itself a literary conceit intended to encourage the enthusiastic reader to conceive of Walpole's wild imaginings as a real past. Strikingly, however, the novel contains no overarching description of the castle as a whole. This disjunction is precisely echoed in the architecture of Walpole's other celebrated creation, his villa at Strawberry Hill (which he sometimes called his 'castle' and which may be the source for some of the layout of Otranto Castle) in which precise but completely disconnected borrowings from medieval monuments were conjoined for effect.

What's significant for Walpole in this novel is that his drama is set in a castle; a building understood to be medieval, in which people can be trapped and subject to the absolute authority of the owner.

Walpole only put his name to the second edition of the novel and, at the same time, inserted onto the title page the words 'a Gothic story'. The adjective has since defined it and the genre of writing it inspired, 'the Gothic Novel'. *The Castle of Otranto* was one of several books important to the revival of popular interest in the Middle Ages that crescendoed in the nineteenth century. Needless to say, however, for those who built or improved castles in the same period, horror was not the driving interest of their architectural patronage. Castles in stone and mortar conveyed a very different message bound up more with the invented history described in Walpole's preface than the drama of his narrative.

Walpole poured jealous scorn on those who shared his interest in the Middle Ages such as Henrietta, Countess of Pomfret or Viscount Egmont. When the latter, a keen antiquary, built his own castle at Enmore, Somerset, in 1751–7, for example, rather than acknowledge a fellow enthusiast, Walpole derided him as 'such a passionate admirer of those noble tenures and customs, that he rebuilt his house . . . in the guise of a castle, moated it round and prepared it to defend itself with cross-bows and arrows, against the time in which the fabric and use of gunpowder shall be forgotten.'

1770
ALNWICK CASTLE
A Royal Entertainment

The direct descent of one of the great patrimonies of medieval England, that of the Percy family, Earls of Northumberland, came to an end in 1670. The estates passed by marriage to Charles Seymour, 3rd Duke of Somerset, then in sequence to his eldest son and granddaughter, Elizabeth. In acknowledgement of this inheritance Elizabeth's husband, the politician Sir Hugh Smithson, assumed the name Percy in 1750. At about the same time he also began to restore one of the major Percy castles in Northumberland, Alnwick. Elizabeth directly encouraged the undertaking and took a leading role in the work. The result was one of the first monumental projects of what is now known as the Gothic Revival. In 1766 the couple were elevated to the title of Duke and Duchess of Northumberland and were still at work at their seat in their titular county. By 1768 their ongoing work to Alnwick was reported to have cost over £10,000. It involved a series of professionals including the architect Robert Adam and the landscape designer familiar as 'Capability' Brown. The renovated castle was admired by others interested in Gothic buildings, as for example a correspondent of Sir Roger Newdigate (who was concurrently rebuilding Arbury Hall, Warwickshire, in the Gothic style) who wrote of it in an undated letter:

Mr. Adams was the architect and has really great merit in keeping up to the style of the old castle, which he has imitated very well. Upon the castle walls are the statues of the warriors of that time [of] the Earl Pierce Eye with a Spear etc. The rooms are all finished with Gothic fretwork – a little modernized, but altogether has a fine effect – the ceilings he has painted in subdued colours in the manner which you sometimes talk of and it gives a gay lively effect to what otherwise would look gloomy.

Undated letter from Charles Parker to Sir Roger Newdigate

THE ranks of sculpted warriors on the battlements have been thinned by time but remain one of the most striking features of the castle. They replaced and augmented a series of medieval fighting figures (see 1520 above). Here the writer understands them to represent the garrison of the castle at the time of the death of Malcolm III of Scotland in 1093. By this date the murder of the king in an ambush (see 1095 above) had been connected to an imagined siege of the castle by the Scots. One version of the story ran that a member of the garrison had offered the keys of the castle to Malcolm on the end of a spear as a token of surrender and then thrust the weapon into the king's eye (hence Earl Pierce Eye). The duchess erected a surviving tower to mark the supposed spot of the murder and also the capture of William the Lion (see 1174 above), evidence of how conscious she was of the history of the place.

After twenty years of restoration and improvements, Alnwick welcomed the youngest brother of George III, the Duke of Cumberland. Aside from the campaigning of his namesake uncle, the commander of Culloden, this was the northernmost visit that any close member of the house of Hanover had ever made. The Duchess of Northumberland recounted the event in her diary:

Thursday 22nd August 1770. – About nine in the evening his royal highness the Duke of Cumberland attended by Lt Col. Deacon, Groom of the Bedchamber, arrived at Alnwick Castle where as he entered the castle gates, he was saluted with 21 Guns and every other mark of respect becoming the Duke and Duchess of Northumberland for their royal visitant. On Sunday his royal highness accompanied by their Graces the Duke and Duchess of Northumberland, the right Honourable Earl Percy and Lord Algernon Percy attended Divine Service at Alnwick church, where an excellent sermon was preached by the Revd Doctor Percy, on their return to the castle, his royal highness received the compliments of the mayor and corporation of Newcastle upon Tyne . . . [and] of the mayor and corporation of Berwick upon Tweed . . . who together with their respective recorders Town clerks etc. were presented to his royal highness and had all the honour of kissing his hand as had many other gentlemen of the county attended by Thomas Charles Bigge esq. high sheriff of Northumberland, they afterwards all dined at a grand entertainment given by the Duke and Duchess of Northumberland where the number of dishes served up was 177 exclusive of the dessert. In short, the magnificence and hospitality displayed on this occasion at Alnwick Castle by its present illustrious possessors, gave a striking picture of the state and splendour of our ancient barons and revived the remembrance of their great progenitors the former Earls of Northumberland.

Duchess of Northumberland, diary

The account reads like a description of the event by a third person, not a diary. That's because Elizabeth regarded this event as a moment of modern history that she was recording like a chronicler. It's significant as well that she compares her own hospitality to that of her medieval Percy ancestors. These figures were, indeed, something of an obsession for Elizabeth, who relished their history and even commissioned surveys of their surviving castles and houses. The family ancestry was illustrated in the interior decoration of the castle. Incidentally, the Rev. Dr Percy, who preached for the royal visitor (but was no relation of the duchess), shared this enthusiasm and clothed the medieval exploits of the family with romance in published ballads such as *The Hermit of Warkworth* (1771).

When the 4th Duke succeeded to the title in 1847 he noted at Alnwick 'a great absence of domestic comfort and a deficiency in those modern conveniences requisite in the residence of a nobleman of His Grace's rank'. With the help of the architect Anthony Salvin, he went on to remodel the entire building at vast expense. Externally, the building was made more archaeologically convincing as a medieval fortress. Internally, the duke created Italianate interiors that provoked criticism in some quarters (see 1857 below).

1777
PEVENSEY, HASTINGS AND BODIAM CASTLES
A Sussex Tour

An engraving of Bodiam Castle, Sussex, published in 1785, soon after the visit by Francis Grose for his great survey. By this date castles were becoming objects of both antiquarian and romantic interest. The figures incorporated here, however, are rustics rather than genteel tourists.

On Saturday, 17 May 1777, a corpulent and convivial former officer of the Surrey Militia, Captain Francis Grose, set out from Wandsworth Common to meet up with the ecclesiastical lawyer, Dr William Burrell, for a tour of Sussex. Both men were eminent antiquarians and the former was now well advanced in a national survey of monuments: The Antiquities of England and Wales, *published between 1772 and 1787, was a successor to the work undertaken by the Bucks earlier in the century. It originally appeared in about a hundred separately issued sections. Accompanying the substantial descriptive and historical text were more than six hundred engravings taken*

from the work of accomplished topographical artists such as Paul Sandby.
Confusingly, this 1777 journey was made to furnish a supplement to this
survey, the original Sussex section having already been published. Because of
his military interest, Grose was more attentive to castles than many of his
fellow antiquaries (who were usually concerned instead with churches). We
take up the journey on Saturday, 14 May, as it is reported in Grose's diary:

Got up at six and after breakfast proceeded in our chaise to
Friston church, of which I made a drawing. There was no font
but some fine monuments . . . From thence walked to Eastdean
. . . [and] proceeded through Southbourne in the chaise to
Westham; the road chalky and very slippery . . . Walked to
Pevensey, a strange rude church; here where I drew the font and
a gravestone, also a slight view of the church. The way to Pevensey
lies through the castle, the shape of the external walls near oval,
the keep of which is moated round, stands on the east side of the
outer area; part of it has lately fallen down. Returned and dined
at the King's Head, Mr Harrison with us. After dinner we were
joined by Mr Baker the curate. A vault lately fell in at the castle,
but it contained only ashes and other rubbish.

Set out in the chaise for Hastings, but the road proving
extremely bad at about five miles from Pevensey mounted our
horses and rode by the sluice houses to Bexhill . . . From
Bulverhythe over a tolerable gravelly road to Hastings Mill. Here
missing our road and turning up to the left by the mill, we passed
a dreadful piece of road like a step ladder consisting of huge loose
stones buried in mud. At length at the close of day arrived safe at
the Swan. Distant from Pevensey only 15 miles, total distance
from Mr Harrison's is 24 miles.

Sunday 25th May. Breakfasted at eight. Walked up the hill to
see the castle, of which I made two drawings. On the west side is
a sallyport of singular construction . . . No marks of the staircase
now remain in the tower described by Mr Green. The shape of
the castle seemingly oval; descended by a lane on the west side
which leads to the limekilns . . . Walked in the afternoon to the
castle with Mr Burrell when I made another view and we took the
following measurements:

Diameter of the twisting staircase 4 feet 4 inches and a half. Inside door of the sallyport 2 feet 9 inches wide, 6 feet 6 inches high . . .

[more measurements]

No trace of buildings in the castle.

THE diary captures some of the realities of travelling as an antiquary in the late eighteenth century. One striking detail is the sheer energy that it required. On the first day alone the two men travelled at least twenty-five miles, with the quality of roads determining whether they moved by chaise, horse or foot. It's clear as well that the castle ruins were in a poor state, hence part of the keep at Pevensey having lately fallen. Added to which they were hard to interpret, presumably because of the vegetation. That's why Grose is tentative about the shape of Hastings Castle. The constant sketching, the whole business of taking measurements and even the diary itself are all means of recording what was seen. Such obsessive attention to detail was thought ridiculous by some but for antiquarians there was no other meaningful record to which they could refer other than their own drawings and notes.

This passage also reveals how the two men garnered information from locals who shared their interests. Mr Harrison, for example, was the owner of a nearby house, Folkington Place (now demolished), and the note of the vault collapse at Pevensey occurs in such a way as to suggest that the curate mentioned it in the course of their meal. Mr Green is presumably Captain William Green, another militia officer with an interest in castles. He constructed a battery at Hastings as part of his duties and supplied Grose with a plan and sketch of the ruins that appeared in *The Antiquities of England and Wales*.

For interest it is worth adding Grose's account of his visit to Bodiam Castle on the same trip at the end of May:

At Sandhurst Green mounted our horses and rode to Bodiam. The church is small and situated on a hill on the left hand side of the road, the village a miserable one consisting of a few straggling cottages. Rode on towards the castle which, being situated in a retired place, we dismounted and walked over the fields.

THE CASTLE

Bodiam Castle stands in a bottom and is encompassed by a stagnant moat overgrown with rushes and chickweed. The castle is a magnificent building not unlike Raglan Castle in Monmouthshire. The great front was on the north side over a kind of bridge or causeway defended by an advanced tower, the ruins of which are now standing. The front is adorned with three shields of arms and the ancient iron portcullis is still suspended under the chief entrance. There was a bridge with a gate or porter's lodge before it. NB. Bodiam Castle is the property of Sir Whistler Webster.

1777, Francis Grose, diary

As this description reveals, Bodiam was out of the way, difficult to access and privately owned. The owner is otherwise known to have kept the ruin locked to deter visitors and, though this description is not explicit, it reads like an external viewing only. By writing about it, however, Grose (and Burrell) were laying the foundations for the future exploration of these sites by much larger numbers of people and particularly those in pursuit of a new aesthetic, the picturesque.

1782
DINEFWR CASTLE
The Castle as a Picture

One of William Gilpin's picturesque views of Dinefwr Castle published in his *Observations on the River Wye*. The picturesque aesthetic was equally an inspiration for owners and architects of new castles.

As well as being an object of antiquarian investigation, castle ruins in the late eighteenth century also began to be appreciated aesthetically. A pioneering figure in this process was the clergyman William Gilpin who in 1768 first wrote about the 'picturesque', which he defined to mean 'a term expressive of that peculiar kind of beauty, which is agreeable in a picture'. In an age where social media and the digital photograph are used to present our lives to advantage, Gilpin's idea has a particular resonance today.

The picturesque was essentially a romantic aesthetic that attempted literally and figuratively to frame nature and impose upon it such visual structures as foreground, middle-distance and distance. Crucially, however, artifice was acceptable if the creating hand could work unseen or undetected. Ruins held a particular appeal for those interested in the picturesque because they lent interest to a landscape but suggested that time and nature had overthrown the transient works of man. The picturesque also helped the tourist traveller appreciate what they saw. As Gilpin explained:

We travel for various purposes – to explore the culture of soils – to view the curiosities of art – to survey the beauties of nature – and to learn the manners of men; their different polities, and modes of life. The following little work proposes a new object of pursuit; that of examining the face of a country by the rules of picturesque beauty

THIS passage introduces the narrative of a journey in South Wales, one of the crucibles of the picturesque movement, made in 1770 (but published twelve years later). It comes from a description of Dinefwr Castle in which Gilpin compares a real prospect with a description of the scene in what was then a celebrated poem by Rev. John Dyer, *Grongar Hill* (1726). In drawing the comparison he reveals the importance of literary description in building up images in the mind's-eye, something that was important to armchair travellers before the age of the camera. The particular passage from the poem relevant here describes the hill on which the distant castle stands:

Ancient towers crown his [the hill's] brow,
That cast an aweful look below;
Whose ragged walls the ivy creeps,
And with her arms from falling keeps;
So both a safety from the wind
In mutual dependence find.

Gilpin comments:

[Dinefwr Castle] . . . is seated on one of the sides of the vale of Towy; where it occupies a bold eminence, richly adorned with wood. It was used, not long ago, as a mansion: but Mr. Rice, the proprietor of it, has built a handsome house in his park, about a mile from the castle; which, however, he still preserves, as one of the greatest ornaments of his place.

This castle also is taken notice of by Dyer in his Grongar-hill; and seems intended as an object in a distance. But his distances, I observed, are all in confusion; and indeed it is not easy to separate them from his foregrounds . . . [There follows a criticism of Dyer's poetic description of the landscape, which fails – in Gilpin's opinion – to corroborate in colour and detail to the view itself.]

The next object he [Dyer] surveys is a level lawn, from which a hill, crowned with a castle, which is meant, I am informed, for that of Dinefwr, arises. Here his great want of keeping appears. His castle, instead of being marked with still fainter colours . . . is touched with all the strength of a foreground. You see the very ivy creeping upon its walls. Transgressions of this kind are common in descriptive poetry. Innumerable instances might be collected from much better poems, than Grongar-hill. But I mention only the inaccuracies of an author, who, as a painter, should at least have observed the most obvious principles of his art. With how much more picturesque beauty does Milton introduce a distant castle:

Towers, and battlements he sees,
Bosomed high in tufted trees.

Here we have all the indistinct colouring, which obscures a distant object. We do not see the iron-grated window, the portcullis, the ditch, or the rampart. We can just distinguish a castle from a tree; and a tower from a battlement . . .

The picturesque scenes, which this place affords, are numerous. Wherever the castle appears, and it appears almost everywhere, a landscape purely picturesque is generally presented. The ground is so beautifully disposed, that it is almost impossible to have bad composition. And the opposite side of the vale often appears as a back-ground; and makes a pleasing distance.

W. Gilpin, *Observations on the River Wye*

Gilpin's ideas about the picturesque were to be developed in a new tradition of small country houses termed villas. These buildings were

Lough Cutra Castle, Co. Galway, was designed by the architect John
Nash in about 1811 for a former soldier Charles Vereker. It exemplifies
his picturesque castle style as developed at Luscombe, Devon, and East
Cowes Castle on the Isle of Wight.

relatively small and so positioned in the landscape both to lend interest
to the approaching view and also to enjoy superb views outwards. One
of the outstanding architects of the picturesque was John Nash, who
worked on some of his commissions with the landscape designer
Humphry Repton. Repton explained the appeal of building 'in the
character of a castle' to clients at Luscombe Castle, Devon, erected
between 1799 and 1804. It could blend:

> chaste correctness of proportion, with bold irregularity of outline;
> its deep recesses and projections producing broad masses of light
> and shadow, while its roof is enriched by turrets, battlements,
> corbels and lofty chimneys, has infinitely more picturesque effect
> than any other style of building . . . Its very irregularity will give
> it consequence . . . [and] extend its site, and make it an apparently
> considerable pile of building
>
> H. Repton, Red Book

These characteristics of asymmetry, contrast, visual interest and the impression of scale helped make the castle style – sometimes medievalising and sometimes Italianate, evoking the serene or 'sublime' views of the seventeenth-century French painter Claude – vastly popular. Meanwhile, the picturesque aesthetic manifestly continues to shape the popular British appreciation of ruins.

1790s
LUDLOW, ARUNDEL, HEDINGHAM
AND SUDELEY CASTLES
The Monograph

As the aesthetic and antiquarian interest in medieval castles gradually intensified, a whole series of monographs and surveys of individual buildings began to appear. Some of these were published by local subscription and were aimed at the growing internal tourist market. In this regard it is important to remember that from 1789, the French Revolution (which showed how vulnerable historic buildings might be), and the ensuing Revolutionary Wars, made travel to Europe intermittently impossible. British tourists increasingly explored their own country with a particular eye for the picturesque. An example of a study aimed in part to serve them was An Historical Account of Ludlow Castle *(1794) by a local attorney, W. Hodges. This contains only two illustrations – an engraved view and a plan of the castle. The main emphasis is on narrating the history of the building but it also describes the ruins. At the end are numerous transcriptions of historic documents relevant to it. As the postscript explains:*

it has frequently been wished that the scattered accounts of Ludlow Castle were compressed within the compass of a few pages, as a guide to the enquiring traveller, and as a refreshment of the memory of the more informed historian. Should the foregoing pages, in the least degree, contribute to the information or amusement of those who may feel, as it were, an interest in the investigation of a noble edifice which every day presents itself to the view, the purpose of the editor will be fully answered.

W. Hodges, *An Historical Account of Ludlow Castle*

WEALTHY castle owners, meanwhile, organised surveys of their own. Such is the case with a magnificent 1787 survey portfolio of Arundel Castle commissioned from James Teasdale by Charles Howard, Duke of Norfolk, the latter a convivial figure with strong antiquarian interests. It comprises a series of detailed views, cross-sections and plans besides a general description of the building, which opens with reference to the legendary founder of the castle, the giant Bevis (see 1290 above).

> Arundel Castle is pleasingly situated upon an elevation which commands a most beautiful and extensive prospect. Who were the founders of this ancient place? History is silent. Traditional opinion says that a Bevis was the first planner of this old pile. Here is still a tower standing which retains his name, which is said to have been his apartment; also a Bevis's Sword which by its unwieldiness, and the hardships it has undergone, bespeak its master to have been of gigantic stature, and a little given to the courageous. But how far fiction or conjecture may bias one's opinion is uncertain.
>
> James Teasdale, *Plans, Elevations and Particular Measurements of Arundel Castle*

Bevis's sword is in fact a fourteenth-century weapon. The Arundel survey may have been produced with the advice of the notable antiquary, Dr William Burrell (see 1777 above). He had been in communication with the future duke in the 1770s about antiquarian matters and eagerly acquired copies of another private survey, of Herstmonceux Castle, from its owner in 1778.

A connection with the Society of Antiquaries, of which both the duke and Burrell were fellows, explains many projects of this kind. Sir Joseph Banks, celebrated as a President of the Royal Society (but also a Fellow of the Society of Antiquaries), commissioned a professional survey of the great tower of Tattershall Castle from one J. L. Johnson in 1783 and Lewis Majendie presented a survey of the keep at Castle Hedingham 'by Mr Henry Emlyn of Windsor, who, by command of his Majesty, so elegantly planned and executed the late magnificent works in St George's Chapel' to the society, which later engraved and published it in 1796. The engraved cross-sections, plans and details of Hedingham were noted by architects and informed, for example, the design of the keep of Penrhyn, one of the most astonishing new castles of the Regency built by the architect Thomas Hopper between 1821 and 1833.

Not all surveys and histories of this kind, however, were connected to the Society of Antiquaries. An interest in ancestry also encouraged the investigation of castles. In 1791, for example, the naval clergyman and topographer Rev. Cooper Willyams produced a luxurious illustrated history of Sudeley Castle. This was not just a labour of love. Willyams was a school friend of the genealogist and heraldic enthusiast Sir Egerton Brydges, who claimed descent from the Brydges of Sudeley. This family had been granted Sudeley Castle by Queen Mary, together with the title of Baron Chandos, which subsequently became extinct. Sir Egerton persuaded his elder brother to lay claim to the title in the House of Lords, one of several such suits in this period (see 1348 above). The ensuing case was a humiliating failure, but this luxurious book was clearly intended to bolster it. After his brother's death, Sir Egerton, evidently still smarting from the judicial result, styled himself 'by the laws of earth Chandos of Sudeley'.

About twenty years later Sudeley was bought by the Duke of Buckingham. His wife also claimed distant descent from the Brydges, which probably explains the purchase. In another act of family piety, she commissioned a survey of the castle from the architect and topographer John Buckler. In addition, she also toyed with the idea of rebuilding it as a residence, though nothing came of the plan.

1801
BELVOIR CASTLE
Romanticising History

Prior to its Regency remodelling (and after its repair following the Civil War), Belvoir Castle, Leicestershire, had been a low and regular building organised around a courtyard. Wyatt redressed it as a spectacular fantasy with a broken roofline of towers, turrets and pinnacles.

On 4 January 1799, the 5th Duke of Rutland celebrated his coming of age with a party for about ten thousand guests at which, as his steward wryly observed, 'all who wished to be drunk were so'. Within a month he was married to the beautiful leader of fashion, Lady Elizabeth Howard. According to tradition, she was horrified at the duke's seat, Belvoir Castle, and almost immediately plans were set in motion to rebuild it. The starting point for the project were proposals drawn up by the duke's father, a spendthrift. He had approached 'Capability' Brown, the celebrated landscape designer. Brown's designs for the castle – referred to as Grecian in style – are now lost. Clearly, however, they were regarded as both dated and staid. The duke turned, therefore, to the fashionable architect of the moment, James Wyatt. Because he was so pressed for work Wyatt initially sent his brother, Samuel, to assess the building. When the two brothers did manage to visit together the duke was absent at Ipswich. The duke's former tutor, Bowyer Edward Sparke, therefore, wrote to him describing the occasion:

The Wyatts arrived at Belvoir on Monday night and I have been over there some part of every day since. The Elder Wyatt proves much more communicative than I had supposed, knowing him to be so great a man; – I am exceeding glad that your Grace has taken his opinion before the work proceeded any further, as his taste is so exactly adapted to a thing of this kind. He at once perceived at a glance of the eye what the nature of the situation requires: – he laughs at the idea of a Grecian building (according to Brown's plan) or indeed of any regular building upon such an eminence, when he says there should be nothing but a castle, or at least what has the appearance of a castle, and the more rough and broken the appearance is, the more striking will be the effect. As I hope so soon to see your Grace I will not enter into any detail of his proposed alterations, which also is the less necessary as I dare to say Mr King (who is abundantly more *au fait* on the subject) would take care to give you every information possible: I am however particularly glad to find that these alterations will not greatly enhance the expense. With regard to the interior I do not find that there is much difference of opinion between them; – the chief thing seems to be that the dining room will be four feet wider than S[amuel] Wyatt had made it: – instead of 38 by 22 it will be 38 by 26, a much better proportion. I believe they leave Belvoir tomorrow but J[ames] Wyatt has had full time enough to examine every particular relative to the situation and to arrange his ideas, which I now long to see on paper.

10 July 1801, Bowyer Edward Sparke
writes to the Duke of Rutland

IN its present form Belvoir Castle still speaks of the spectacular ambition of James Wyatt's vision, not to mention the depth of the Duke of

Rutland's purse; as eventually completed from 1801 it absorbed the astonishing sum of £200,000. Wyatt's assessment highlights many of the qualities spoken of by Repton (see 1782 above). Classical architecture was constrained by proprieties, but a castle could be a fantasy. In persuading patrons to build in this extravagant manner, it helped that the Regency had no qualms about creating luxurious interiors in a different style to the outward form of the building. This disjunction between the interior and exterior was a striking novelty that grew in popularity as the nineteenth century progressed.

At Belvoir, for example, there were Gothic interiors, some of them completed after the death of Wyatt in 1816 under the direction of an illegitimate half-brother of the duke, the clergyman and amateur architect John Thoroton. The main room for entertainment, however, was named the Elizabeth Saloon after the duchess. She blazed a trail in Britain for decoration in the style of Louis XIV and furnished the room with boiserie, or wood panelling, and furniture brought from Paris, some of it believed to have come from the house of Madame de Maintenon, the morganatic wife of Louis XIV. Such decoration was stupendously expensive – the panelling alone cost 1,450 guineas – but it had a vainglorious appeal for the nobility of a kingdom that had just emerged triumphant from the Napoleonic Wars. It also evoked France before the chaos of the Revolution; a consolation to Britain's nobility.

The duchess had a strong interest in the history of her husband's family, the Manners. An exquisitely bound commonplace book of hers incorporates drawings made by her of Belvoir and the earlier Manners' home at Haddon, Derbyshire, as well as poems on both places. The latter, a largely medieval house, had long been a secondary family residence. Now it became popular among tourists to the Peaks and began to be consciously preserved and furnished as a historic Manners property, where old family furniture and tapestries were relegated to splendid effect. To animate Haddon, particular historical episodes were located within it, such as the supposed elopement of Dorothy Vernon (a subject later celebrated in an operetta, *Haddon Hall* (1892), by Arthur Sullivan, but not with a libretto by W. S. Gilbert; the two men had quarrelled). The emphasis was on the building as a glorious fossil of ancestry. In Elizabeth's own words about Haddon in a verse signed and dated 1812:

For all is hush'd and echo'ed through thy halls,
No voice of mirth, is heard within thy walls,
But tho' thou art <u>deserted</u> now; and drear,
Haddon to *Manners* must be ever *dear.*

The Rutlands were not alone among the very greatest families to create heirloom houses in this way. The Earls of Carlisle treated Naworth Castle, Cumberland, in much the same way (as a counterpart to Castle Howard) and the Dukes of Devonshire used the 1590s Hardwick Hall, Derbyshire, as their ancestral building, while splendidly modernising their seat at Chatsworth.

1806
LOWTHER CASTLE
Industrial Wealth

Lowther Castle, Cumbria, the seat of the Lowther family from the twelfth century and extravagantly rebuilt from 1806 by the twenty-five-year-old architect Robert Smirke. Its then owner, William, was made Earl of Lonsdale (the second creation) the following year and was fabulously rich, having inherited the town of Whitehaven, collieries, considerable English property and sugar plantations and slaves from a cousin, who had a reputation for ruthless miserliness. By careful use of materials from the estate the estimated cost of the new castle was reduced from an eye-watering £150,000 to £70,000. This frontage faces Penrith, a relationship that speaks of the authority the earl exercised over this town.

SMIRKE was the third architect to work on the castle project (the commission having been previously passed through the hands of James Wyatt and George Dance). Smirke adopted a strictly symmetrical composition around a central block with a dominating tower. This was at odds with the rambling and irregular designs favoured by architects such as John Nash. There are eighteenth-century castles that resemble Smirke's design, such as Inveraray, Argyll, begun in 1744, but the immediate source for this was Kew Castle, begun for George III by James Wyatt. Kew was never finished but its shell was blown up by George IV, as an expression of filial loathing. In the aftermath of the French Revolution, the regular exterior implied less an aesthetic delight with the picturesque than an interest in the castle as a celebration of established social hierarchy and order in the face of war and the disquieting effects of industrialisation.

The building essentially comprises a series of connected rectangular blocks on different scales with turrets set at every corner. In front of it there is an apron wall with towers and a small gatehouse; the latter possesses a distinctly tapering outline that gives the impression of squat strength. The apron encloses a turning circle large enough for a carriage. Notice that the front door of the castle is enclosed by a covered porch that could accommodate such a vehicle and allow visitors to enter the house without exposing themselves to the elements, a relative novelty in British architecture.

Smirke made his name at Lowther and undertook further castle commissions, notably Eastnor, Herefordshire, for another Tory peer, Lord Somers, its main front based on Warwick Castle. In the early twentieth century the Lowther family fortunes declined and the contents of the castle were auctioned in 1947. The roof was removed in 1957 and the building obscured by trees. Since the 1990s the castle ruins and gardens have been magnificently opened up and restored.

1809
HAWARDEN CASTLE
The Character of a Castle

A sketch of Hawarden Castle in 1809 during the course of its transformation by the architect Thomas Cundy from a neoclassical country house into a castle. The house, originally known as Broadlane Hall, was built in 1749–57 at a cost of £2,624 (which sets in context the relative cost of Lowther). Henceforth it became known as Hawarden Castle, the name linking it to the ruins of an important thirteenth-century castle of that name on a hill immediately beside it. This had been occupied until the Civil War and ordered for demolition by Parliament in December 1645. The battlements, towers and name of the new building asserted a connection and continuity with the adjacent ruins.

THE drawing illustrates just how cosmetic the trappings of fortification might be. As well as transforming the outward style of the building, this change also, importantly, made the overall composition of the building asymmetric.

At Hawarden the eighteenth-century interiors were completely untouched by these external changes. The smoking chimneys perhaps suggest that the family continued to live here during the course of work. A superficial refacing of this kind was much cheaper than reconstruction; it took less time; and it was less intrusive. This approach, therefore, was widely adopted in the modernisation of gentry houses across the kingdom until architectural tastes began to change again in the 1840s.

Even then, however, a building on the scale of Highclere, Hampshire, could be castellated in this way as late as 1842. Highclere Castle was remodelled by Charles Barry, the architect of the new Palace of Westminster. The patron of this project was the 3rd Earl of Carnarvon, a vigorous opponent of political reform. As he wrote to a friend on 22 January 1831: 'Wherever I go I hear one pervading feeling of discontent towards existing institutions and I fear a restless desire for extensive changes . . . I question much whether the gale that will eventually sweep aristocracy from the face of this country has not set in.' To noblemen of this persuasion, castles were a reassuring statement of Britain's inherited political and social order. They also outwardly expressed the deep historic roots of its unwritten constitution. Gothic did the same, which is why it was the chosen style of the new Palace of Westminster when it was rebuilt by Barry after the fire of 1834 as the seat of Britain's recently reformed Parliament.

1819
CONISBROUGH CASTLE
Walter Scott's Castles

The keep of Conisbrough Castle, Yorkshire, was a hugely ambitious creation of cut stone probably built in the 1180s. To the eye of many mid-nineteenth-century antiquarians including Walter Scott, however, this tower with its 'six huge external buttresses' was a monument to the 'Dark Ages' of the Anglo-Saxon world.

The novels of Sir Walter Scott had a profound effect on the popular perception of the Middle Ages in Britain. Scott had serious antiquarian interests and prided himself on the accuracy with which he presented historic buildings. By making them the setting for stories that a nineteenth-century readership found so compelling, however, he additionally made both the people and places of the past seem real. In this passage taken from his novel Ivanhoe *(1819) he describes the arrival of Richard I, Coeur-de-Lion, with his companions at the castle of Conisbrough (or Coningsburgh), Yorkshire. Notice that he separates the antiquarian analysis of the ruin as he knew it from his re-imagining in the narrative of the novel itself. The Heptarchy is a reference to the seven kingdoms of Anglo-Saxon England:*

the King, attended by Ivanhoe, Gurth, and Wamba, arrived, without any interruption, within view of the Castle of Coningsburgh, while the sun was yet in the horizon.

There are few more beautiful or striking scenes in England, than are presented by the vicinity of this ancient Saxon fortress. The soft and gentle river Don sweeps through an amphitheatre, in which cultivation is richly blended with woodland, and on a mount, ascending from the river, well defended by walls and ditches, rises this ancient edifice, which, as its Saxon name implies, was, previous to the Conquest, a royal residence of the kings of England. The outer walls have probably been added by the Normans, but the inner keep bears token of very great antiquity. It is situated on a mount at one angle of the inner court, and forms a complete circle of perhaps twenty-five feet in diameter. The wall is of immense thickness, and is propped or defended by six huge external buttresses which project from the circle, and rise up against the sides of the tower as if to strengthen or to support it. These massive buttresses are solid when they arise from the foundation, and a good way higher up; but are hollowed out towards the top, and terminate in a sort of turrets communicating with the interior of the keep itself. The distant appearance of this huge building, with these singular accompaniments, is as interesting to the lovers of the picturesque, as the interior of the castle is to the eager antiquary, whose imagination it carries back to the days of the Heptarchy. A barrow, in the vicinity of the castle, is pointed out as the tomb of the memorable Hengist; and various monuments, of great antiquity and curiosity, are shown in the neighbouring churchyard.

When Coeur-de-Lion and his retinue approached this rude yet stately building, it was not, as at present, surrounded by external fortifications. The Saxon architect had exhausted his art in rendering the main keep defensible, and there was no other circumvallation than a rude barrier of palisades.

A huge black banner, which floated from the top of the tower, announced that the obsequies of the late owner were still in the act of being solemnized. It bore no emblem of the deceased's birth or quality, for armorial bearings were then a novelty among the Norman chivalry themselves and were totally unknown to the Saxons. But above the gate was another banner, on which the figure of a white horse, rudely painted, indicated the nation and rank of the deceased, by the well-known symbol of Hengist and his Saxon warriors

Walter Scott, *Ivanhoe*

THE irony of Scott's careful attempt at historical accuracy is that he was, in fact, largely mistaken in his understanding of Conisbrough. At the time *Ivanhoe* was published, antiquaries did still believe that many castle buildings dated to the Anglo-Saxon or even the Roman past, but these ideas were completely discredited by the early twentieth century. In fact, the keep at Conisbrough was probably being built in the 1180s, shortly before Scott had Richard I arriving here. Likewise, the figure of Hengist (the brother of Horsa, the reputed leaders of the German people who invaded Britain in the fifth century and established the royal house of Kent) is now regarded by some historians as a mythical figure invented by the twelfth-century historian Geoffrey of Monmouth. The historical accuracy of Scott, however, is in some ways beside the point. Just by writing about these places he established them in the popular consciousness and made their history seem human.

The changes that followed could be rapid and transformative. Another location that figured in *Ivanhoe*, for example, was Ashby de la Zouch, Leicestershire. Two years after the novel was published, in 1821, it was proposed to name a new spa complex in the town 'Ivanhoe Baths'. Construction began the following year and the numbers of visitors to the town was sufficient to prompt the publication of the first guidebook in 1824. This offered a real location for the completely fictional joust that the novel described as taking place here. Two years later, the landowner responsible for the ruins of Ashby de la Zouch Castle (which Scott correctly noted in the novel had been built after the period of the story) repaired them for visitors to enjoy.

More generally, Scott's novels fuelled a wider interest in populating historic buildings and locating celebrated events within them (see 1801 above). It's also apparent in the growing popularity of historical paintings focused on the medieval – rather than simply the Classical – past. Scott also helped establish some parts of the popular framework of British history; for example, he coined the phrase the 'Wars of the Roses' as the name of the fifteenth-century dynastic struggle between the houses of York and Lancaster.

1819
GWRYCH CASTLE
A Nationalist Castle

In 1819 work began on a rambling new castle on the north coast of Wales just outside Abergele, Conwy. Gwrych Castle was conceived by its young builder, Lloyd Hesketh Bamford-Hesketh, as a monument to his Welsh mother and her ancestors, the Lloyds of Gwrych. Her family's ancestral seat in Abergele had been recently damaged by fire and was ripe for rebuilding. Lloyd was born in 1788 and had been fascinated by castles since his childhood. He evidently wanted this building to be a riposte to the medieval castles built in North Wales by Edward I from 1277 during the conquest of the principality and, in preparation for the design, he visited and measured the ruins of castles associated with the native Welsh, such as Ewloe, Flintshire, and Dolwyddelan, Conwy.

LLOYD Hesketh Bamford-Hesketh was largely his own architect but he planned the castle from 1816 with Thomas Rickman, the architect who

first categorised the different phases of Gothic architecture. The castle comprises a main block or keep, just visible to the right, and a series of terraces retained against the hillside by walls and eighteen towers. It's carefully laid out with relation to the landscape and there are spectacular views to and from the castle, which overlooks the sea. It was Rickman who advised on some striking economies in the construction of the building, notably the use of Gothic cast-iron windows painted to look like masonry, which were much cheaper to make than stone ones.

Gwrych Castle was begun in the same year as Thomas Telford's first great suspension bridge over the Menai Strait just a few miles away. The concurrence is a reminder of the economic and industrial might that underpinned British architecture in this period.

Gwrych fell into ruin only in the 1990s and was devastated by vandals and arsonists. It's a chastening reminder that even prominent historic buildings are not guaranteed a future in twenty-first-century Britain. The castle has since been the object of a heroic restoration project by the Gwrych Castle Preservation Trust, which bought the building and its immediate surroundings in 2018. It has since made an improbable appearance in the 2020 reality TV show, *I'm a Celebrity – Get Me Out of Here!*

1824
WINDSOR CASTLE
Imperial Splendour

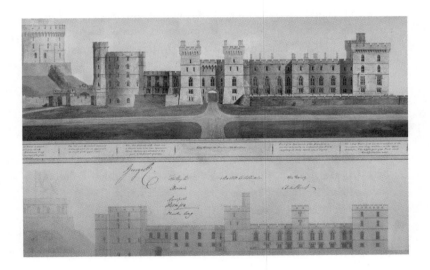

One of Wyatville's drawings for the remodelling of Windsor Castle. The lower section shows the south front and Round Tower of Windsor Castle as they existed in 1824 and the upper their proposed enhancement. The authorising signatures include those of George IV, the Duke of Wellington and the Prime Minister, Lord Liverpool.

In 1820, after ten years of madness and seclusion, George III died and was buried at Windsor. His son, George IV, had hitherto enjoyed the company of Whigs and reformers, chiefly to annoy his father. Now he abandoned his old friends and became an arch Tory, keen to celebrate tradition. His coronation set a breathtaking standard, with its opulence and consciously historicist costume astonishing European observers. George IV also determined to have an architectural competition to renew Windsor Castle as his principal seat.

THE CASTLE

The brief was set out in a memorandum drafted by the king's artistic advisor, Sir Charles Long, for the prime minister on 13 February 1824. It's divided into sections dealing with the approach, external appearance and interior arrangement. This excerpt is from the second:

The character of this castle should be that of simplicity and grandeur, and as well from its history, as from the imposing style of building belonging to that period; I should say that the period of Edward III is that which should generally predominate, not however excluding the edifices of earlier periods, where we find anything of grand or picturesque effect – Conway, Carnarvon, Raglan, Bodiam, Haddon, and many others, will furnish the most useful examples. In considering Windsor in this point of view, the architect will find as much to restore as to invent; for the castle has so much in it which belongs to these times, that it may be considered even now as its principal character. The alterations which have been since adopted have been generally made in periods less favourable to castle architecture . . . And here I must observe, that the style of alteration which I should most dread is that of *modern Gothic architecture*. By modern Gothic architecture I mean that which has been adopted in some of the most costly mansions which have recently been erected – in which the repetition of small towers appears to me to destroy the grandeur of the edifice without adding at all to its beauty . . . and does not belong to any period of castle architecture that I am acquainted with.

I am fully aware . . . That it might be necessary to relax in some degree from the strict severity of this [Edward III's] style, in some parts of the building . . . But as castles afterwards became less important as places of defence . . . the stern grandeur of the castle character yielded in some degree to the more elegant and decorative style of the inhabited mansion. Among the best specimens of the mixed character Raby, Lumley, Thornbury, Warwick, Oxburgh, Wingfield Manor, Brancepeth, Hampton Court in Herefordshire etc. I would recommend that the style of some of these examples should be applied [to] . . . the state apartments and those [parts of the castle] occupied by His Majesty.

... In an old castle there should be some predominant feature,
and the keep seems to me to furnish such a feature in Windsor
Castle ... I would add to this tower 20 or 30 feet ... The other
parts of the castle should be kept comparatively low

1824, Sir Charles Long's memorandum

THE castle exterior conceived by Sir Charles – and inspired by an impressive
list of architectural exempla, evidence of burgeoning antiquarian interest
– is essentially that which greets the twenty-first-century visitor. It was
realised by the architect Jeffry Wyatt, who, eager to aggrandise himself in
the light of this commission, and with royal permission, assumed the
name Wyatville and the motto 'Windsor'. No expense was spared in this
project and by 1834/5 the stupendous sum of £771,000 had been spent
on restoring and beautifying Windsor (while destroying much of Charles
II's work; see 1683 above). Even more astonishing is the fact that no one
really complained about the cost; in Wyatville's efficient hands such
opulence seemed appropriate for the seat of a monarch ruling over what
was unambiguously the richest and most powerful nation in the world.
Having prevailed – as Prince Regent – over Napoleon, moreover, George
IV thought it only appropriate his apartments be vaingloriously decorated
in the French style. Nevertheless, the chambers used for the Order of the
Garter ceremonies were in a Gothic idiom.

Soon after George IV's death, on 5 June 1831 the well-connected
Charles Greville dined at Windsor, where he admired the transformed
building and mused on the change between the court of George IV and
his brother and successor, William IV. The weirdness of the occasion
shines through the diary entry:

On Friday we dined at the Castle; each day the King asked a crowd
of people from the neighbourhood. We arrived at a little before
seven; the Queen was only just come in from riding, so we had to
wait till near eight. Above forty people at dinner, for which the
room is not nearly large enough; the dinner was not bad, but the
room insufferably hot. The Queen was taken out by the Duke of
Richmond, and the King followed with the Duchess of Saxe
Weimar, the Queen's sister. He drinks wine with everybody, asking
seven or eight at a time. After dinner he drops asleep. We sat for a

short time. Directly after coffee the band began to play; a good band, not numerous, and principally of violins and stringed instruments. The Queen and the whole party sat there all the evening, so that it was, in fact, a concert of instrumental music. The King took Lady Tavistock to St. George's Hall and the ballroom, where we walked about, with two or three servants carrying lamps to show the proportions, for it was not lit up. The whole thing is exceedingly magnificent, and the manner of life does not appear to be very formal, and need not be disagreeable but for the bore of never dining without twenty strangers . . . What a *changement de décoration*; no longer George IV, capricious, luxurious, and misanthropic, liking nothing but the society of listeners and flatterers, with the Conyngham tribe and one or two Tory Ministers and foreign Ambassadors; but a plain, vulgar, hospitable gentleman, opening his doors to all the world, with a numerous family and suite, a Whig Ministry, no foreigners, and no toad eaters at all. Nothing can be more different, and looking at him one sees how soon this act will be finished, and the scene be changed

Charles Greville, *Memoirs*

In fact, William IV's reign lasted six more years and, in 1837, the scene was indeed transformed by the accession of a young woman, Victoria, to the throne. When Greville's diaries were posthumously published she was outraged: 'The tone in which he speaks of royalty is unlike anything which one sees in history, even of people hundreds of years ago, and is most reprehensible.'

1831
CROTCHET CASTLE
The Pursuit of Gentility

Having bought the site of a medieval castle at Benington Lordship, Hertfordshire, the solicitor George Proctor transformed the ruins in 1835–8 with the construction of an imagined castle including this gateway made out of artificial stone. In this endeavour Proctor seems like a character reared to life from Peacock's novel.

At the opening of this satirical novel, Crotchet Castle *(1831), we are introduced to the eponymous castle of the title. It's in fact a comfortable suburban house or villa, erected by a man of Scottish and Jewish ancestry who has risen through doubtful speculation from poverty to wealth. He is, in short – uncomfortably – everything that a Regency reader would have been predisposed to ridicule. Having become wealthy, his chief concern is to make himself respectable. To this end he changes his name and assumes a coat of arms. The 'sharp' crest and the absurd charges on the shield – empty bladders; gold; naked swords; and a wig stand – emphasise his dishonesty as well as the emptiness, corruption and vanity of his claim to these emblems of gentility. He also names his villa a castle. In this case, the point of reference is not in fact to a medieval castle (as a modern reader might assume). Instead, a link is made back to the most exiguous remains of a Roman fort. The clear implication of the description is that the remains are a fiction. There is no description of the villa itself but it is evidently modern and commodious. Possibly it possessed a battlement or two but nothing else.*

Ebenezer Mac Crotchet, Esquire, was the London-born offspring of a worthy native of the 'north countrie', who had walked up to London on a commercial adventure, with all his surplus capital, not very neatly tied up in a not very clean handkerchief. [Ebenezer] . . . derived from his mother the instinct, and from his father the rational principle, of enriching himself at the expense of the rest of mankind, by all the recognised modes of accumulation on the windy side of the law . . . he had married an English Christian, and, having none of the Scotch accent, was ungracious enough to be ashamed of his blood. He was desirous to obliterate alike the Hebrew and Caledonian vestiges in his name, and signed himself E. M. Crotchet, which by degrees induced the majority of his neighbours to think that his name was Edward Matthew. The more effectually to sink the Mac, he christened his villa Crotchet Castle, and determined to hand down to posterity the honours of Crotchet of Crotchet. He found it essential to his dignity to furnish himself with a coat of arms, which, after the proper ceremonies (payment being the principal) he obtained videlicet: Crest, a Crotchet rampant, in A sharp: Arms, three empty bladders, turgescent, to show how opinions are formed; three bags of gold, pendent, to show why they are maintained; three naked swords, tranchant, to show how they are administered; and three barbers' blocks, gaspant, to show how they are swallowed . . .

He was not without a plausible pretence for styling his villa a Castle, for, in its immediate vicinity, and within his own enclosed domain, were the manifest traces, on the brow of the hill, of a Roman station, or Castellum, which was still called the Castle by the country people. The primitive mounds and trenches, merely overgrown with greensward, with a few patches of Juniper and box on the vallum, and a solitary ancient beach surmounting the place of the Praetorium, presented nearly the same depths, heights, slopes, and forms, which the Roman soldiers had originally given them. From this castellum Mr Crotchet christened his villa. With his rustic neighbours he was of course immediately and necessarily a Squire: Squire Crotchet of the Castle.

Thomas Love Peacock, *Crotchet Castle*, Chapter 1

ANCESTRY remained an obsession for those who aspired to – or were already possessed of – gentility in the early nineteenth century. Snobbery and social exclusivity certainly had a part to play in this interest but there was more to it than that. Ancestry was something that justified the exercise of power; a quality urgently to be acquired by anyone who wanted political or social authority. As an expression of this need the art of heraldry enjoyed a particular resurgence in this period. Heraldry had never disappeared as a mark of social distinction but its last great flowering had been in the early seventeenth century. Now interest in it revived once more and the expensive services of heralds were employed in fleshing out the most extravagant of ancestral claims (see 1348 and 1790s above). Elaborate heraldic displays also appeared in the work of fashionable architects such as Sir John Soane, whether Gothic in character – as with the 'Saxon Library' at Stowe, Buckinghamshire, with a panel of 726 coats by the artist P. Sonard of 1806 – or Classical, such as the 1820s Tribune of Wootton, Buckinghamshire. At Borris House, Co. Carlow, Thomas Kavanagh not only castellated his house but in 1817 commissioned a magnificently illuminated *Pedigree* that traces the history of his family and the line of the kings of Leinster, to 1670 BC. Beside such claims, Mr Crotchet's association of his house with the merely Roman past seems modest.

The comedy of *Crotchet Castle* derives partly from heated debates between the principal characters over society, the human condition and the nature of progress. Each has strong and contrasting views including:

Mr Chainmail, a good-looking young gentleman . . . with very antiquated tastes. He is fond of old poetry, and is something of a poet himself. He is deep in monkish literature, and holds that the best state of society was that of the twelfth century, when nothing was going forward but fighting, feasting, and praying, which he says are the three great purposes for which man was made. He laments bitterly over the inventions of gunpowder, steam, and gas, which he says have ruined the world. He lives within two or three miles, and has a large hall, adorned with rusty pikes, shields, helmets, swords, and tattered banners, and furnished with yew-tree chairs, and two long old worm-eaten oak tables, where he dines with all his household, after the fashion of his favourite age.

The character of Mr Chainmail echoes that of Don Quixote as described in the hugely influential eponymous novel by Cervantes (published in two parts in 1605 and 1615), which made universally familiar the idea of a man turned mad by an obsession with chivalry and the medieval past. *Crotchet Castle* ends, absurdly, with a mob of 'Captain Swing' rioters – a reference to agrarian disturbances in 1830 involving the smashing of threshing machines – arriving at Mr Chainmail's hall, his 'fortress of beef and ale', where he lives communally in the medieval manner with his household (and can accordingly find no wife). The guests settle their usually insurmountable differences and seize the weapons from the wall to drive the 'jacquerie' away. In all sorts of ways, reality would soon answer this parody.

1839
EGLINTON CASTLE
Chivalry Revived

A detail of the Great Drawing Room ceiling at Taymouth Castle, Perthshire, completed in time for Queen Victoria's visit in 1842 with sumptuous decoration devised by James Gillespie Graham in conjunction with A. W. N. Pugin and painted by the London decorator Crace. It breathes the spirit of the Eglinton Tournament.

The revival of interest in the Middle Ages in the nineteenth century was not simply an academic pursuit. It was also a romantic one and – for those who yearned to revive the spirit of King Arthur's court – it seemed only natural to organise tournaments as a means of displaying their prowess and chivalry. By far the most celebrated event of this kind took place at Eglinton Castle, Ayrshire, partly to make up for the cancellation of Queen Victoria's coronation banquet and its associated ceremonies. The three-day tournament in August

1839 was famously dogged by bad weather but it drew together a stellar cast of young aristocrats as well as a vast public audience. As a souvenir Account of the Tournament at Eglinton *(1839), luxuriously illustrated with coloured engravings, dramatically states:*

The world has been startled from its lethargy. After centuries of repose, each distinguished beyond its predecessor for an increasing tendency to utilitarian dullness, the age of chivalry, with its splendid pageants, has again come round; and the eyes of the lover of the romantic have been favoured with the sight of a real tournament.

THE volume is prefaced with a 'sketch of chivalry', outlining the ideals behind this code of behaviour, a history of the Eglinton family, and a description of the castle, a medieval building in origin but one, in fact, completely modernised and remodelled between 1798 and 1803 by the Edinburgh architect John Paterson:

The Castle of Eglinton stands in the midst of a beautiful and extensive park, richly wooded, on the south side of the Water of Lugton, a stream which, by the help of art, is made to meander in the most delightful manner through the domain. Part of it is a very ancient edifice, and the modern additions have been built to harmonize – the whole wearing a fine castellated aspect. The entrance hall is hung round with armour of all descriptions . . .

From the entrance hall, a door opens into the armoury, which on this occasion presented a strange scene – corselets, shields, gorgets, greaves, breast-pieces, helmets, and coats-of-mail, with saddles and trappings for horses lying strewed about in every direction.

No apartment within the premises being capable of banqueting so many guests, a large pavilion, about 375 feet in length and 45 in breadth, was erected in the rear of the Castle, having communication with the drawing room by a stair erected for the purpose. This magnificent hall was . . . beautifully festooned with laurel and choice exotics. Each side of the grand staircase leading into this saloon was decorated with French tapestry and splendidly wrought needle-work . . . Over the archways of the hall and banquet room were the arms of Lord Eglinton. The proscenium was adorned also with evergreens and variegated lamps, surrounded by the union flag of England . . . The Ground enclosed for the lists was admirably adapted for the purpose. It is a beautiful piece of level lawn, stretching from east to west about 600 yards in length by 250 in breadth, inclosing nearly four acres, and bounded on the north by a gentle rising ground, on which the spectators were admitted to view the jousting . . . On the south side of the lists was the pavilion erected for the guests of the Earl, calculated to hold about 1200 people; in the centre of which was the seat appropriated for the Queen of the Tournament.

Spirits ran high in anticipation of the opening procession as the crowds – reputed to number 100,000 – were regaled with music played by the band of the 78th Highlanders:

In the stands were assembled the greater part of the rank, fashion, and beauty of Scotland, arrayed in the gayest and most brilliant attire . . . The fancy costumes were chiefly of the reigns of Henry VIII and Elizabeth . . . But this splendour was extremely short-lived. Twelve o'clock was the time fixed for the procession to leave the Castle; and at that hour accordingly all eyes were turned to the place from which it was to proceed. The cavalcade did not make its appearance; but in its stead came the rain. At first it fell slow and small, as if compounding between rain and sleet; and, as the wind began to arise about the same time, it was hoped that the clouds might yet be carried off; and comforting themselves with this expectation, the crowd began to make what defence they could against the storm, and patiently to wait the commencement of the sports. The splendour of the scene then began to disappear, as if by magic. In the place where a few minutes before the whole glittered with drapery of all the colours of the rainbow, there was now presented nothing but one dull, unvarying scene of silk and cotton umbrellas.

The later days of the tournament were more successful and brought together enthusiasts for the Middle Ages from the Countess of Charleville (an admirer of Walpole's Strawberry Hill and the builder, with her husband, of a castle modelled on it and Warwick Castle at Charleville, Co. Offaly) to Prince Louis Napoleon, soon to be Napoleon III (who fought in full armour with a broadsword at Eglinton and went on to restore Carcassonne, Aude, and Pierrefonds, Oise, in France). It speaks of the spirit of the occasion, moreover, that in the same year Joseph Nash published the first volume in *The Mansions of England in the Olden Time* (1839–49), a luxuriously produced series that accurately illustrated historic interiors inhabited by figures in period – and also usually Tudor – costume.

Those involved in the Eglinton tournament knew their pursuit strayed to the brink of fantasy. Certainly, the lavish fancy dress underlined the removal of the occasion from reality and there were, besides, plenty of hostile critics who poured scorn upon it. Yet in some ways this demonstrative entertainment put on by the immensely rich for their pleasure is completely authentic of the Middle Ages. After all, when Edward III invited the citizens of London to Windsor to watch his favoured circle joust and fight in a sumptuous costume (see 1344 above) he was doing something very similar to the young and beautiful circle at Eglinton in 1839.

1 8 4 1
MODERN CASTLES
An Offence to True Principles

Over the first six weeks of 1841, the architect and polemicist Augustus Welby Northmore Pugin compiled The True Principles of Pointed or Christian Architecture. *The book caused a sensation, lending energy to the ongoing resurgence of interest in medieval architecture familiarly known as the Gothic Revival. Pugin was a Catholic convert of romantic sensibility and the focus of his interest was the reconciliation of Protestant England with its medieval past, social, architectural and religious.*

In this book he set out the principles by which Gothic could correctly be applied to any building or fitting, from a fireplace or curtain to a house. Among the eponymous principles of its argument was the assertion that 'there should be no features about a building which are not necessary for convenience, construction or propriety'. Also, that ornament should enrich only essential structure. Small surprise, therefore, that modern castles (which he pairs with modern abbeys, another fashionable idiom for new houses), just like that of Eglinton, Hawarden or Lowther, are singled out for particular derision.

national feelings and national architecture are at so low an ebb, that it becomes an absolute duty in every Englishman to attempt their revival. Our ancient architecture can alone furnish us with the means of doing this successfully; but, unfortunately, those who profess to admire pointed architecture, and who strive to imitate it, produce more ridiculous results than those who fly to foreign aid. What can be more absurd than houses built in what is termed the castellated style? Castellated architecture originated in the wants consequent on a certain state of society: of course the necessity of great strength, and the means of defence suited to the military tactics of the day, dictated to the builders of ancient castles the most appropriate style for their construction. Viewed as historical monuments, they are of surprising interest, but as models for our imitation they are worse than useless. What absurdities, what anomalies, what utter contradictions do not the builders of modern castles perpetrate! How many portcullises which will not lower down, and drawbridges which will not draw up ! – how many loop-holes in turrets so small that the most diminutive [chimney] sweep could not ascend them! – On one side of the house machicolated parapets, embrasures, bastions, and all the show of strong defence, and round the corner of the building a conservatory leading to the principal rooms, through which a whole company of horsemen might penetrate at one smash into the very heart of the mansion! – for who would hammer against nailed portals when he could kick his way through the greenhouse? In buildings of this sort, so far from the turrets being erected for any particular purpose, it is difficult to assign any destination to them after they are erected, and those which are not made into chimneys seldom get other occupants than the rooks. But the exterior is not the least inconsistent portion of the edifices, for we find guard-rooms without either weapons or guards; sally-ports, out of which nobody passes but the servants, and where a military man never did go out; donjon keeps, which are nothing but drawing-rooms, boudoirs, and elegant apartments; watch-towers, where the housemaids sleep, and a bastion in which the butler cleans his plate: all is a mere mask, and the whole building an ill-conceived lie.

A. W. N. Pugin, *The True Principles of Pointed or Christian Architecture*

BY Pugin's analysis modern castles were an absurdity in part because they answered archaic social needs and circumstances – such as the need for defence – that no longer pertained (though, curiously, Pugin fortified his first house at St Marie's Grange, Wiltshire, built in 1835 following his conversion to Catholicism; he remained fearful of mob violence in later life). Also, because the architectural ornament they incorporated was completely superfluous to their function; turrets were useful as chimneys but nothing more, so were occupied by birds. It was a further source of outrage that they were not actually defensible given the needs of a modern gentleman's seat to possess – say – a greenhouse.

Most twentieth-century scholars of castles have concurred with Pugin's charges and have confidently drawn a clear distinction between medieval castles that were functional and subsequent castles that are not. Pugin, however, later changed his mind on this point and advocated another idea about the application of medieval precedent to modern buildings. This was the principle of 'development' by which the forms and ornament of Gothic could be adapted to any modern purpose, from a railway station to a country house (see 1857 below). He would also restore a medieval castle at Alton, Staffordshire, for his outstanding patron, the Earl of Shrewsbury.

To complicate matters further, the publication of *True Principles* anticipated a period of political uncertainty and social unrest surrounding the repeal of the Corn Laws. In response some landowners began to build fortifications that really did aim to resist attack, not by a modern army but by the mob.

1844
PECKFORTON CASTLE
Back to the Future

Peckforton Castle, Cheshire, built in 1844–50, in a perspective view by the architect, Anthony Salvin, dated 1845. The builder of Peckforton was John Tollemache, created 1st Lord Tollemache in 1876, a Tory of imperious temperament, Evangelical conviction and immense physical strength. He fathered twenty-four children (twenty-three boys and one girl), of which twelve survived him, and lived to the age of eighty-five. He was also a fierce opponent of the repeal of the Corn Laws, owned five West Indian sugar plantations and accommodated his Cheshire tenants with unusual, if decidedly patrician, generosity. Salvin came to him with outstanding experience in the restoration of castles and had previously worked on Tollemache's other house, Helmingham Hall, Suffolk.

SALVIN created for his patron a building in the idiom of an Edwardian castle of about 1300. In this regard its details are accurately observed. The tower visible to the extreme right, for example, is possessed of spur bases, a feature of numerous castle buildings in the southern March of Wales from about 1260, including Chepstow and Goodrich. It was austerely detailed both internally and externally and the symmetrical outline is composed for picturesque effect. Tollemache insisted that the building contain no central heating and also built his own chapel, where he could manage divine service after his own simple preferences without the interference of the bishop.

The castle sits prominently on a hilltop and it faces the ruins of an early thirteenth-century castle, Beeston. This was not simply a Romantic castle, however. Its situation, scale and fortifications also undoubtedly reflect concerns about social unrest; Peckforton was begun in the same year that Engels started work on *The Condition of the Working Class in England* and proceeded through the Irish Famine and the Year of Revolutions in 1848. As this view shows, the castle was without a garden, only ditches, another mark of its serious purpose. No correspondence about the castle between the patron and builder survives but the new building is known to have cost £67,847. From this commission, Salvin went on to restore the Tower of London and also Alnwick Castle.

It was not uncommon for domestic buildings to be fortified against mobs in this period. The perimeter of Wollaton Park, Nottinghamshire, for example, was fortified for Lord Middleton by Sir Jeffry Wyatville in the 1820s. Nor were such precautions necessarily paranoid; nearby Nottingham Castle, a seat of the 4th Duke of Newcastle, a staunch opponent of political reform, was sacked by a mob in 1831 when news arrived in the city that the Reform Bill had been rejected by the House of Lords. It was in fear of the Chartists that the Duke of Wellington presided over the renovation of the defences of the Tower of London from 1845.

1854
CHIRK CASTLE
A Housekeeper's Tour

This conscious and slightly over-blown description of a visit to Chirk Castle illustrates the experience of the well-to-do as they travelled for pleasure across Britain and visited country seats in the mid-nineteenth century before the advent of the bicycle or the motor car. It was written by George Borrow as part of his account of a recreational journey through Wales with his wife and daughter. Borrow cut a striking figure, standing 6 foot 3 inches and with white hair. He was an inveterate traveller, having worked for the British and Foreign Bible Society, and also a polyglot. Welsh was among his spoken languages, as his conversation with the family guide, John Jones, reveals:

The scenery was now very lovely, consisting of a mixture of hill and dale, open space and forest, in fact the best kind of park scenery. We caught a glimpse of a lake in which John Jones said there were generally plenty of swans, and presently saw the castle, which stands on a green grassy slope, from which it derives its Welsh name of Castell y Waen; gwaen in the Cumrian language signifying a meadow or unenclosed place . . . A noble edifice it looked, and to my eye bore no slight resemblance to Windsor Castle.

Seeing a kind of ranger, we inquired of him what it was necessary for us to do [to visit], and by his direction proceeded to the southern side of the castle, and rung the bell at a small gate. The southern side had a far more antique appearance than the western; huge towers with small windows, and partly covered with ivy, frowned down upon us. A servant making his appearance, I inquired whether we could see the house; he said we could, and that the housekeeper would show it to us in a little time but that at present she was engaged. We entered a large quadrangular court . . . [with] . . . a kennel, chained to which was an enormous dog, partly of the bloodhound, partly of the mastiff species, who occasionally uttered a deep magnificent bay. As the sun was hot, we took refuge from it under the gateway . . . Here my wife and daughter sat down on a small brass cannon, seemingly a six-pounder, which stood on a very dilapidated carriage . . . As my two loved ones sat, I walked up and down, recalling to my mind all I had heard and read in connection with this castle. I thought of its gallant defence against the men of Oliver [Cromwell]; I thought of its roaring hospitality . . . and I thought of the many beauties who had been born in its chambers, had danced in its halls, had tripped across its court, and had subsequently given heirs to illustrious families.

At last we were told that the housekeeper was waiting for us. The housekeeper, who was a genteel, good-looking young woman, welcomed us at the door which led into the interior of the house. After we had written our names, she showed us into a large room or hall on the right-hand side on the ground floor, where were some helmets and ancient halberts, and also some pictures of great personages. The floor was of oak, and so polished and slippery, that walking upon it was attended with some danger. Wishing that John Jones, our faithful attendant, who remained timidly at the doorway, should participate with us in the wonderful sights we were about to see, I inquired of the housekeeper whether he might come with us. She replied with a smile that it was not the custom to admit guides into the apartments, but that he might come, provided he chose to take off his shoes; adding, that the reason she wished him to take off his shoes was, an apprehension that if he kept them on he would injure the floors with their rough nails. She then went to John Jones, and told him in English that he might attend us, provided he took off his shoes; poor John, however, only smiled and said 'Dim Saesneg!' [no English!]

'You must speak to him in your native language,' said I, 'provided you wish him to understand you – he has no English.'

'I am speaking to him in my native language,' said the young housekeeper, with another smile – 'and if he has no English, I have no Welsh.'

'Then you are English?' said I.

'Yes,' she replied, 'a native of London.'

. . . I then told John Jones the condition on which he might attend us, whereupon he took off his shoes with great glee and attended us, holding them in his hand.

We presently went upstairs, to what the housekeeper told us was the principal drawing-room, and a noble room it was, hung round with the portraits of kings and queens, and the mighty of the earth . . . Many were the rooms which we entered, of which I shall say nothing, save that they were noble in size and rich in objects of interest . . . The candle of God, whilst we wandered through these magnificent halls, was flaming in the firmament, and its rays, penetrating through the long narrow windows, showed them off, and all the gorgeous things which they contained to great advantage. When we left the castle we all said, not excepting John Jones, that we had never seen in our lives anything more princely and delightful than the interior.

George Borrow, *Wild Wales*

THE Borrows travelled with all the confidence of the genteel and prosperous. They knew it was possible that the castle might be shut but unspoken in this account is the fact that they were self-evidently the right kind of people – by dress and demeanour – to get in if it was open. Once within the castle courtyard Mr Borrow – in the manner of a Romantic – tries to use the building to animate his imagination and bring to his mind's eye the personalities who had lived here as well as their personal dramas. The great dog adds a touch of life to the scene and the wait in the cool shade suggests that while they might get access to the building they were not important enough to interfere with the business of the housekeeper.

The treatment of John Jones underlines the social gulf that divides him not only from the family but even from the housekeeper, a senior servant. Her inability to speak Welsh, moreover, implies that the household she ran was entirely cosmopolitan or at least English-speaking. It's possible to imagine, therefore, that relations with the local tenantry might have been strained. She does allow John in, however, though there must have been something slightly absurd about him accompanying the party while clutching his hobnail boots in his hands.

SPECIMENS OF ANCIENT ART
Restoration and Preservation

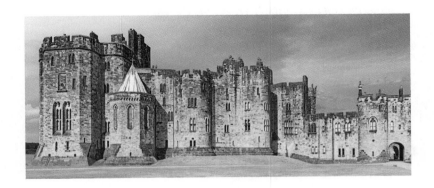

The early fourteenth-century inner bailey or keep of Alnwick Castle, Northumbria, as reworked by Anthony Salvin. Scott was offended by the spectacular Italianate interiors that the Duke of Northumberland created inside this newly medievalised buiding. A twenty-first-century visitor, however, can still marvel at them.

The towering figure of the Gothic Revival, with a claim to being both the most prolific, as well as the most celebrated, architect of Victorian Britain, was George Gilbert Scott. In his recollections, published in 1879, he writes of being inspired early in his career by the writings of A. W. N. Pugin (see 1841 above), which 'excited me almost to fury'. Like Pugin, he detested the falsehood of modern castles. As part of a treatise, Remarks on Secular and Domestic Architecture *(1857), he regretted their continued popularity. In a swipe at Peckforton (see 1844 above), moreover, he thought it absurd that the largest and most 'learnedly executed Gothic mansion of the present day is not only a castle in name . . . but . . . a real and carefully constructed mediaeval fortress.'*

All this, however, is merely to repeat Pugin and later in the same book he addresses a quite different issue. This is the modern treatment of occupied, historic castles. In it he ventured an idea that in some ways was no less radical than Pugin's early advocacy of Gothic. It was that the historic parts of these buildings should be preserved. Hitherto it had been perfectly acceptable to tear down old buildings. Now, however, Scott – well versed in the restoration of historic churches – suggested that where they were particularly well preserved, they ought to be sacred as monuments to the past and modernised in character. To make the point he concludes by criticising the recent restoration of Alnwick Castle by the Duke of Northumberland and the creation of Italianate interiors within the walls of a great medieval fortress.

I have, at the commencement of this work, expressed myself in strong terms as hostile to modern castle-building, as being on the very face of it grossly frivolous and unreal. The case, however, is different when we come to the restoration of ancient castles. These possess the same claims upon preservation and conservative restoration which I have advocated for other works which are at once relics of antiquity and specimens of ancient art. They should be most religiously protected, and so far – and so far only – as is necessary, from time to time, receive such repairs as are required for their conservation . . . The historical interest attached to them overrides any practical inconvenience which may arise from their having been built for other than their present uses . . .

We do not, however, by asking this one sacrifice to antiquarian feeling, imply the remotest wish that the modern lord of an ancient castle should forego any of the conveniences or comforts of his day . . . I would rather glory in shewing, in the fittings of his apartments, how marvellously the [castle] style is open to adaptation to every conceivable requirement – so much so, as positively to luxuriate in shaping itself to everything which taste, comfort, or modern discovery may suggest. It is a task almost too charming to be hoped for, to carry out this glorious idea, – to restore in all its nobility a stern Edwardian castle, scrupulously preserving all its external grandeur, restoring in their pristine form such of its apartments as the hall, the chapel, and others which may have come down to us unaltered, but fitting up the rest in the true spirit and inspiration of the noble style of art which produced the lordly structure, while so shaping it as to suit the wants, the feelings, and taste of its present occupant as perfectly as its first builder met the requirements of its then feudal and warlike lord. Yet this is no fantastic dream, – it is just what our style will effect, if rightly handled.

A truly lamentable error has recently been fallen into at Alnwick Castle ... The present Duke of Northumberland conceived the princely idea of its thorough restoration, – a work which, so far as the exterior is concerned, would appear to have been exceedingly well carried out by his architect, Mr. Salvin. At this point, however, his Grace appears to have become alarmed, and to have asked himself whether he was to sacrifice his future comforts, and the luxuries of modern life, and to be immured within the stern apartments of a feudal fortress. The true answer is obvious – that nothing of the kind was necessary, but that, on the contrary, he had before him the noblest opportunity, perhaps, ever offered of bending the beautiful style of the fourteenth century to meet the usages and refinements of the nineteenth. It positively takes one's breath away to think of so glorious an opportunity ... [but] his Grace became enamoured of the interiors of the Renaissance palaces, and fostered the infelicitous idea of making his ancestral residence a feudal castle without and a Roman palazzo within; and this is now being actually carried into effect, in a manner so liberal and so costly as only to render one's grief the more poignant, that a scheme conceived in so princely a spirit should be ruined by so unfortunate an error.

G. G. Scott, *Remarks on Secular and Domestic Architecture*

SCOTT's views about castles were directly drawn from his experience as the restorer of churches and reflect his confidence in the principle of 'development', by which historic forms could be turned to contemporary purpose. His comments, moreover, about the importance of stylistic consonance between the interior and exterior of a castle are in complete contrast to those of the Regency (see 1801 and 1809 above). It was a disjunction that other visitors to castles commented about in the period: 'A complete adaptation to modern uses and splendour disappoints one in the interior,' sniffed William Howitt at Raby Castle, Co. Durham, in his *Visits to Remarkable Places* (1890). A few owners of castles anticipated Scott's ideas about the sacred quality of historic fabric; a striking case in point would be the treatment of Sudeley Castle, Gloucestershire, from 1838 by John and William Dent, where the ruined parts of the building were strictly preserved rather than rebuilt. That, however, didn't make his comments on castles any less radical or important. History was becoming sacrosanct.

1874
CARDIFF AND COCH CASTLES
Medievalism and Scholarship

Cardiff Castle, Glamorgan. The outer wall incorporates the remains of a Roman fort. Visible here are William Burges's additions to the medieval buildings, including the new clock tower, and, to the extreme right, the base of the castle motte. The restored Castell Coch served as a summerhouse to the castle on the edge of the estate.

In 1874 a reporter for The Architect *magazine, described simply as 'Rambler', gave an enthusiastic account of the redevelopment of Cardiff Castle by the 3rd Marquess of Bute. The marquess owned the docks that gave the town its purpose and prosperity but his intense interests were focused from his childhood on the Middle Ages (he was the model for the eponymous hero of Benjamin Disraeli's popular novel* Lothair, *published in 1870). In 1865, at the age of eighteen, he met the architect William Burges – who also enjoyed a reputation as an archaeologist – and there began a relationship that would transform Cardiff Castle. He commissioned from Burges a report on the restoration of the south wall of the castle, which incorporated fabric from the Roman fort on the site. Burges suggested restoring this but additionally proposed a huge clock tower to dominate the city and incorporate domestic chambers for the marquess. By 1874 the tower had been realised and further major alterations, funded by Lord Bute's vast fortune, were in train:*

The new tower, besides being the timepiece of the neighbourhood, is the distinguishing mark of Cardiff viewed from a distance. No stranger passes by without stopping to stare at, if not examine, it; and a few of the Cardiff folk are even yet sufficiently accustomed to its outlines to regard it without a little wonderment mixed with their contempt. There is no ancient tower in Britain resembling it, few abroad; and, though in character essentially Mediaeval, it is practically modern. Perhaps the coloured statues of the planets, seven in all, and placed at the side of each clock face, are the principal cause of astonishment to the casual pedestrian . . .

Cardiff Tower has the merit of explaining itself both in construction and decoration . . . the summer smoking room is cool, lofty, well-lighted, and commands a magnificent view over plain, hill and water; no bachelor could covet a more enviable bedroom than the tower holds; and if there be many modern works of architecture in this country containing as much thoughtful art within a space of equal dimensions as it is to be found cut and depicted on the fine walls of Cardiff Tower, England is more favoured than many of its children suppose. The decorations are not only legible, but to read them is a treat to educated people; the thoughts and occupations of the owner are translated in the things surrounding him; there is style in them – not the style of the multitude, but of a grand seigneur, who, from circumstances, has more sympathy with the past than with the present; who is poet enough to choose poetical subjects for the decoration of his favourite rooms; and who, blessed with vast hereditary possessions, chooses to make a little world of them and live in it.

'Rambler', *The Architect*

IN 1868, while the castle works at Cardiff were under way, the marquess courted controversy by becoming a Catholic and in 1872 married a granddaughter of the Duke of Norfolk, the senior Catholic peer of the realm, Hon. Gwendolen Fitzalan Howard. Shortly before this, in 1871, he commissioned further reports from Burges on two castles on his estates, Rothesay, Bute, and Castell Coch, about six miles from Cardiff. He went on to restore the former as a ruin. The report on the latter, however, concludes:

> There are two courses open with regard to the ruins; – one is to leave them as they are and the other to restore them so as to make a country residence for your occasional occupation in the summer.
>
> In the former case all that is wanted are a few repairs sufficient to keep the walls together, the foundations having been already made secure.
>
> In the case of a restoration being effected the first and most necessary thing required would be to make careful measurements to a half inch scale of every existing portion of the ruins – The measurer should be provided with a copy of this report to ascertain how far the restoration does or does not work in with what remains.
>
> 27 December 1872, William Burges Castell Coch report

There can never have been much doubt as to the outcome. The ruins were investigated and recorded and in 1875 a new Castell Coch began rising from the ground on the footings of the old. Burges extrapolated every detail that he could from the remains but many details of his reconstruction – notably the high-pitched roofs over the towers, which he deemed 'romantic' – went beyond the available evidence. In such cases, however, he put forward reasoned arguments for his designs and marshalled the comparative evidence, including manuscript illuminations. He was particularly influenced by buildings he had seen in his Continental travels and, perhaps, to accentuate the undoubted French character of the resulting building, the marquess planted the only commercial vineyard in Victorian Britain on the slopes beneath it.

To contemporary eyes, this project was not a fantasy – which is what many modern observers assume – but a work of archaeological re-creation that brought this building into modern use. Writing in 1884, G. T. Clarke, for example, the outstanding Victorian scholar of castles, judged it to be 'very complete indeed, in excellent taste, and in strict accordance with what has been ascertained of the original structure'. It was also merely the first in a whole series of projects undertaken by the marquess, variously to excavate, record or repair other historic buildings through the 1880s and 1890s. In Wales, these included Caerphilly Castle, and Greyfriars and Blackfriars in Cardiff and, in Scotland, Whithorn Priory, Galloway; Falkland Palace; St Andrew's Cathedral Priory, Fife; Greyfriars, Elgin; Pluscarden Abbey, Morayshire; and St Blane's, Kingarth, Bute.

Undoubtedly through Gwendolen's connections, these projects seem to have fired a related series of castle restoration projects by another retiring aristocrat with intellectual interests. Henry, 15th Duke of Norfolk, rebuilt his family seat at Arundel Castle between 1875 and 1909 to the designs of a herald, J. C. Buckler. From 1880 he also purchased the nearby ruins of Amberley Castle, formerly the possession of the Bishops of Chichester, and began to restore that.

There were, meanwhile, others who also bought castles in a similar spirit. Baron Armstrong of Cragside, inventor, engineer and arms manufacturer, for example, was reported to have purchased Bamburgh Castle, Northumberland, in 1893 in order 'to restore all the parts that have fallen into decay in accordance with the original design'. Over the next decade he perhaps spent as much as £1 million on the project.

1899
KENILWORTH CASTLE
Mass Tourism

Two women enjoy the ruined splendours of Kenilworth Castle, Warwickshire, from The Shakespeare Country, *published by* Country Life *in 1899. In the nineteenth century, travel – and therefore tourism – in Britain was incrementally transformed by three innovations. First, the railway consigned coaching to oblivion, then the bicycle revived the road system. Bicycles allowed for the exploration of the countryside in a completely new way and gave women, in particular, a degree of independence unimaginable before. Finally, the car, initially the preserve of the rich, opened up the countryside yet further. Haddon Hall, Derbyshire, for example, had forty thousand visitors in 1905.*

The Shakespeare Country was aimed at this new tourist audience and incorporated a map of the Midlands to allow for the exploration of its riches. The text and title implied that the soul of England resided in this landscape and its buildings.

Far from being a mouldering pile, the photograph shows how self-consciously Kenilworth was presented to the visiting public. Not only has the shell of the building been cleared of rubble and fitted with steps for ease of circulation, but the wall in the middle distance is partly rebuilt and is crowned by specimens of carved masonry. Meanwhile, the ruins are lightly clothed in vegetation, a Romantic effect that suggests neglect but actually demands regular and careful maintenance. In evidence of the weight of visitors, notice the degree of wear on the steps and also the formidable turning barrier of spikes below the left window aimed to deter climbing on the ruins.

By happy coincidence, the American author and Anglophile, Henry James, visited Kenilworth at about the time this photograph was taken and his account perfectly captures a sense of what visitors came for and what they found:

There is no better way to plunge *in medias res* [in the centre of something], for the stranger who wishes to know something of England, than to spend a fortnight in Warwickshire. It is the core and centre of the English world; midmost England, unmitigated England. The place has taught me a great many English secrets; I have been interviewing the genius of pastoral Britain. From a charming lawn – a lawn delicious to one's sentient boot-sole – I looked without obstruction at a sombre, soft, romantic mass whose outline was blurred by mantling ivy. It made a perfect picture, and in the foreground the great trees over arch to their boughs, from left and right, so as to give it a majestic frame. This interesting object was the castle of Kenilworth. It was within distance of an easy walk, but one hardly thought of walking to it, any more than one would have thought of walking to a purple-shadowed tower in the background of a [painting by] Berghem or a Claude. Here were purple shadows and slowly shifting lights, with a soft-hued, bosky country for the middle distance.

Of course, however, I did walk over to the castle; and of course the walk led me through leafy lanes and beside the hedgerows that make a tangled screen for large lawn-like meadows. Of course too, I am bound to add, there was a row of ancient pedlars outside the castle-wall, hawking twopenny pamphlets and photographs. Of course, equally, at the foot of the grassy mound on which the ruins stand were half a dozen public-houses and, always of course, half a dozen beery vagrants sprawling on the grass in the moist sunshine. There was the usual respectable young woman to open the castle-gate and to receive the usual sixpenny fee. There were the usual squares of printed cardboard, suspended upon venerable surfaces, with further enumeration of twopence, threepence, fourpence. I do not allude to these things querulously, for Kenilworth is a very tame lion – a lion that, in former years, I had stroked more than once. I remember perfectly my first visit to this romantic spot; how I chanced upon a picnic; how I stumbled over beer-bottles; how the very echoes of the beautiful ruin seemed to have dropped all their h's. That was a sultry afternoon; I allowed my spirits to sink and I came away hanging my head. This was a beautiful fresh morning, and in the interval I had grown philosophic. I had learnt that, with regard to most romantic sites in England, there is a constant cockneyfication with which you must make your account. There are always people on the field before you, and there is generally something being drunk on the premises.

Henry James, *English Hours*

When James published this account, Kenilworth was essentially a well-visited picturesque ruin. Some owners of ruins, however, were inspired to a more rigorous preservation and presentation of such remains to the public.

1 9 1 1
TATTERSHALL CASTLE
Saving Britain's Heritage

Lord Curzon led a most extraordinary life; perhaps his only significant disappointment was that he never became prime minister. He travelled widely and as Viceroy of India was actively involved both in reshaping the Archaeological Survey of India and repairing such celebrated monuments as the Taj Mahal in Agra. As a result of this experience, he came to view historic monuments not only as intrinsically valuable but as monuments to the history of the nation and the empire. In 1911 he became involved in a controversy over the treatment of a castle ruin that underlined his own and changing public attitudes to historic buildings in Britain. He succinctly narrated the story – which underlines the complexity of the international art market at the time – as follows:

The famous old red-brick castle of Tattershall in Lincolnshire, and the four sculptured stone mantelpieces which were made for it by its founder Lord Cromwell in 1440 . . . were sold by the family to whom they had belonged for centuries in 1910. Subsequently, upon the purchaser of the estate becoming bankrupt, they passed into the hands of a Lincoln bank, to whom the estate had been mortgaged, and were sold by them in 1911. The castle was presently acquired by an American syndicate of speculators, who looked only to profit. The mantelpieces were sold separately from the castle and were bought by a London firm of art dealers, and again disposed of by them to a German dealer with partners in America, where it has all along been intended to offer them for sale.

The attention of the public having been called to the sale of the castle and to the abstraction of the mantelpieces, which were carried off by the dealers to London, and an abortive attempt to save both having been made by the National Trust for Places of

Historic Interest, I was led in the past autumn to look into the question by my interest in archaeological matters, and my strong feeling against the destruction or spoliation of one of the foremost and most splendid of our national monuments.

Finding that there was a very serious and imminent danger that the Castle might be pulled down, or otherwise ruined, by the American syndicate, and learning that there was an interval of 24 hours in the course of which it could still be recovered by the payment of a certain profit to them, I intervened to rescue it.

The Marquis of Curzon of Kedleston, *Tattershall Castle*

Following his intervention, the Tattershall fireplaces were returned amidst public celebration, the carts carrying them draped in Union Jacks. Curzon went on to restore the castle in an Arts and Crafts vein and opened it to the public. He further articulated his views of heritage in 1913 when he spoke in support of the Ancient Monuments Act in Parliament:

The whole attitude of this country and of the civilised world in general has changed towards archæology in recent years. We regard the national monuments to which this Bill refers as part of the heritage and history of the nation. They are part of the heritage of the nation, because every citizen feels an interest in them although he may not own them; and they are part of the history of the nation, because they are documents just as valuable in reading the records of the past as is any manuscript or parchment deed . . . The case in England is different from what it is in any other country I know, and for this reason. These ancient monuments are dear, not only to ourselves, but to our offspring who have gone out from this country to our Dominions beyond the seas . . . Therefore we have a duty in keeping them up which is not only a national duty but may be described as an Imperial duty.

The Marquis of Curzon of Kedleston in
parliamentary debate

Four years later, in 1917, Lord Curzon bought the ruins of Bodiam Castle, Sussex, having been beguiled by their beauties many years before.

His initial intention was to redevelop Bodiam as a residence. Indeed, at this time, by virtue of the motor car, a number of castles in easy striking distance of London were being redeveloped as weekend homes by the wealthy. Crucially, however, he changed his mind.

In the summer of 1919, he commenced a year of research and excavations with a staff of around twenty-five men under the direction of William Weir, with whom he had also worked at Tattershall. At Bodiam Curzon again dredged the moats, repaired the fabric and recorded the building in great detail. That in turn encouraged him to set out the history of the building to the public and open a museum on the site. His impressive research on both Tattershall and Bodiam was posthumously published in two lavish volumes. In the latter book he reminisces about Bodiam:

At one time I contemplated restoring, in the sense of rebuilding, a portion of the interior of the castle, and making it again practicable for residence, and I had plans prepared for the purpose. But on reflection I felt that a new gem does not usually do honour to an old setting; I realised that while gaining something I should sacrifice more; I remembered what [the French architect and restorer] Viollet-le-Duc had done with Pierrefonds and in a lesser degree with Carcassonne; and I desisted from what would have been an interesting architectural experiment, but might easily have degenerated into an archaeological crime.

Perhaps in preserving and dedicating the remains of the castle to the public for all time, and in writing this book about their history, I may have rendered a rather better service both to sentiment and to learning.

The Marquis of Curzon of Kedleston,
Bodiam Castle, Sussex

Nor was Lord Curzon simply concerned with medieval buildings. He thoughtfully restored the eighteenth-century state apartments at his seat of Kedleston Hall, Derbyshire, and furnished the seventeenth-century interiors of Montacute House, Somerset. And he had a flair for temporary architecture as well, having acted as the impresario both of the 1911 Imperial Durbar at Delhi and the 1919 Peace Parade in London that gave birth to the Whitehall Cenotaph. In his treatment of castle ruins, however, his activities follow on from those of the Marquess of Bute (see 1874 above) and imitate in some regards – but with greater sensibility, perhaps – the contemporary work of the state, acting through the Office of Works, to preserve archaeological monuments.

1921
FARLEIGH HUNGERFORD
State Restoration

Farleigh Hungerford, Somerset, as it appears today with the walls stripped of vegetation, the footings of walls cleared and large areas of historic cobbling, as well as the masonry facing of the castle ditches, laid bare to archaeological scrutiny. The management of ruins is vastly expensive however it is undertaken.

In 1915, while commanding a regiment on the Western Front, Lord Cairn completed the transfer of the ruins of Farleigh Hungerford Castle, Somerset, to the guardianship of the state. It was one of a steadily growing number of important medieval ruins entering state care at this time, many of them offered out of a sense of public duty. After the war, the Office of Works began to clear and repair the site. The department aimed to present ruins as evidential – rather than merely evocative – vestiges of the past. To this end vegetation was cut down, wall footings revealed and any structure deemed irrelevant to the defining history of the building cleared away. This left the medieval fabric secure and naked to interrogation.

Less than a mile away from Farleigh Hungerford, at Iford Manor, the eminent architect and garden designer Harold Peto watched this treatment of the ruins with complete horror. He wrote twice to Country Life *objecting to the 'deplorable method of restoration' being adopted. The magazine's architectural editor, Avray Tipping (who jointly authored Lord Curzon's posthumously published book on Tattershall: see 1911 above), wrote an article that nicely sums up the issue:*

The treatment of Farleigh Castle . . . opens up the question of what are right and wrong methods of preserving historic ruins. Such remains of the past make appeal to mental phases that are distinct and in some measure divergent – the artistic and the archaeological. The former is insistent upon the picturesque aspect and the quality given by time. It is not much disturbed by additions to or subtractions from the fabric, by its further decay or even by a smothering of ivy. The latter does not mind, may even be pleased with the complete removal of all tone and texture and growths that nature and age have produced, but it exclaims at any effacement of forms and details that represent and tell of past purpose and style. Some men have a tendency and training towards the one phase, some towards the other. Only a few combine both, but to them alone should be entrusted the care of ancient monuments, and even with them the balancing of the two scales is a task needing thought and judgement . . .

It is a matter of importance if we consider the constantly increasing activities of the Office of Works in this domain, and we will, therefore, shortly consider what Farleigh Castle was, what it is, and what it should be

Tipping then goes on to consider a tower or bastion, only the lower section of which had then been restored:

The upper part of the bastion is full of the picturesqueness and the sentiment of age. There is the poetry of tone and texture in high degree. It is warm and living. But the icy touch of a mechanical and bureaucratic age is creeping up it, and for the first few feet of its height and over the whole of the adjacent curtain wall it looks as if a free hand have been given to an engineer expert in the most modern forms of concrete construction. In anyone sensitive to quality in building the first glimpse produces a shudder and a conviction that the government department in charge has stamped out all individuality, all sense of personal tenderness and respect for beauty, at this hitherto favourite spot in our land of lovely landscape and ancient homes. Is there any such expensively drastic and charm-destructive process necessary or called for at Farleigh? . . .

There has evidently been an earnest desire to do right. But it is borne in upon the visitor that through some lapse the narrow path has been taken. That the wide way with broad human outlook has been missed. That a prompt retracing of steps is called for, so that, to the very large extent which is quite compatible with maintenance, the warm and speaking spirit of nature should be allowed to continue to vitalise and render sympathetic these walls and towers that are still capable of throbbing in remembrance of the doughty deeds and tragic lives of the ancient Hungerfords

Henry Avray Tipping, *Country Life*

STRIKING a balance between the aesthetic and archaeological treatment of historic buildings remains as difficult as ever. Looking at the activities of the Office of Works, and its successor body, the quango and now the charity, English Heritage, Tipping might have thought that his observations had been ignored. In reality, however, the desire to preserve the character of state monuments has undoubtedly grown stronger over time. In part that's because the damaging long-term consequences of intervention have become ever clearer, in particular the problems created by exposing sensitive fabric to the weather. Added to which, the costs of maintaining ruins have spiralled. That's one reason why, by the 1990s, a castle of the importance of Wigmore, Herefordshire, was conserved by English Heritage without clearance.

Such treatment is in striking contrast to state restoration projects of medieval buildings in other parts of Europe. While work was under way at Wigmore, for example, Trim Castle, Co. Meath, in the Republic of Ireland, and Falaise Castle, Calvados, France, saw ruined keeps of the twelfth century flamboyantly restored with new roofs and floors using stridently modern materials. The latter project certainly looks misjudged.

1923
BLANDINGS CASTLE
The Castle as Idyll

Blandings Castle, the seat of the 'amiable and boneheaded peer' Lord Emsworth, is the setting of several of the comic novels of P. G. Wodehouse. This imaginary castle represents a peculiarly English vision of a castle in the twentieth century – the medieval fortress softened by time into an idyll. Life inside it, moreover, is a seemingly perpetual house party. Almost everyone is short of ready money, yet the cast of characters has little to do beyond fall in love with each other. For an occupant of Blandings, motoring down to London for the day is the very height of engagement with the world, even if it is only to lay a bet on the 2.30 at Ascot.

The demi-Eden of Blandings Castle is an important foil for the plots that Wodehouse narrates. Its very unworldliness suffuses everything that happens within it with a sense of innocence. It also makes the ordinary seem jarring and unwelcome. In this case, the ordinary is represented by the private secretary of the Earl of Emsworth, the 'Efficient Baxter'. A diamond necklace has just been stolen and he is – quite justifiably – suspicious of several of the house guests. When woken by strange noises in the garden in the middle of the night, he steps out in his pyjamas to investigate. His undetected quarry, however, slips back into the house and locks him out:

To find oneself locked out of a country-house at half-past-two in the morning in lemon-coloured pyjamas can never be an unmixedly agreeable experience, and Baxter was a man less fitted by nature to endure it with equanimity than most men. He was a fiery and an arrogant soul, and he seethed in furious rebellion against the intolerable position into which fate had manoeuvred him. He even went so far as to give the front door a petulant kick. Finding, however, that this hurt his toes and accomplished no useful end, he addressed himself to the task of ascertaining whether there was any way of getting in – short of banging the knocker and rousing the house, a line of action which did not commend itself to him. He made a practice of avoiding as far as possible the ribald type of young man of which the castle was now full, and he had no desire to meet them at this hour in his present costume. He left the front door and proceeded to make a circuit of the castle walls; and his spirits sank even lower. In the Middle Ages, during that stormy period of England's history when walls were built six feet thick and a window was not so much a window as a handy place for pouring molten lead on the heads of visitors, Blandings had been an impregnable fortress. But in all its career it can seldom have looked more of a fortress than it did now to the Efficient Baxter.

One of the disadvantages of being a man of action, impervious to the soft emotions, is that in moments of trial the beauties of nature are powerless to soothe the anguished heart. Had Baxter been of a dreamy and poetic temperament he might now have been drawing all sorts of balm from the loveliness of his surroundings. The air was full of the scent of growing things; strange, shy creatures came and went about him as he walked; down in the woods a nightingale had begun to sing; and there was something grandly majestic in the huge bulk of the castle as it towered against the sky. But Baxter had temporarily lost his sense of smell; he feared and disliked the strange, shy creatures; the nightingale left him cold; and the only thought the towering castle inspired in him was that it looked as if a fellow would need half a ton of dynamite to get into it . . . The clock over the stables struck three.

P. G. Wodehouse, *Leave it to Psmith*

THE reader is expected to delight in the Efficient Baxter's predicament and his complete inability to laugh at the absurdity of his position. Oblivious to his fury and the passage of time, the castle defies the cares of the world and locks them out. In this sense, the idyll of Blandings is perhaps the antithesis of Doubting Castle in *The Pilgrim's Progress* (see 1678 above). There can be little doubt, however, that John Bunyan would not have approved; it savours too much of the idle rich.

1925
ST DONAT'S CASTLE
Purchasing History

In the early twentieth century, American money and enthusiasm created a hugely lucrative international market for historic fittings and buildings (see 1911 above). One of the most insatiable collectors of the period was William Randolph Hearst, a newspaper tycoon. He began work in 1919 to Hearst Castle, California, a magpie creation assembled without any regard for cost from the transported elements of European buildings. In 1925 he decided to buy a castle in England and wired the following telegram to his London newspaper office:

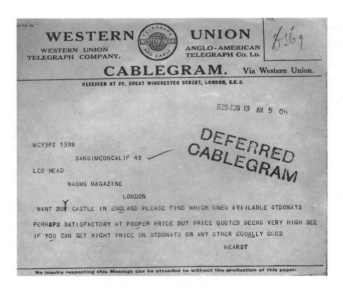

A copy of the telegram survives in the Country Life archive and the following week, 22 August, a leader in the magazine explains why:

Far away from here, in America, Mr W. R. Hearst, the owner of many newspapers, saw – and greatly admired – the pictures of St Donat's Castle in the advertisement pages of *Country Life*. As the result, the Hearst organisation in London has had instructions to buy it on his behalf . . . Mr Hearst has not been hitherto credited with any great affection for this country. Perhaps he will come to like it better now that he has so romantic a home in it.

HEARST was, indeed, through his papers, a fierce critic of Britain, but he lavished money on his new castle at St Donat's. The castle had recently been modernised by Thomas Garner and G. F. Bodley (working separately for the industrialist and collector Morgan Williams) but Hearst took things further, furnishing it with architectural elements from other medieval buildings. Hearst bought incredibly well, to the despair of some observers, but that was the whole point; everything was commodified in his mind and had to be the best.

It's noteworthy that Hearst was not the only buyer for St Donat's. Two months later, on 31 October, an advertisement was placed in *Country Life*: 'Wanted by an American gentleman of large means, to purchase a castle possessed of character and interest, such as that attaching to St Donat's Castle (Wales) recently sold . . . any position within about eight hours of London.' Nor was such enthusiasm unique to Americans. In 1882 Randal Berkeley unexpectedly found himself heir to the earldom of Berkeley and its namesake seat, Berkeley Castle, Gloucestershire. As he awaited his inheritance, he moved to Oxford to pursue his interests in scientific research. There he bought a small house overlooking the city on Boar's Hill and, independent of the university, attached a laboratory to it. Then in 1904–6 he employed the architect Ernest George (a partner of Harold Peto, see 1921 above) to encastellate it and create what is presently known as Foxcombe Hall. Having inherited Berkeley Castle in 1920, he transformed the building, restoring the interior, importing fittings and modernising it with bathrooms and electricity.

1930
CASTLE DROGO, DEVON
A New Ancestral Seat

Castle Drogo, Devon, as photographed by Country Life, *1945. The castle is set dramatically on a granite outcrop and was built between 1911 and 1930 by the architect Edwin Lutyens for the wealthy tea merchant and owner of the Home and Colonial Stores, Julius Drewe. It was Drewe who insisted that his new house take the form of a castle. Also that it stood close to the village of Drewsteignton, which he regarded as his ancestral home.*

LUTYENS responded to his brief by creating a bold and abstracted external design to the castle inspired by Tudor architecture. There are serried grids of windows and cleverly arranged recessions of plane in the walls that heighten the impression of monumentality. They are built of granite.

The building is not battlemented but there are arrow-loops in the parapets. To the left is the chapel with a crowning bellcote that evokes in miniature the forms of the war memorials, including the Cenotaph on Whitehall, which made Lutyens a household name after World War I. Lutyens had had considerable experience working on castles. He had previously overseen the restoration of the sixteenth-century Lindisfarne Castle, Northumberland, as a summerhouse for the editor of *Country Life*, Edward Hudson. And while working on Drogo he was also concurrently engaged in the restoration of the sixteenth-century Lambay Castle on an island in Dublin Bay. Work to Drogo finished in 1930 before the original plans were completed and a year before Drewe's death. Drewe lost his son and heir in World War I and his enthusiasm for this project died afterwards.

1940
WORLD WAR II
An Explosive Miscalculation

Kelburn Castle, Ayrshire, the scene of the explosion described by Waugh. The graffiti executed by four Brazilian artists in 2007 is eye-catching. Such interventions are often reported as controversial but they generate publicity and the vast majority of people seem to relish them.

The conquest of Norway in April 1940 and the fall of France the following month opened up Britain to the immediate threat of invasion. Up and down the country coastal fortifications as well as inland lines of defence were constructed to slow any enemy advance and frustrate airborne assault. Castles often occupied readily defensible or prominent sites. At Pevensey, Sussex, pillboxes were built into the ruins and the dramatic coastal fort of Dunstanburgh, Northumberland, fell within a landing zone that was additionally fortified with tank traps, minefields and lines of wire. The night-time detonation of mines by foxes was a problem and caused at least one short-lived invasion scare.

Some castles, meanwhile, had never passed out of military use. Dover, for example, remained an important military base. Because it stood within long-distance artillery range of occupied France, much of its activity was pushed underground into a complex of Napoleonic tunnels that was rapidly extended on multiple layers. It was from the safety of this tunnel system that the Dunkirk evacuation of the British Expeditionary force was planned. After the war the lowest functioning level of tunnels was fitted out as the headquarters for the regional government of Kent in the event of a nuclear war. They were only abandoned and officially acknowledged to exist in the 1980s. Mothballed with their period office furniture they are a sinister thing to see.

Wherever wartime alterations touched historic fabric the Ministry of Works had to be consulted. Even faced with the exigencies of war, for example, an officer at Carlisle wrote punctiliously on 20 March 1941 about a new anti-aircraft position in the castle, which still served as a barracks:

In order to give a full field of fire for the AA post on the top of the keep, the Castle, Carlisle, it is intended to build a 'light machine-gun' platform of wood. The material available is old railway sleepers, and the appropriate weight of the platform with gun and two men of crew will be 25cwts.

To which came the obliging reply:

Sir, I am directed by the Minister of Works and Buildings to acknowledge the receipt of your recent letter . . . The ministry have no objection to offer to the proposal providing that a suitable base is used on which to erect the gun platform as without the base there is a danger that the lead rolls on the flat roof would suffer damage

BUT it wasn't just castles that had become ruins or barracks that were touched by the war. Even before the outbreak of hostilities, the government had surveyed the entire housing stock of the British Isles to identify all properties that might be large enough to accommodate official bodies and soldiers. Large buildings were subsequently requisitioned across the country for every kind of wartime purpose. Anecdotes abound about the consequences but this is my favourite from a letter written by the novelist Evelyn Waugh, who was now in the army, to his wife:

Darling

It was a great joy to get a letter from you . . . no. 3 commando were very anxious to be chums with Lord Glasgow so they offered to blow up an old tree stump for him and he was very grateful and he said don't spoil the plantation of young trees near it because that is the apple of my eye and they said no of course not we can blow a tree down so that it falls on a sixpence and Lord Glasgow said goodness you are clever and he asked them all to lunch for the great explosion. So Col. Durnford-Slater DSO said to his subaltern, have you put enough explosive in the tree. Yes, sir, 75lbs. Is that enough? Yes sir I worked it out by mathematics it is exactly right. Well better put a bit more. Very good sir.

And when Colonel D. Slater DSO had had his port he sent for the subaltern and said subaltern better put a bit more explosive in that tree. I don't want to disappoint Lord Glasgow. Very good sir.

Then they all went out to see the explosion and Colonel DS DSO said you will see that tree fall flat at just that angle where it will hurt no young trees and Lord Glasgow said goodness you are clever.

So soon they lit the fuse and waited for the explosion and presently the tree, instead of falling quietly sideways, rose 50 feet into the air taking with it half an acre of soil and the whole of the young plantation.

And the subaltern said Sir I made a mistake, it should have been 7 1/2 lbs not 75.

Lord Glasgow was so upset he walked in dead silence back to his castle and when they came to the turn of the drive in sight of his castle what should they find but that every pane of glass in the building was broken.

So Lord Glasgow gave a little cry and ran to hide his emotion in the lavatory and there when he pulled the plug the entire ceiling, loosened by the explosion, fell on his head.

This is quite true. E

31 May 1942, Evelyn Waugh writes to his wife, Laura

Kelburn Castle, Ayrshire, the scene of this disaster, enjoyed renewed celebrity in 2007 when four Brazilian artists were invited to decorate the exterior with striking graffiti.

1949
GODSEND AND COURANTSDAIR CASTLES
Decay, Neglect and Obscurity

Dodie Smith is perhaps most celebrated today as the author of The Hundred and One Dalmatians *(1956) but her heart-warming book* I Capture the Castle *(1949) now enjoys considerable popularity in its own right. It's in the form of a diary, written by seventeen-year-old Cassandra, and set against the backdrop of two castles: a Norman motte, Bellemotte, which is just a hill, and the moated castle that succeeded it, Godsend. The latter well represents the fate of countless smaller castles across Britain that fell out of use from the seventeenth century onwards and became farms or were divided up as cottages. The Arts and Crafts movement began to restore and make these buildings genteel once more from the 1880s but even today the process is not complete. In the novel an artistic family has retired to one such castle – inspired by Wingfield Castle, Suffolk – in the 1930s, where they live completely removed and in abject poverty. The book memorably begins:*

I write this sitting in the kitchen sink. That is, my feet are in it; the rest of me is on the draining board, which I have padded with our dog's blanket and the tea cosy. I can't say that I'm really comfortable, and there is a depressing smell of carbolic soap, but this is the only part of the kitchen where there is any daylight left. And I have found that sitting in a place where you have never sat before can be inspiring . . .

Drips from the roof are plopping into the water-butt by the back door. The view through the windows above the sink is excessively drear. Beyond the dank garden in the courtyard are the ruined walls on the edge of the moat. Beyond the moat, the boggy ploughed fields stretch to the leaden sky.

Dodie Smith, I Capture the Castle

DEPRESSING as Godsend may be in the rain, it was a fortunate survivor in comparison to Courantsdair Castle, in Osbert Lancaster's short story published the previous year, 1948, about an inept knight, William de Littlehampton, who is compelled to go on crusade against his wishes and finds unexpected success. The opening is deliberately absurd and plays on the idea of medieval castles as essentially functional buildings and, therefore, devoid of human comforts.

Once upon a time, in the reign of King Richard Coeur-de-Lion to be precise, there lived in Sussex a certain landowner known as William de Littlehampton. He was exceedingly rich, the lord of five manors with the rights of soccage, corkage and drainage between Chanctonbury Ring and Bognor-supra-Mare and in addition he enjoyed the rare privilege of fishing for sturgeon in the river Arun. (In fact there are no sturgeon in the river Arun but this was nevertheless regarded as a very rare distinction.) His principal residence was the castle of Courantsdair, a large, prominently situated building completely equipped with drawbridge, moat, bailey, keep, posterns, dungeons and all the usual twelfth-century fittings and enjoying a magnificent view of the South Downs and the English Channel. Unfortunately, though immensely strong it had already been built over a hundred years and even by twelfth-century standards was considered more than a little uncomfortable. The fires smoked without stopping, the wind whistled round the great hall through a dozen cracks and none of the window shutters fitted properly, which was all the more noticeable as none of the windows had any glass. William who every year from the beginning of November to the end of May had a constant succession of colds, coughs, bronchitises and influenzas, was fully aware of these defects and had made several attempts to make his home a little more up to date, but he had never yet succeeded in overcoming the resistance of his mother, a remarkably tough old lady of sixty-eight of whom, I am sorry to say, he was very much afraid. Whenever he suggested putting a screen across the entrance to the kitchen or hanging some arras on the walls of his bedroom his mother promptly reminded him that his dear father had never had any such sissy fittings in his day, and what was good enough for old Sir Dagobert should certainly be quite good enough for his son. William invariably agreed, apologised deeply for having raised the matter and tried hard to suppress his sneezes for the rest of the evening in case his mother should think he was playing for sympathy

Where Osbert Lancaster's satire has real teeth is in his account of the afterlife of this building at the very end of the story. In the aftermath of World War II, country houses and their estates were vanishing rapidly, largely as a result of a punitive tax regime. There is real bathos, therefore, to the short modern history of the castle at the end of the book:

Today more than seven centuries have passed since all these things took place and small trace now remains of any of the figures in this tale. The ruins of the castle of Courantsdair were long conspicuous, but were finally sold by the father of the present Lord Littlehampton some years ago in order to pay death duties, and the site is now covered by the Chateau Housing Estate. Today the only remaining indication of that once formidable pile is to be found in Nos. 18 to 25 Acacia Road which, being rather hastily erected on the side of the old moat, are quite exceptionally damp in winter.

Osbert Lancaster, *The Saracen's Head*

Time does have a brutal way of reducing the past and for all the castles that either remain in occupation or are managed as visitor attractions and ruins, the story of the vast majority created in the centuries since the Norman Conquest is ultimately of neglect, decay and obscurity.

1969
CAERNARFON CASTLE
The Investiture of the Prince of Wales

The Prince of Wales is invested by his mother, the Queen, in Caernarfon Castle, with the symbols of his estate including a coronet, rod, ring and mantle in 1969. The medievalising ceremony and stylish furniture were developed under the presiding hand of Lord Snowdon.

On an overcast afternoon on 1 July 1969, the Prince of Wales was invested by the Queen, his mother, as Earl of Chester and Prince of Wales at Caernarfon Castle. He had spent the previous two months getting to know Wales and to learn Welsh. The train bringing him to the ceremony arrived at a specially constructed temporary platform close to the town at 2 p.m. and he travelled to the castle by carriage, wearing for the occasion the uniform of the Colonel in Chief of the Royal Welsh Regiment and the Order of the Garter. The event itself was consciously medieval in inspiration with the interior of the castle dressed with heraldry and converted into an auditorium under the presiding hand of the Earl of Snowdon. In the centre stood a perspex awning, a protection from the weather also intended – like the backless thrones beneath – to improve sight-lines and facilitate television filming. Letters patent conferring the name, style, title and dignity of Prince of Wales and Earl of Chester were read out in English and then Welsh. Afterwards the prince was symbolically girt with a sword, crowned with a coronet and received a gold ring, gold rod and ermine-lined mantle. After a loyal address the prince responded. His speech, less a short preface, began in Welsh and was as follows:

It is with a certain sense of pride and emotion that I have received these symbols of office, here in this magnificent fortress, where no one could fail to be stirred by its atmosphere of time-worn grandeur, nor where I myself could be unaware of the long history of Wales in its determination to remain individual and to guard its own particular heritage. A heritage that dates back into the mists of ancient British history, that has produced many brave men, Princes, poets, bards, scholars and more recently, great singers, a very memorable 'goon' and eminent film stars. All these people have been inspired in some way by this heritage.

The prince then switched to English:

I hope and trust that in time I shall be able to offer my own contribution and to do that I seek your cooperation and understanding.

Speaking for myself, as a result of my two-month stay in this country, I have come to see far more in the title I hold than hitherto. I am more than grateful to the people of this Principality for making my brief stay so immensely worthwhile and for giving me such encouragement in the learning of the language.

I know that social conditions have changed since 50 years ago and, of course, are still changing. The demands on a Prince of Wales have altered, but I am determined to serve and to try as best I can to live up to those demands, whatever they might be in the rather uncertain future. One thing I am clear about and it is that Wales needs to look forward without forsaking the traditions and essential aspects of her past. The past can be just as much a stimulus to the future as anything else. By the affirmation of your loyalty today for which I express my gratitude, this will not simply be a faint hope.

Charles, Prince of Wales, speaking at his installation

THE prince's words at his installation articulate the idea of a role shaped by tradition and identity yet responsive to change. It's one that Caernarfon Castle – as an open ruin dressed for the occasion – perfectly reinforced.

The investiture of 1969 was closely modelled on the first ceremony of its kind at which the future Edward VIII (and later Duke of Windsor) was created Prince of Wales at Caernarfon on 13 July 1911 – hence the prince's reference to social change over the last fifty years. Many of the sensitivities apparent in 1969 were prefigured on that occasion, which took place in a tense political atmosphere immediately after the coronation of George V. For this reason it was one of the first royal events recorded on film. A crucial figure involved in organising the 1911 ceremony was the then Chancellor of the Exchequer and future prime minister, Lloyd George. He partly grew up in his mother's home, Llanystumdwy, Caernarvonshire, and coached the seventeen-year-old prince to speak some words of Welsh for the occasion.

The connection of the investiture to the castle harks back to the late thirteenth century. Edward I's queen, Eleanor of Castile, was sent, heavily pregnant, to Caernarfon and was delivered there on 25 April 1284 of a son, the future Edward II. The birth of the child here was undoubtedly an act of policy because the castle and town had been begun less than a year earlier as the new capital of Wales and the whole place must have been a building site. As early as the sixteenth century, the story was told that when Edward I heard of the birth he gathered the Welsh leaders together at Rhuddlan. There they demanded that he appoint a prince of their own country, who was beyond reproach and spoke neither French nor Saxon as his native tongue. Agreeing to their every demand, Edward I smugly proffered them the baby. Since the baby spoke no language at all, the king explained, his first words could be in Welsh if they chose. Edward of Caernarfon was not in fact created Prince of Wales until 1301, but the story may contain a germ of truth.

1997
WINDSOR CASTLE
The Rebuilding of St George's Hall

St George's Hall, Windsor Castle, as rebuilt in 1997 following a devastating fire on 20–21 November 1992. The blaze spread from the Private Chapel and was finally extinguished after fifteen hours, by which time it had inflicted damage to 115 rooms at a cost of about £38,000 for every minute it burned. The restoration of Windsor Castle that followed is a reminder that neither the Gothic Revival nor castle-building are dead in Britain. It was completed in five years at a cost of £37 million, 70 per cent of which was raised by opening Buckingham Palace to the public.

NO sooner was the fire out than controversy erupted in the press as to what should now happen to Windsor. The spectrum of opinion embraced everything from faithful reconstruction to the creation of a strikingly modern architectural intervention within the castle. There was even the suggestion that parts of the building might be left ruinous. Questions were also raised about the management of Windsor: should it be run as a museum and who should take responsibility for it?

By June 1993 the crucial decisions underpinning the restoration for the castle had already been taken. Acting on the advice of the newly established Windsor Castle Restoration Committee, chaired by the Duke of Edinburgh (which in turn acted on the advice of a design subcommittee chaired by the Prince of Wales), the decision was taken that a group of rooms less severely affected by the fire would be restored to their form in George IV's reign and according to the designs of the architect Jeffry Wyatville. This restoration work was awarded to Donald Insall Associates.

Meanwhile, the Sidell Gibson Partnership was invited in June 1994 to draw up new designs for St George's Hall and the chapel where the fire had started. The appointment of Sidell Gibson, a small and relatively little-known architectural practice, came as a surprise to many and when their designs, drawn up by Giles Downes in a Gothic idiom, were presented to the press they received a mixed welcome. The *Daily Telegraph* described them as conceived in the manner of a theme park and characterised them as 'Ruritanian'. *Country Life* denounced such 'architectural bigotry' and pointed out that Gothic design had been maintained as a living and vibrant tradition into the twentieth century in Britain.

In St George's Hall a great deal of care was taken to infuse the new interior with ornaments appropriate to its role as a ceremonial meeting place of the Order of the Garter. A huge new oak roof by Capps and Capps was erected over the entire space and ornamented with several hundred shields bearing the arms of the Garter knights in an organic Perpendicular Gothic style. At one end a wooden screen was designed to double as a throne dais. Its detailing includes handles in the form of the patron saint of the order, St George, and the Dragon. Above the screen are a series of the Queen's Beasts presented by the Corporation of the City of London and carved by Ray Gonzalez. The photograph also shows the sixteenth-century armour of the King's Champion – now removed – that was erected at the suggestion of Prince Philip against the backdrop of a circular device with the motto of the Order of the Garter gifted to the queen by the Commonwealth. This device was inspired by a medieval lock plate on a door in St George's Chapel, Windsor.

The new interiors stood ready for a ball to celebrate the golden wedding anniversary of the Queen and Prince Philip on 20 November 1997. A week earlier they also hosted a party to thank the 1,500 contractors and craftsmen involved in the project.

1 9 9 7
HOGWARTS CASTLE
The Modern Gothic Castle

Castles not only remain in occupation across Britain today but they feature widely in popular books and films, particularly in fiction and fantasy. An excellent representative example is Hogwarts Castle, the school setting of much of the action in the so-called Harry Potter series of novels by J. K. Rowling. The novels are in fact strikingly short of architectural description because Hogwarts is really a fantastical backdrop that the reader can imagine to suit themselves. It is, indeed, a castle in the tradition of the Gothic novel (see 1764 above); a place removed where anything can happen and magic, excitement and fear lurk. In the following passage, Harry Potter is arriving with a group of children for the start of their first term. They are being led by a huge member of staff, the gentle half-giant, Hagrid, and the description focuses not on the detail of the building but its presence and drama as they approach it:

Slipping and stumbling, they followed Hagrid down what seemed to be a steep, narrow path. It was so dark either side of them that Harry thought there must be thick trees there. Nobody spoke much. Neville, the boy who kept losing his toad, sniffed once or twice.

'Yeh'll get yer firs' sight o' Hogwarts in a sec,' Hagrid called over his shoulder, 'jus' round this bend here.'

There was a loud 'Oooooh!'

The narrow path had opened suddenly on to the edge of a great black lake. Perched atop a high mountain on the other side, its windows sparkling in the starry sky, was a vast castle with many turrets and towers.

'No more'n four to a boat!' Hagrid called, pointing to a fleet of little boats sitting in the water by the shore. Harry and Ron were followed into their boat by Neville and Hermione.

'Everyone in?' shouted Hagrid, who had a boat to himself,
'Right then – FORWARD!'

And the fleet of little boats moved off all at once, gliding
across the lake, which was as smooth as glass. Everyone was silent,
staring up at the great castle overhead. It towered over them as
they sailed nearer and nearer to the cliff on which it stood.

J. K. Rowling, *Harry Potter and the Philosopher's Stone*

IN the light of such limited description, it's fascinating to see the way in
which Hogwarts Castle has been reared into life for the series of films
based on the novels. The overarching views of the school – as it has been
conjured into being by digital special effects – are actually based on
Durham Cathedral, with its crossing and western towers (but with other
buildings attached). To lend drama to this composition, high-pitched
roofs and spires have been added, along with additional turrets and
pinnacles to enliven the roof level.

Medieval ecclesiastical buildings were also used to shoot many of the
interior scenes of the early films, including the cloisters of Durham
Cathedral, Gloucester Cathedral and Lacock Abbey, formerly a medieval
convent. The interior used for the dining hall of the school, meanwhile,
was that of Christ Church, Oxford, built by Cardinal Wolsey in the
1520s. Indeed, the only castle that actually appears in the films is
Alnwick, Northumberland, which was used for some outdoor scenes.
Medieval ecclesiastical architecture generally looks more immediate and
obviously Gothic than its secular counterpart, and in their preference for
it, the set designers of the Harry Potter films follow in a long tradition
that stretches back to artists and architects of the eighteenth century
(and beyond).

Over the course of filming, however, the series has gradually moved
away from real buildings altogether. That aligns the visualisation of
Hogwarts with the mainstream of castles that have recently appeared in
fantasy films. These use special effects to create buildings of very dramatic
appearance. Nearly all are elevated and integral with a spectacular
landscape feature, usually a ragged mountain, and possess a busy outline
of towers and turrets. *Game of Thrones* (2011–19), for example, has
furnished a whole series of fantastical castles that conform in deliberately
varied ways to this essential description.

Other visual conventions are regularly applied to such buildings. Some castles are dark in colour, windowless and without surrounding greenery, the seats of evil powers. Examples would include Minas Morgul or Barad-dûr in the films based on J. R. R. Tolkien's *Lord of the Rings* directed by Peter Jackson (2001–3). Others are welcoming and splendid, with brightly coloured walls, balconies and gardens, such as Cair Paravel in *The Chronicles of Narnia* (2005, 2008 and 2010) based on the novels of C. S. Lewis. Castles – or something very like them – even feature in futuristic space films, as with Theed Palace in *Attack of the Clones* (2002) from the Star Wars series, as well as in computer games.

2009
DOVER CASTLE
Recreating the Past

In 2009 work was completed to a reconstruction of the interiors of the keep at Dover as they might have appeared in 1184, during a visit to the castle by its builder, Henry II. Full-blooded recreations of this kind, often underpinned by informed scholarship, have a very long history stretching back to the Gothic Revival (see 1874 above). They tend to look their age quite quickly. Many of those undertaken in castles over the last thirty years or so – as for example at Leeds Castle, the Bloody Tower at the Tower of London, Tretower, Chepstow and Stirling Castle – have simply involved dressing rooms in period style. Other visitor attractions, such as Warwick Castle, have used waxwork mannequins further to enliven rooms for visitors.

THE reconstruction of every object in this room is based on rigorous academic research and undertaken with close attention to detail. Both the bed and scissor frame chair to the left, for example, are based on twelfth-century manuscript images and the evidence of surviving medieval furnishing. Dressing rooms in this way makes it much easier to understand castles as residences and challenges the popular perception of these buildings as no more than barrack-like fortresses (see 1949 above).

For all the work and scholarship they involve, however, such displays should not be viewed uncritically. Nor should the undoubted quality, workmanship and interest of the furnishings make us lose sight of how much we see is wishful invention. Henry II definitely visited Dover Castle in 1184 but this room may not have been structurally complete (see 1181 above). Nor, if it was, is there any evidence that it was configured or furnished in this way. Added to which, the present floor and brick vault date to the eighteenth century, a reminder that such a presentation of the room effectively bypasses much of its history. The fireplace to the right, meanwhile, dates to the fifteenth century.

It's a compounding problem that Henry II himself was a king of immense power whose personal possessions were undoubtedly of huge intrinsic value. Such things are impossible to afford or to recreate today. Strangely, therefore, were a twelfth-century visitor to be shown this room and told that it was the accommodation of Henry II, he or she might well regard it as comfortless and threadbare. In this way, even the best recreations can paradoxically create rooms that nobody from the past would recognise.

2012
LANCASTER CASTLE
An Empty Prison

In January 2011 the Ministry of Justice announced that the prison in Lancaster Castle would close. When the last inmates left a few weeks later, in March 2011, about nine hundred years of continuous judicial use came to an end and the buildings were returned to their ancient owner, the Duchy of Lancaster. This photograph shows the main prison yard soon afterwards. The justice secretary was quoted in the Lancashire Telegraph *as saying: 'The decision to close any prison is a difficult one but one that we have had to make. Closing outdated and expensive prisons is an important step in our strategy to provide a secure and modern, fit-for-purpose prison estate, while improving efficiency and value for the taxpayer.' Lancaster was the last medieval castle in Britain to operate as a prison (after Oxford, which closed in 2006).*

THE closure of the prison made Lancaster Castle accessible for the first time. By the time this photograph was taken, some of the more visually intrusive security fixtures had already been removed. The main prison yard roughly corresponds to the bailey of the medieval castle and is dominated by the medieval keep. Aside from this, most of the buildings visible here were created during the modernisation of the prison from 1788 by the architect Thomas Harrison and later J. M. Gandy. Lancaster was at the time an immensely wealthy city – made rich in part by the slave trade – and it built in accordance with its means in the Gothic style deemed appropriate to the castle. Gaols had hitherto been largely holding places for those awaiting justice; the decision of the court promised release or punishment (though debtors might be resident for long periods and paid for the pleasure). By the late Georgian period, however, prisons had to accommodate increasing numbers of long-term inmates. Consequently, Lancaster Castle was expanded with segregated cells respectively for men, women and debtors. The women's cells were in the tower just visible to the left of the photograph and were arranged on the 'panopticon' principle, allowing for easy surveillance.

Overlooking the castle yard from the back of the women's cells is a statue of Justice, one breast exposed, holding a sword and scales. A high fence and gate with the bald inscription 'HMP Lancaster Castle' define an exercise space within this. A clock tower to the right regulated prison life. The yard is partly enclosed to the right and rear by ranges of debtors' cells. The latter occupy the former site of the medieval castle hall. They screen a large, purpose-built court complex including the immense amphitheatre of Shire Hall, a Crown Court and a Grand Jury Room (connected to the condemned hold for public executions). In combination with the prison this is one of the most complete collections of Georgian judicial buildings in Britain.

The associations of Lancaster Castle are not uplifting but they are testimony to the phenomenal staying power of some castles. Also, the strange way in which these buildings can exist in plain sight and yet for any number of reasons be inaccessible to the vast majority of people, even those who pass by them on a daily basis.

EPILOGUE
THE DISNEY CASTLE . . . AND THE FUTURE

SINCE 1985 every one of the scores of films produced by Walt Disney has been prefaced by a short sequence illustrating a castle with a fantastical outline of towers, turrets, steep roofs and a central gateway. This castle of the screen was inspired by Cinderella's Castle, a central feature of Disneyland, California, an amusement park that first opened in 1955 (and is now imitated in various different forms across the world). At first the film image of the castle was a silhouette, but over the past fifteen years or so it has been rendered much more vividly. The opening sequence that includes it has been endlessly varied to suit the theme of the particular film it prefaces but it remains broadly the same.

The viewer stares into a star-laden sky. Suddenly, there is an illusion of rapid downward movement through clouds and a wide landscape with a river running through it appears in half-light. Animating the scene is a sailing ship and steam train. Then, as the camera continues to descend, a fluttering standard rises into view. It is rapidly revealed as the topmost pinnacle of a castle. Fireworks explode around the building as the camera draws away and drops to ground level. The castle is mountain-shaped with pale, floodlit walls and a busy outline of high-pitched roofs in blue slate. In the centre of the building is an open gate, its portcullis clearly visible but raised. Entering this opening a river flows right through the building. To either side of the castle there extend into the landscape long causeways lit with lamps. Apart from the continuing display of fireworks there is no sign of any movement or activity. An arc of light crosses the sky above the castle, the music surges and the film begins.

Many theories have been advanced as to the particular inspiration of the Disney Castle. Whether it imitates, say, a particular chateau on the Loire, Ludwig of Bavaria's Neuschwanstein begun in 1869, or the

352

fabulous medieval illustrations of the *Très Riches Heures* of the Duc de Berry, however, is in some ways beside the point. This building is really meant to entice us into the imagined world of the ensuing film, which it prefigures.

The sources for it properly lie in the spectacular and fantastical scene-setting decoration that appeared in super cinemas of the 1930s, such as the Gothic splendours of the Granada Tooting (1931) or the 'Mermaid's Palace' of the New Victoria, Westminster (1930). Like them, the Disney Castle doesn't advance the plot or even directly connect with it. Instead, it simply sharpens the appetite of our imagination for the feast to come.

The Disney Castle seems an appropriate subject with which to end this book, in part simply because it offers a twenty-first-century vision of a castle and is familiar to so many people. It's also fascinating, however, because it illustrates yet another thought-provoking perspective on the idea of the castle.

To a European audience familiar with these buildings either as ruins in the landscape or as residences, the most obvious point of reference for any image of a castle they see is the historical past. Yet to a North American audience – which the Disney Castle was created first and foremost to delight – as well as to a much wider global audience, many of whom may never have actually seen a castle at all, the point of association is not with the past or anything tangible at all. Instead, it is with fairy tales and the fantastical.

These associations – the historical and the imaginary – are not exclusive, not least because, as we have seen, there is a long tradition in Europe of associating castles with legend. They are, however, different. And that highlights perhaps the most marvellous quality of the castle: the idea of one is instantaneously recognisable to a huge proportion of the global population today, irrespective of their cultural background, yet it speaks to everyone with a slightly different emphasis. Like a mirror, the idea of the castle isn't really consistent at all but it ends up reflecting what we put in front of it. For this reason alone the castle surely not only has a rich history – as this book has tried to illustrate – but an equally rich future.

BIBLIOGRAPHY

NOTE ON THE BIBLIOGRAPHY

This select bibliography is structured according to the chronology of the book. Each entry begins with the full citation in bold for the quotations in the order in which they appear. There then follow references to other sources cited and books and articles that further explore – or lead on from – the themes discussed.

J. Goodall, *The English Castle*, London and New Haven, 2011, supplies a much fuller bibliography and also discusses many of the themes explored here. I have only cited it below where it has a particular bearing on the discussion.

For those interested in pursuing reading with relation to a particular castle I would recommend:
www.gatehouse-gazetteer.info
A. Emery, *Greater Medieval Houses of England and Wales*, 3 vols, Cambridge, 1996–2006
J. R. Kenyon, *Castles, Town Defences and Artillery Fortifications in the United Kingdom and Ireland: A Bibliography, 1945–2006*, Donington, 2008
D. J. C. King, *Castellarium Anglicanum: An Index and Bibliography of the Castles in England, Wales and the Islands*, 2 vols, Millwood, NY, 1983

For descriptions of buildings by county:
N. Pevsner et al., *The Buildings of England* and *The Buildings of Wales*, Harmondsworth; London and New Haven, 1951–
The Castle Studies Group Journal presents annual summaries of excavations, news and studies on the subject of castles in Britain and beyond.

Both the guidebooks of Cadw and English Heritage offer excellent accounts of buildings in state care.

THE WORD 'CASTLE'

Caesar. *The Conquest of Gaul*, trans. S. A. Handford, Harmondsworth, 1951, 133
***Vulgate Gospel of Luke* 10:38 (Douay-Rheims translation, 1611)**
***The Anglo-Saxon Chronicles*, trans. and ed. M. Swanton, London, 2000, 173–4**
R. A. Brown, 'The Norman Conquest and the Genesis of English Castle Building', *Château Gaillard*, 3 (1969), 131–46
A. Wheatley, *The Idea of the Castle in Medieval England*, Woodbridge, 2004
London, Lambeth Palace, MS 1212, fol. 188, Treaty of Westminster enrolled in *Regesta Regum Anglo-Normannorum, 1066–1154*, vol. 2: *1100–1135*, ed. C. Johnson and H. A. Cronne, Oxford, 1956, 203, no. 1475

BIBLIOGRAPHY
655 BAMBURGH
Anglo-Saxon Fortifications

Bede, *Ecclesiastical History of the English People*, trans. L. Sherley-Price, revised L. E. Latham, rev. edn, Harmondsworth, 1990, 168

E. Fernie, *The Architecture of the Anglo-Saxons*, London, 1983

J. Goodall, *The English Castle*, London and New Haven, 2011, 53–7

A. Williams, 'A Bell House and a Burh-Geat: Lordly Residences in England before the Conquest', in *Anglo-Norman Castles*, ed. R. Liddiard, Woodbridge, 2003, 23–40

1066 PEVENSEY AND HASTINGS
The Norman Landing

The Gesta Normannorum ducum of William of Jumièges, Orderic Vitalis and Robert of Torigni, ed. and trans. E. M. C. van Houts, vol. 2, Oxford, 1995, 159–67

The Anglo-Saxon Chronicles, trans. and ed. M. Swanton, London, 2000, 199

The Gesta Guillelmi of William of Poitiers, trans. and ed. R. H. C. Davis and M. Chibnall, Oxford, 1998, 116–17

Wace, *The Roman de Rou*, ed. A. J. Hoden and trans. G. S. Burgess, Jersey, 2002, 240–41

R. Porter, *Pevensey Castle*, London, 2020 (English Heritage Red Guide)

1066 HASTINGS CASTLE
A Campaign Castle

P. A. Barker and K. J. Barton, 'Excavations at Hastings Castle, 1968', *Archaeological Journal*, 134 (1977), 88

N. J. G. Pounds, *The Medieval Castle in England and Wales*, Cambridge, 1990, 15–20

1068 YORK, WARWICK AND NOTTINGHAM CASTLES
The Subjugation of England

The Ecclesiastical History of Orderic Vitalis, ed. and trans. M. Chibnall, vol. 2, Oxford, 1968, 216–19

R. A. Brown, *The Normans and the Norman Conquest*, London, 1969

D. J. C. King, *The Castle in England and Wales: An Interpretative History*, London, 1988

Symeon of Durham, *Libellus de Exordi*, ed. and trans. D. Rollason, Oxford, 2000, 183–5

1081 TOWER OF LONDON
Building in Stone

Photograph by the author / 2020

The White Tower, ed. E. Impey, New Haven and London, 2008

E. Fernie, *The Architecture of Norman England*, Oxford, 2000

J. Goodall, *The English Castle*, New Haven and London, 2011, 77–84

BIBLIOGRAPHY

1086 RICHMOND CASTLE
Interpreting Domesday

The Anglo-Saxon Chronicles, trans. and ed. M. Swanton, London, 2000, 216
Domesday Book, vol. 30: *Yorkshire*, ed. M. L. Faull and M. Stinson, vol. 2, Chichester, 1986, sn Ct.a 45
L. Butler, 'The Origins of the Honour of Richmond and its Castles', *Château Gaillard*, 16 (1992), 69–80
R. Liddiard, *Castles in Context: Power, Symbolism and Landscape, 1066–1500*, Bollington, 2005

1095 BAMBURGH AND TYNEMOUTH
Early Baronial Castles

The Anglo-Saxon Chronicles, trans. and ed. M. Swanton, London, 2000, 230–31
R. Bartlett, *England Under the Norman and Angevin Kings, 1075–1225*, Oxford, 2000
H. H. E. Craster, *A History of Northumberland*, vol. 8, The Parish of Tynemouth, Newcastle and London, 1907, 99–100
N. J. G. Pounds, *The Medieval Castle in England and Wales: A Social and Political History*, Cambridge, 1990

1137–53 HEREFORD CASTLE
Castle Building in the Anarchy

The Anglo-Saxon Chronicles, trans. and ed. M. Swanton, London, 2000, 264–5
Gesta Stephani, ed. and trans. K. R. Potter, Oxford, 1976, 72–3
R. Shoesmith with P. J. Pikes, 'The Early Castle, the City Walls and Gates', in *The Story of Hereford*, ed. A. Johnson and R. Shoesmith, Eardisley, 2016, 36–7
P. Dalton, *Conquest, Anarchy and Lordship: Yorkshire, 1066–1154*, Cambridge, 1994

1139 ROGER OF SALISBURY
Castle-Building by Royal Favour

Gesta Stephani, ed. and trans. K. R. Potter, Oxford, 1976, 48–9
William of Malmesbury, *Gesta Regum Anglorum*, ed. and trans. R. A. B. Mynors, R. M. Thomson and M. Winterbottom, vol. 1, Oxford, 1998, 738–9
J. Ashbee, 'Cloisters in English Palaces in the 12th and 13th Centuries', *Journal of the British Archaeological Association*, 159 (2006), 71–90
J. McNeill, *Old Sarum*, London, 2006 (English Heritage Red Guide)
R. A. Stalley, 'A 12th-Century Patron of Architecture: A Study of the Buildings Erected by Roger, Bishop of Salisbury, 1102–39', *Journal of the British Archaeological Association*, third series, 34 (1971), 62–83

1141 CASTLE HEDINGHAM, ESSEX
The Mark of an Earl

Photograph Country Life Picture Library / Paul Highnam / 2016
P. Dixon and P. Marshall, 'The Great Tower at Hedingham Castle: A Reassessment', *Fortress*, 18 (1993), 16–23

BIBLIOGRAPHY

J. Goodall, 'Castle Hedingham', *Country Life*, 2 and 9 November 2016, 44–9 and 58–63

P. Marshall, 'The Ceremonial Function of the Donjon in the 12th Century', *Château Gaillard*, 20 (2000), 141–51

G. H. White, 'King Stephen's Earldoms', *Transactions of the Royal Historical Society*, fourth series, 13 (1930), 51–82

1144–9 DURHAM CASTLE
A Castle Described

Laurence of Durham, *Dialogi Laurentii Dunelmensis Monachi ac Prioris*, ed. J. Raine, Surtees Society, 70, Durham, 1878, 11–12

P. Barker and R. Higham, *Timber Castles*, London, 1992, 118–19

E. Impey, 'A Castle in the Air? The Building, Arms, Action and Incident on the Eleventh-Century "Castle" Capital from Westminster Hall', *Arms & Armour*, 13 (2016), 1–23

c. 1150 THE PRINCIPLES OF CASTLE DESIGN
A Sermon

Sermon XVII: In Assumptione Beate Mariae in *Patrologiae Latinae Cursus Completus*, ed. J. P. Migne, Paris, 1844–64, 195, col. 303–4

A. Wheatley, *The Idea of the Castle in Medieval England*, Woodbridge, 2004, 78–111

1158 CARDIFF CASTLE
Injustice and Hostage-Taking

'The Itinerary through Wales', trans. Sir Richard Colt Hoare in *The Historical Works of Giraldus Cambrensis*, ed. T. Wright, London (1894), 379–80 and 399–400

R. R. Davies, *The Age of Conquest: Wales 1063–1415*, Oxford, 1990

1174 BROUGH AND ALNWICK CASTLES
Capturing a King

Jordan Fantosme's Chronicle, ed. and trans. R. C. Johnston, Oxford, 1981, 86–97, 102–13 and 130–35

J. Bradbury, *The Medieval Siege*, Woodbridge, 1992

L. Keen, 'The Umfrevilles, the Castle and the Barony of Prudhoe, Northumberland', *Anglo-Norman Studies*, 5 (1982), 177–81

1181 DOVER CASTLE
A Pilgrimage Route

Photograph Country Life Picture Library / Will Pryce / 2010

The Great Tower of Dover Castle, History, Architecture and Context, ed. P. Pattison, S. Brindle and D. M. Robinson, Swindon, 2020

R. A. Brown, 'Royal Castle Building in England, 1154–1216', *English Historical Review*, 70 (1955), 353–98

BIBLIOGRAPHY

1190 YORK CASTLE
The Massacre of the Jews

William of Newburgh, *Historia Rerum Anglicarum*, in *The Church Historians of England*, ed. J. Stevenson, London, 1853–8, vol. 4, part ii, 568–71

Christians and Jews in Angevin England: The York Massacre of 1190, Narratives and Contexts, ed. S. Rees Jones and S. Watson, York, 2013

C. Coulson, *Castles in Medieval Society: Fortresses in England, France and Ireland in the Central Middle Ages*, Oxford, 2003

1204 DUBLIN CASTLE
Mandates for a New Castle and a Royal Hall

Historical and Municipal Documents of Ireland A.D. 1172–1320, ed. J. T. Gilbert, London, 1870, 61

Calendar of Close Rolls of the Reign of Henry III, 1242–47, London, 1916, 23

C. Manning, ' "But you are first to build a tower" – The Bermingham Tower, Dublin Castle', *Ulster Journal of Archaeology*, 74 (2017–18), 145–54

T. McNeill, *Castles in Ireland: Feudal Power in a Gaelic World*, London and New York, 1997

T. Borenius, 'The Cycle of Images in the Palaces and Castles of Henry III', *Journal of the Warburg and Courtauld Institutes*, 6 (1943), 40–50

1215 THE FALL OF ROCHESTER CASTLE
The Fat of Forty Pigs

Memoriale fratris Walteri de Coventria, ed. W. Stubbs, Rolls Series, 58, vol. 2, London, 1873, 226–7

T. D. Hardy, *Rotuli Litterarum Clausarum in Turri Londinensi Asservati*, vol. 1, London, 1833, 238b

D. Carpenter, *The Minority of Henry III*, London, 1990

J. Goodall, 'The Great Tower of Rochester Castle', in *Medieval Art, Architecture and Archaeology at Rochester*, ed. T. Ayers and T. Tatton-Brown, British Archaeological Association Conference Transactions, 28, Leeds, 2006, 274

1241 TOWER OF LONDON
Fighting Royal Tyranny

Matthew Paris, *Chronica Majora*, ed. H. R. Luard, Rolls Series, 57, vol. 4, 93–4, as quoted in E. Impey, 'The Western Entrance to the Tower of London, 1240–1241', *Transactions of the London and Middlesex Archaeological Society*, vol. 48 (1998), 59–76

G. Keevill, *The Tower of London Moat: Archaeological Excavations, 1995–9*, Oxford, 2004, 45–78

1265 DOVER CASTLE
The Baron's War

Household Roll of Eleanor de Montfort, Countess of Leicester and Pembroke, ed. and trans. L. J. Wilkinson, Pipe Rolls Society, new series 63, Woodbridge, 2020, nos. 407, 409, 413, 418, 419, 435, 438

BIBLIOGRAPHY

'Chronicon Vulgo Dictum Chronicon Thomae Wykes', in *Annales Monastici*, ed. H. R. Luard, Rolls Series, 36, vol. 4, London, 1869, 178
Close Rolls of the Reign of Henry III, 1247–1251, London, 1922, 8
C. M. Woolgar, *The Great Household in Late Medieval England*, London and New Haven, 1999

1277 CASTLE BUILDING
Pressing Labour for the King

Calendar of Patent Rolls, 1272–81, London, 1901, 213
The History of the King's Works: The Middle Ages, ed. R. A. Brown, H. M. Colvin and A. J. Taylor, vol.1, London, 1963, 183, 193–422
The Impact of the Edwardian Castles in Wales, ed. D. M. Williams and J. R. Kenyon, Oxford, 2010

1288 MONTGOMERY CASTLE
Trying on a New Cloak

Quoted from A. J. Taylor, 'An Incident at Montgomery Castle on New Year's Day, 1288', *Archaeologia Cambrensis*, 116 (1967), 159–64

1290 WINCHESTER CASTLE
The Great Hall and King Arthur's Round Table

Photograph by John Crook / 2005
King Arthur's Round Table: An Archaeological Investigation, ed. Martin Biddle et al., Woodbridge and Rochester, NY, 2000
R. S. Loomis, 'Edward I, Arthurian Enthusiast', *Speculum*, 28 (1953), 114–27
The Rows Rol, ed. W. Courthope, London, 1845, no. 46

1296 BEAUMARIS CASTLE
A Progress Report

National Archives E 101 / 5 / 18 no. 11, quoted from *History of the King's Works*, ed. R. A. Brown, H. M. Colvin and A. J. Taylor, vol. 1, London, 1963, 398–9
J. Ashbee, *Beaumaris Castle*, Cardiff, 2017 (Cadw guidebook)
M. Hislop, *James of St George and the Castles of the Welsh Wars*, Barnsley, 2020
A. J. Taylor, 'Master James of St Georges', *English Historical Review*, 65 (1950), 433–57

c. 1300 SEAL OF ROCHESTER
The Image of the Castle

Society of Antiquaries of London, seal impression
J. Cherry, 'Imago Castelli: The Depiction of Castles on Medieval Seals', *Château Gaillard*, 15 (1992), 83–90
T. A. Heslop, 'English seals in the 13th and 14th centuries', in J. Alexander and P. Binski, *The Age of Chivalry: Art in Plantagenet England, 1200–1400*, exhibition catalogue, Royal Academy, London, 1987, 114–7 and 493–8

BIBLIOGRAPHY

1300 CAERLAVEROCK CASTLE
Edward I's Subjection of Scotland

The Siege of Carlaverock, ed. and trans. N. H. Nicolas, London, 1828, 61
Documents Illustrative of the History of Scotland, ed. J. Stevenson, Edinburgh, 1870, vol. 2, 481–3
M. Prestwich, *Edward I*, London, 1988, 469–516
M. Prestwich, *The Three Edwards: War and State in England, 1272–1377*, London, 1980
Knights of Edward I, ed. C. Moor, 5 vols, Harleian Society, London, 1929–32, 80–84

1303 CONWY CASTLE
A Miracle in a Moat

Vatican Latin MS 4015, fols 188–203, unpublished translation by J. Ashbee (the text also appears in Bollandists' *Acta Sanctorum*, Die Secunda Octobris, Antwerp, 1765, 626–8)
J. Ashbee, *Conwy Castle*, Cardiff, 2007, 60–61 (Cadw guidebook)
J. Ashbee and S. J. Ridyard, 'The Resuscitation of Roger of Conwy: A Cantilupe Miracle and the Society of Edwardian North Wales', *Journal of Medieval History*, 41 (2015), 309–24
K. D. Lilley, 'The Landscape of Edward I's New Towns: Their Planning and Design', in *The Impact of the Edwardian Castles in Wales*, ed. D. M. Williams and J. R. Kenyon, Oxford, 2010
J. Richard, *The Castle Community: The Personnel of English and Welsh Castles, 1272–1422*, Woodbridge, 2002
J. H. Ross and M. Jancey, 'The Miracles of St Thomas of Hereford', *British Medical Journal*, 295 (19–26 December 1987), 1590–94
N. Saul, *Decorated in Glory: Church Building in Herefordshire in the Fourteenth Century*, Eardisley, 2020

c. 1320 THE CASTLE OF LOVE
Court Entertainment

British Library, Ms Additional 42130, fol. 75v
A. Wheatley, *The Idea of the Castle in Medieval England*, Woodbridge, 2004, 103–8

1323 TOWER OF LONDON
St Peter in Chains

Calendar of Close Rolls of the Reign of Edward II, 1323–1327, 13 and 132–3
M. Lewis, 'A Traitor's Death? The Identity of A Drawn, Hanged and Quartered Man from Hulton Abbey, Staffordshire', *Antiquity*, 82 (2008), 113–24
I. Mortimer, *The Greatest Traitor: The Life of Sir Roger Mortimer, Ruler of England, 1327–30*, London, 2003
M. Prestwich, 'English Castles in the Reign of Edward II', *Journal of Medieval History*, 9 (1982), 159–78

BIBLIOGRAPHY

1330 NOTTINGHAM CASTLE
A Palace Coup

The Chronicle of Geoffrey le Baker of Swinbrook, trans. E. Preest and ed. R. Barber, Woodbridge, 2012, 41–2

W. M. Ormrod, *The Reign of Edward III*, London and New Haven, 1990

C. Shenton, 'Edward III and the Coup of 1330', in *The Age of Edward III*, ed. J. S. Bothwell, York, 2001, 13–34

J. Vale, *Edward III and Chivalry: Chivalric Society and its Context, 1270–1350*, Woodbridge, 1982

1342 BERKELEY CASTLE
The Noble Life

John Smyth, *The Lives of the Berkeleys*, ed. J. Maclean, vol. 1, Gloucester, 1883, 301–2, 306, 308–9, 324–5

M. Keen, *Chivalry*, London and New Haven, 1984

C. Given-Wilson, *The English Nobility in the Late Middle Ages*, London, 1987

J. R. V. Barker, *The Tournament in England, 1100–1400*, Woodbridge, 1986

1344 WINDSOR CASTLE
Arthur's Round Table and the Order of the Garter

Adam Murimuth, Continuatio Chronicarum, ed. E. M. Thompson, Rolls Series, 50, London, 1889, 155–6

R. Barber, R. Brown and J. Munby, eds, *Edward III's Round Table at Windsor*, Woodbridge, 2007

R. Barber and J. Barker, *Tournaments: Jousts, Chivalry and Pageants in the Middle Ages*, Woodbridge, 1989

N. Saul, 'Chivalry and St George, 1327–57', in *Windsor Castle: A Thousand Years of a Royal Palace*, ed. S. Brindle, London, 2018, 82–93

C. Shenton, 'Edward III and the Symbol of the Leopard', in *Heraldry, Pageantry and Social Display in Medieval England*, ed. P. Coss and M. Keen, Woodbridge, 2002, 69–81

1348 STAFFORD CASTLE
A Castle-Building Contract

Quoted from M. J. B. Hislop and A. M. Hislop, 'Master John Burcestre and the Castles of Stafford and Maxstoke', *Transactions of the South Staffordshire Archaeological and Historical Society*, 33 (1993), 14–20

J. S. Bothwell, 'Edward III, the English Peerage and the 1337 Earls: Estate Redistribution in Fourteenth-Century England', in *The Age of Edward III*, ed. J. S. Bothwell, York, 2001, 35–52

L. F. Salzman, *Building in England Down to 1540*, reprinted with additions and corrections, Oxford, 1967

J. Darlington, ed., *Stafford Castle: Survey, Excavation and Research, 1978–98. Volume I: The Surveys*, Stafford, 2001

BIBLIOGRAPHY

AFTER 1360 A PAPER CASTLE
Sir Gawain Seeks Hospitality

Sir Gawain and the Green Knight, trans. M. Smith, London, 2018, 66–8, with the original words supplied from an edition ed. and trans. W. R. J. Barron, Manchester, 1974, 68–71
R. Barber, *King Arthur: Hero and Legend*, rev. edn. Woodbridge, 1973
T. H. White, *The Sword in the Stone*, London, 1938 (novel)

1375 THE TOMB OF BISHOP WYVILLE OF SALISBURY
Symbols of Lordship

Rubbing by Derrick Chivers photographed by A. C. Cooper / 2011
The original epitaph is recorded in R. Symonds, *Diary of the Marches of the Royal Army during the Great Civil War*, ed. C. E. Long, Camden Society, old series, 74, London, 1859, 136–7
J. Alexander and P. Binski, *The Age of Chivalry: Art in Plantagenet England, 1200–1400*, exhibition catalogue, Royal Academy, London, 1987, 231
J. Goodall, *The English Castle*, London and New Haven, 2011, 1–4

1381 TOWER OF LONDON
Kissing a Queen and Beheading an Archbishop

The Chronica Maiora of Thomas of Walsingham, 1376–1422, **trans. D. Preest, Woodbridge, 2005, 124–6**
Froissart Chronicles, ed. and trans. G. Brereton, Harmondsworth, 1968, 219–20
Peasants' Revolt, ed. R. B. Dobson, 2nd edn, London, 1983
N. Saul, *Richard II*, New Haven and London, 1997

1386 SANDWICH
The Capture of a Timber Castle

The Chronica Maiora of Thomas of Walsingham, 1376–1422, **trans. D. Preest, Woodbridge, 2005, 241, with original words supplied from Thomas Walsingham, Historia Anglicana, ed. H. T. Riley, Rolls Series, 28, vol. 2, London, 1864, 147**
D. Knoop, G. P. Jones and N. B. Lewis, 'Some New Documents Concerning the Building of Cowling Castle and Cobham College', *Archaeologia Cantiana*, vol. 46 (1934), 167–76
Knighton's Chronicle 1337–1396, ed. and trans. G. H. Martin, Oxford, 1995, 348–9
J. R. Kenyon, 'Early Artillery Fortifications in England and Wales: A Preliminary Survey and Reappraisal', *Archaeological Journal*, 138 (1981), 205–41

1399 FLINT CASTLE
The Capture of Richard II

A Metrical History of the Deposition of Richard II attributed to Jean Creton, ed. and trans. J. Webb, *Archaeologia*, 20 (1814), 151–72
D. J. C. King, 'The Donjon of Flint Castle', *Chester and North Wales Architectural, Archaeological and Historic Society Journal*, 45 (1958), 61–9
N. Saul, *Richard II*, New Haven and London, 1997

BIBLIOGRAPHY

1401 CONWY CASTLE
Recapturing a Royal Castle

The Chronicle of Adam Usk, 1377–1421, ed. and trans. C. Given-Wilson, Oxford, 1997, 129

Royal and Historical Letters during the Reign of Henry IV, ed. and trans. F. C. Hingeston, vol. 1, London, 1860, 69–72

R. R. Davies, *The Revolt of Owain Glyn Dŵr*, Oxford, 1995

1403 ALNWICK AND WARKWORTH CASTLES
The Pretence of Loyalty

Proceedings and Orders of Privy Council, ed. H. Nicolas, vol. 1, London, 1834, 213–15 and 275–6

J. C. Hodgson, *A History of Northumberland*, vol. 5, Newcastle, 1899, 37–40

1414 KENILWORTH CASTLE
A Retreat from Formality

Memorials of Henry V, ed. C. A. Cole, London, 1858, 100–101, as translated in M. W. Thompson, 'Reclamation of Waste Ground for the Pleasance at Kenilworth Castle, Warwickshire', *Medieval Archaeology*, 8 (1964), 222–3

British Library Add Ms. 35295, fol. 266. Strecche's text as quoted in *The First English Life of Henry V*, trans. C. L. Kingsford, Oxford, 1911, xliii–xliv

Unpublished transcription by R. K. M. Morris of National Library of Wales, Chirk Castle MS F 13310

For the tent see W. H. St John Hope, 'The Funeral, Monument and Chantry Chapel of King Henry V', *Archaeologia*, 65 (1914), 144–5

1439 TATTERSHALL CASTLE
Building in Brick

W. D. Simpson, 'The Building Accounts of Tattershall Castle, 1434–72', *Lincoln Record Society*, 55 (1960), 25, 56, 32 and 73

N. J. Moore, 'Brick', in *English Medieval Industries*, ed. J. Blair and N. Ramsey, London, 1991, 227–9

W. H. St John Hope, 'The Funeral, Monument and Chantry Chapel of King Henry V', *Archaeologia*, 65 (1914), 144–5

T. P. Smith, *The Medieval Brickmaking Industry in England, 1400–1450*, British Archaeological Reports British Series, 138, Oxford, 1985

c. 1450 RICHMOND CASTLE
Castleguard

British Library Cotton Faustina B.VII, fol.85v

L. Butler, 'The Origins of the Honour of Richmond and its Castles', *Château Gaillard*, 16 (1992), 69–80

The Paston Letters, 1422–1509, ed. J. Gairdner, vol. 4, London, 1904, no. 691

C. Richmond, *The Paston Family in the Fifteenth Century: Fastolf's Will*, Cambridge, 1996, 200

BIBLIOGRAPHY

1462 ALNWICK, BAMBURGH AND DUNSTANBURGH CASTLES
A Northern Campaign

The Paston Letters, 1422–1509, ed. J. Gairdner, vol. 4, London, 1904, no. 533

E. Bateson, *A History of Northumberland*, vol.1, Newcastle-upon-Tyne, 1893, 43–8

C. Ross, *Edward IV*, London, 1974

R. L. Storey, *The End of the House of Lancaster*, London, 1966

1474 A LICENCE TO CRENELLATE AND IMPARK
William, Lord Hastings

Calendar of the Charter Rolls, 1427–1516, vol. 6, London, 1927, 242

San Marino, California, Huntington Library, Map Drawer 11 U2 (formerly HAM Box 22, [3]), fol. 14r. The operation continued until the sequence of accounts ceased in 1477–8

A. H. Thompson, 'The Building Accounts of Kirby Muxloe Castle, 1480–4', *Transactions of the Leicestershire Archaeological Society*, 11 (1913–20)

For Bagworth see Leland, *Itinerary*, vol. 1, 20

Thomas More, 'The History of King Richard the Thirde (1513)', in *The Works of Sir Thomas More*, London, 1557, 53–5

1485 WARWICK CASTLE
Castles, Lineage and History

British Library, Add MS 48976 and published as *The Rows Rol*, ed. W. Courthope, London, 1845, nos. 13, 18, 42 and 59

M. Hicks, *False, Fleeting, Perjur'd Clarence*, Gloucester, 1992, 169

A. Payne, 'The Beauchamps and the Nevilles', in *Gothic: Art for England, 1400–1547*, ed. R. Marks and P. Williamson, exhibition catalogue, Victoria and Albert Museum, London, 2003, 219–33

1494 DURHAM CASTLE
A Prince Bishop's Palace

Historiae Dunelmensis Scriptores Tres: Gaufridus de Coldingham, Robertus de Graystanes et Willielmus de Chambre, ed. J. Raine, Surtees Society, 9 (1839), 146–7

C. Davies (2010, September 23). Fox [Foxe], Richard (1447/8–1528), administrator, bishop of Winchester, and founder of Corpus Christi College, Oxford. *Oxford Dictionary of National Biography*. Retrieved 28 February 2021, from https://www.oxforddnb.com/view/10.1093/ref:odnb/9780198614128.001.0001/odnb-9780198614128-e-10051

R. Pears, 'Bishop Tunstall's Alterations to Durham Castle, 1536–48', *Antiquaries Journal*, 99 (2019), 161–85

Lord Darcy quoted in *Victoria County History: Durham*, vol. 3, London, 1928, 27

A. Wood, *Athenae Oxonienses*, London, 1721, 665

BIBLIOGRAPHY

1506 CAREW CASTLE
Garter Day with St David and St George

A transcript of Henry Rice's biography of his ancestor appears in *The Cambrian Register for 1795*, London, 1796, 123–34

P. Brears, *Cooking and Dining in Medieval England*, Totnes, 2007

D. J. C. Cathcart-King and J. C. Perks, 'Carew Castle, Pembrokeshire', *Archaeological Journal*, 119 (1962), 304–5

1520 DOVER CASTLE
A Diplomatic Encounter

Bodleian Library, MS Ashmole 116, fols 100–3 as transcribed in J. G. Russell, *The Field of Cloth of Gold*, New York, 1969, 209

S. Anglo, *Spectacle, Pageantry and Early Tudor Policy*, Oxford, 1969

H. Colvin et al., *History of the King's Works*, vol. 3, London, 1975, 248

Lieutenant Hammond, *A Relation of a Short Survey of the Western Counties (1635)*, ed. L. G. Wickham Legg, Camden Miscellany, 16, London, 1936, 24

1521 THORNBURY CASTLE
A Ducal Seat

National Archives E36/130, fol. 19

J. Goodall, *The English Castle*, London and New Haven, 2011, 411–15

P. Henderson, *The Tudor House and Garden*, New Haven and London, 2005

M. Howard, *The Early Tudor Country House: Architecture and Politics, 1490–1550*, London, 1987

S. Thurley, *The Royal Palaces of Tudor England*, New Haven and London, 1993

1522 AND 1536 FARLEIGH HUNGERFORD CASTLE
Murder and poison

Coram Rege Roll membrane 17 and Cotton MS Titus B.I, fol. 388. as transcribed in *The Antiquary*, December 1880, 233–5

M. A. Everett Wood, *Letters of Royal and Illustrious Ladies*, London, 1846, 271–5

C. Kightly, *Farleigh Hungerford*, London, 2006, 17–18 (English Heritage Red Guide)

1539 DEAL CASTLE
Resisting Invasion

British Library, Cotton MS Augustus, I. i, fol. 20

H. M. Colvin et al., *History of the King's Works*, vol. 4 pt ii, London, 1982, 455–65

A. Saunders, *Fortress Britain: Artillery Fortification in the British Isles and Ireland*, Liphook, 1989, 34–52

1540 BELVOIR CASTLE
A Castle Restored

The manuscripts of His Grace the Duke of Rutland preserved at Belvoir Castle, vol. 4, London, 1905, 305, 310–11, 337 and Belvoir Castle Mss accounts

J. Goodall, 'Belvoir Castle, Leicestershire', *Country Life*, 19 June 2019, 74–9

R. K. Morris, 'Monastic Architecture: Destruction and Reconstruction', in *Archaeology of Reformation*, ed. Gaimster and Gilchrist, 235–51

BIBLIOGRAPHY

1545 WRESSLE CASTLE
A Study in Paradise

The itinerary of John Leland in or about the years 1535–1543, ed. L. Toulmin-Smith, vol. 1, London, 1907, 52–3
Letters and Papers: Henry VIII, vol. 12, pt 2, London, 1891, 205–6
The Earl of Northumberland's Household Book. Regulations and Establishment of the Household . . . at his Castles of Wressle and Leckonfield (1512), ed. T. Percy, London, 1905
M. Purcell, *The Country House Library*, New Haven and London, 2017

1553 FRAMLINGHAM CASTLE
Securing the Succession

R. Wingfield, *Vita Maria Anglicanae regina*, ed. D. MacCulloch, Camden Miscellany, 28, 4th ser., vol. 29, 1984, 255–65
Medieval Framlingham: Select Documents, 1270–1524, ed. J. Ridgard, Suffolk Record Society, 27, Woodbridge, 1985, 129–58

1554 COOLING CASTLE
The Spanish Marriage

Calendar of State Papers Domestic Series of the reign of Mary I, 1553–1558, revised edn., ed. C. S. Knighton, London, 1998, no. 57, as transcribed in W. A. Scott Robertson, 'Coulyng Castle', *Archaeologia Cantiana*, vol. 11 (1877), 141–2
B. Cope, 'Sir Thomas Wyatt's Assault on Cooling Castle, 30th January, 1554', *Archaeologia Cantiana*, vol. 39 (1927), 167–76
N. Saul, *Death, Art and Memory in Medieval England: The Cobham Family and their Monuments, 1300–1500*, Oxford, 2001

1559 TOWER OF LONDON
The Knights of the Bath

Bodleian Library, Ashmole MS 862 fols 299–300 as transcribed by Anna Keay in *The White Tower*, ed. E. Impey, New Haven and London, 2008, 338 and 163–5

1562 PONTEFRACT CASTLE
Royal Heritage

The National Archives MR 1/16/1
H. Colvin et al., *History of the King's Works*, vol. 3, London, 1975, 179–81
I. Roberts, *Pontefract Castle: Archaeological Excavations, 1982–86*, Yorkshire Archaeology, 8, Leeds, 2002

1575 KENILWORTH CASTLE
A Royal Visit

Transcribed respectively in J. Nichols, *Progresses and Public Processions of Queen Elizabeth*, London, 1823, 486–91 and 430–31

366

BIBLIOGRAPHY

The Elizabethan Garden at Kenilworth Castle, ed. A. Keay and J. Watkins, Swindon, 2013

E. Goldring, *Robert Dudley, Earl of Leicester, and the World of Elizabethan Art*, New Haven and London, 2014

1588 THE HOUSE OF WOLLATON
A Biblical Device

Photograph Country Life Picture Library / Paul Highnam / 2014
M. Girouard, *Elizabethan Architecture*, New Haven and London, 2009, 209–45
M. Girouard, *Robert Smythson and the Elizabethan Country House,* New Haven and London, 1983
M. Airs, *The Making of the English Country House, 1500–1640*, London, 1975

1598 TOWER OF LONDON
A Foreign Tourist

P. Hentzner, *A Journey into England*, ed. H. Walpole, trans. R. Bentley (1757), 37–9
D. Carpenter, *Henry III 1207–1258*, New Haven and London, 2020
A. Keay, *The Elizabethan Tower of London: The Haiward and Gascoyne Plan of 1597*, London Topographical Society, 158 (2001)

1618 BERKELEY CASTLE
A Tale of a Toad

John Smyth, *The Lives of the Berkeleys*, ed. J. Maclean, vol. 1, Gloucester, 1883, 291
John Smyth, *A description of the Hundred of Berkeley*, ed. J. Maclean, vol. 2, Gloucester, 1885, 93

1622 NAWORTH CASTLE
Cannibalising a Castle

Edmund Sandford, *A Cursory relation of all the Antiquities and familyes in Cumberland*, ed. R. S. Ferguson, and Westmorland Antiquarian and Archaeological Society, Tract Series no. 4, Kendal, 1890, 44–45
Selections from the Household Books of Lord William Howard, ed. G. Ornsby, Surtees Society, 68, Durham, 1878, 194
E. Chappell, 'New Light on the "Little Men" of Naworth Castle', in *Late Gothic England: Art and Display*, ed. R. Marks, Donington, 2007, 70–80

1634 LUDLOW CASTLE
An Exhortation to Virtue

A Mask Presented at Ludlow Castle 1634 on Michaelmas Night, London, 1637
B. K. Lewalski, 'Milton's *Comus* and the Politics of Masquing', in *The Politics of the Stuart Court Masque*, ed. D. Bevington and P. Holbrook, Cambridge, 1998, 296–315
B. Ravelhofer, *The Early Stuart Masque: Dance, Costume, and Music*, Oxford, 2006

BIBLIOGRAPHY

1635 WINCHESTER CASTLE
The Ceremony of the Court of Eyre

Lieutenant Hammond, *A Relation of a Short Survey of the Western Counties*, ed.
L. G. Wickham Legg, Camden Miscellany, 16, London, 1936, 51–5

1645 SCARBOROUGH CASTLE
The Fall of the Keep

The Memoirs and Memorials of Sir Hugh Cholmley of Whitby, 1600–57, ed. J.
Binns, Yorkshire Archaeological Society Record Series, vol. 153, 1997–8, 154–7

1648–9 KENILWORTH CASTLE
Vanishing Monuments

Engraving by W. Hollar in W. Dugdale, *The Antiquities of Warwickshire*,
London, 1656, facing 249
Order in Council as quoted in E. Carey-Hill, 'The Hawkesworth papers, 1601–60',
Birmingham Archaeological Society transaction and proceedings, 54 (1929–30), 33
San Marino, California, Huntington Library, HAP BOX 19 (7)
S. Porter, *Destruction in the English Civil War*, Stroud, 1994

1649 SKIPTON, APPLEBY, BROUGH AND BROUGHAM CASTLES
A Patrimony Restored

'The Life of Me Lady Anne Clifford', in *Anne Clifford's Autobiographical
Writing, 1590–1676*, ed. J. L. Malay, Manchester, 2018, 115–16
J. Goodall, 'Lady Anne Clifford and the Architectural Pursuit of Nobility', in *Lady
Anne Clifford: Culture, Patronage and Gender in 17th-Century Britain*, ed. K. Hearn
and L. Hulse, Yorkshire Archaeological Society Occasional Paper no. 7 (2009), 73–86
H. Summerson, M. Trueman and S. Harrison, 'Brougham Castle, Cumbria',
Cumberland and Westmorland Antiquarian and Archaeological Society Research Series,
8 (1998)

1665 ROCHESTER CASTLE
Exploring a Ruin

The Diary of Samuel Pepys, ed. R. Latham and W. Matthews, vol. 6 (1665),
Berkeley and Los Angeles, 2000, 249 and vol. 8 (1667), 311
M. W. Thompson, *The Decline of the Castle*, Cambridge, 1987

1667 CAPHEATON
Replacing Castles

Unpublished contract, private collection
N. Cooper, *Houses of the Gentry, 1480–1680*, New Haven and London, 1999
J. Goodall, 'Capheaton Hall, Northumberland', *Country Life*, 7 March 2018, 52–7
R. Pears and R. Hewlings, 'Capheaton Hall in the Eighteenth Century', *Georgian
Group Journal*, 22 (2014), 1–20

BIBLIOGRAPHY

1670 WINDSOR CASTLE
Armour as Architecture

The Diary of John Evelyn, ed. E. S. de Beer, London, 1959, 545
A. Keay and R. Harris, 'The White Tower 1642–1855', in *The White Tower*, ed. E. Impey, New Haven and London, 2008
S. Thurley, 'The Baroque Castle', in *Windsor Castle: A Thousand Years of a Royal Palace*, ed. S. Brindle, London, 2018, 216–39

1678 DOUBTING CASTLE
The Capture and Escape of Christian and Hopeful

J. Bunyan, *The Pilgrim's Progress*, London, 1678, 182–6
R. Greaves (2004, September 23). Bunyan, John (bap. 1628, d. 1688), author. *Oxford Dictionary of National Biography*. Retrieved 28 February 2021, from https://www.oxforddnb.com/view/10.1093/ref:odnb/9780198614128.001.0001/odnb-9780198614128-e-3949
John Bunyan and his England, 1628–88, ed. A. Laurence, W. R. Owens and S. Sim, London, 1990

1683 WINDSOR CASTLE
A Baroque Stronghold and Palace

The Diary of John Evelyn, ed. E. S. de Beer, London, 1959, 742–3
A. Keay, *The Magnificent Monarch*, London, 2008, 177–82
S. Thurley, 'The Baroque Castle', in *Windsor Castle: A Thousand Years of a Royal Palace*, ed. S. Brindle, London, 2018, 216–39
S. Thurley, *Palaces of Revolution: Life, Death and Art at the Stuart Court*, London, 2021
J. F. Turrell, 'The Ritual of Royal Healing in Early Modern England: Scrofula, Liturgy and Politics', *Anglican and Episcopal History*, 68, no. 1 (March 1999), 3–36

1697 WARWICK CASTLE
All Mere Fiction

C. Fiennes, *Through England on a Side-Saddle in the Time of William and Mary*, ed. Mrs Griffiths, London, 1888, 95
D. Hey (2004, September 23). Fiennes, Celia (1662–1741), traveller. *Oxford Dictionary of National Biography*. Retrieved 28 February 2021, from https://www.oxforddnb.com/view/10.1093/ref:odnb/9780198614128.001.0001/odnb-9780198614128-e-37414

1715 BLENHEIM CASTLE
A Grateful Nation's Gift

C. Campbell, *Vitruvius Britannicus*, London, 1715, 5 and plates 59–60
Photograph by the author, 2021
K. Downes, *Vanbrugh*, London, 1977
G. Worsley, 'Sir John Vanbrugh and the Search for a National Style', in *Gothic Architecture and its Meanings, 1550–1830*, ed. M. Hall, Reading, 2002

BIBLIOGRAPHY

J. Cornforth, 'Drayton House, Northamptonshire', *Country Life*, 27 May 1965, 1286–9

J. Cornforth, 'Castles for a Georgian Duke', *Country Life*, 8 October 1992, 58–61

1726 NEWARK CASTLE
The Jaws of Time

Samuel Buck, engraving / 1726
R. Hyde, *A Prospect of Britain: The Town Panoramas of Samuel and Nathaniel Buck*, London, 1994
R. Hyde (2004, September 23). Buck, Samuel (1696–1779), topographical draughtsman, engraver, and print publisher. *Oxford Dictionary of National Biography*. Retrieved 28 February 2021, from https://www.oxforddnb.com/view/10.1093/ref:odnb/9780198614128.001.0001/odnb-9780198614128-e-3850

1730 STAINBOROUGH AND WENTWORTH CASTLES
The Monument to Ancestry

Thomas Badeslade, *Vitruvius Britannicus*, vol. 4, London, 1739, engraving / 1730
T. Richardson, *The Arcadian Friends: Inventing the English Landscape*, London, 2007

1745 CARLISLE CASTLE
A Jacobite Defence

***Carlisle in 1745: Authentic Account of the Occupation of Carlisle in 1745*, ed. G. Mounsey, London, 1846, 158, 160, 167, 168**
G. Smith, 'Account of the Rebels' March into England and the Loss of Carlisle', *Gentleman's Magazine*, 16 (May 1746), 233–5
J. Riding, *Jacobites: A New History of the '45 Rebellion*, London, 2016
E. Douet, *British Barracks, 1600–1914*, London, 1998

1764 THE CASTLE OF OTRANTO
The Gothic Novel

Horace Walpole, *The Castle of Otranto*, London, 1765, 21–3
Horace Walpole's Strawberry Hill, ed. M. Snodin, New Haven and London, 2009
M. Lewis, *The Monk*, London, 1798 (novel)
M. Shelley, *Frankenstein*, London, 1818 (novel)
B. Stoker, *Dracula*, London, 1897 (novel)
T. Mowl, ' "Against the Time in Which the Fabric and Use of Gunpowder Shall Be Forgotten": Enmore Castle, Its Origins and Its Architect', *Architectural History*, 33 (1990), 102–19

1770 ALNWICK CASTLE
A Royal Entertainment

Warwick County Records 136B/2133 as transcribed in M. McCarthy, 'Sir Roger Newdigate: Drawings for Copt Hall, Essex, and Arbury Hall, Warwickshire', *Architectural History*, 16 (1973), 33, note 38
The Diaries of a Duchess, ed. J. Greig, London, 1926, 141–3

BIBLIOGRAPHY

A. Aymonino, *Enlightened Eclecticism: The Grand Design of the 1st Duke and Duchess of Northumberland*, New Haven and London, 2021

G. Worsley, *Classical Architecture in Britain: The Heroic Age*, New Haven and London, 1995, 175–95

1777 PEVENSEY, HASTINGS AND BODIAM CASTLES
A Sussex Tour

British Library Add. MS 17398, ff.103–26 as transcribed in J. Farrant, *Sussex Depicted*, Sussex Record Society, 85 (2001), 118–21

C. Coulson, 'Some Analysis of the Castle of Bodiam, East Sussex', *Ideals and Practice of Medieval Knighthood*, 4 (1992), 51–107

R. Sweet, *Antiquaries: The Discovery of the Past in 18th-Century Britain*, Hambledon and London, 2004

1782 DINEFWR CASTLE
The Castle as a Picture

W. Gilpin, *Observations on the River Wye, and several parts of South Wales, &c. relative chiefly to picturesque beauty: made in the summer of the year 1770*, London, 1782, 1 and 59–62

Red Book, private collection as quoted in G. Tyack, 'Domestic Gothic', in *John Nash: Architect of the Picturesque*, ed. G. Tyack, Swindon, 2013, 42

Uvedale Price, *Essays on the Picturesque*, 2 vols, London, 1810

1790s LUDLOW, ARUNDEL, HEDINGHAM AND SUDELEY CASTLES
The Monograph

W. Hodges, *An Historical Account of Ludlow Castle*, Ludlow, 1794, 104

Plans, Elevations and Particular Measurements of Arundel Castle in Sussex, ed. F. W. Steer, Arundel, 1976, 15

L. Majendie, *Vetusta Monumenta*, vol. 3, London, 1796, 1

J. Munby, '"Out of his Element": Mr Johnson, Sir Joseph Banks and Tattershall Castle', *Antiquaries Journal*, 94 (2014), 253–89

C. Willyams, *The History of Sudeley Castle*, London, 1791

J. C. Buckler, Sudeley Castle MS, Private Collection

1801 BELVOIR CASTLE
Romanticising History

Unpublished correspondence, private collection

J. Goodall, 'Belvoir Castle, Leicestershire', *Country Life*, 12 June 2019, 72–8

J. Robinson, *James Wyatt, Architect to George III*, New Haven and London, 2012

1806 LOWTHER CASTLE
Industrial Wealth

Photograph Country Life Picture Library / Paul Highnam / 2018

J. M. Robinson, 'Lowther Castle, Cumbria', *Country Life*, 26 September 2018, 58–63

J. Goodall, 'Eastnor Castle, Herefordshire', *Country Life*, 28 November 2012, 66–71

BIBLIOGRAPHY

1809 HAWARDEN CASTLE
The Character of a Castle

Anon., Broadlane Hall, 1809, private collection / Country Life Picture Library
J. Goodall, 'Highclere Castle, Hampshire', *Country Life*, 11 September 2019, 46–52

1819 CONISBROUGH CASTLE
Walter Scott's Castles

W. Scott, *Ivanhoe*, Chapter 41, Edinburgh and London, 1819
R. Hill, *Time's Witness: History in the Age of Romanticism*, London, 2021
E. King, *Munimenta Antiqua; or, Observations on Ancient Castles including Remarks on the Whole Progress of Architecture, Ecclesiastical as well as Military, in Great Britain: and on the Corresponding Changes in Manners, Laws and Customs etc.*, 4 vols, London, 1799–1804
H. Sands, H. Braun and L. C. Loyd, 'Conisbrough and Mortemer', *Yorkshire Archaeological Journal*, 32 (1936), 147–59

1819 GWRYCH CASTLE
A Nationalist Castle

Photograph Country Life Picture Library / Paul Highnam / 2020
M. Binney, 'Gwrych Castle, Conwy', *Country Life*, 18 July 2019, 58–63
T. Rickman, *An Attempt to Discriminate the Styles of English Architecture*, London, 1817

1824 WINDSOR CASTLE
Imperial Splendour

British Library Add. MS38371, fols 1–8 as transcribed in *The History of the King's Works*, vol. 6, 1782–1851, ed. J. Mordaunt Crook and M. H. Port, London, 1973, 381–3
The Greville Memoirs: A Journal of the Reigns of King George IV, King William IV and Queen Victoria, ed. H. Reeve, vol. 2, London, 1888, 150–52
S. Brindle, 'The Great Rebuilding 1820–40', in *Windsor Castle: A Thousand Years of a Royal Palace*, ed. S. Brindle, London, 2018, 318–39
Queen Victoria quoted in C. Hibbert (2008, January 03). Greville, Charles Cavendish Fulke (1794–1865), political and social diarist. *Oxford Dictionary of National Biography*. Retrieved 28 February 2021, from https://www.oxforddnb.com/view/10.1093/ref:odnb/9780198614128.001.0001/odnb-9780198614128-e-11515

1831 CROTCHET CASTLE
The Pursuit of Gentility

T. L. Peacock, *Crotchet Castle*, London, 1831, Chapters 1 and 10
G. Tyack, 'Domestic Gothic', in *John Nash: Architect of the Picturesque*, ed. G. Tyack, Swindon, 2013, 35–55

BIBLIOGRAPHY

1839 EGLINTON CASTLE
Chivalry Revived

J. Aikman, *Account of the Tournament at Eglinton*, Edinburgh, 1839, 5 and 9

M. Girouard, *The Return to Camelot: Chivalry and the English Gentleman*, New Haven and London, 1981

J. Nash, *The Mansions of England in the Olden Time*, 4 vols, London, 1839–49

J. Hill, 'Charleville, Co. Offaly', *Country Life*, 26 October 2016, 60–65

E. Viollet-le-Duc, *An Essay on the Military Architecture of the Middle Ages*, trans. M. Macdermott, London, 1860

1841 MODERN CASTLES
An Offence to True Principles

A. W. N. Pugin, *The True Principles of Pointed or Christian Architecture*, London, 1841, 57–9

R. Hill, *God's Architect: Pugin and the Building of Romantic Britain*, London, 2007

1844 PECKFORTON CASTLE
Back to the Future

A. Salvin, watercolour perspective of Peckforton Castle, 1845, RIBA Archive PB106/11(15)

J. Allibone, *Anthony Salvin: Pioneer of Gothic Revival Architecture, 1799–1881*, Columbia, 1987, 98–106

M. Girouard, *The Victorian Country House*, New Haven and London, 1979

1854 CHIRK CASTLE
A Housekeeper's Tour

G. Borrow, *Wild Wales: Its People, Language and Scenery*, vol. 2, London, 1862, 244–50

J. Anderson, 'Remaking the Space: The Plan and the Route in Country-House Guidebooks from 1770 to 1815', *Architectural History*, 54 (2011), 195–212

1857 SPECIMENS OF ANCIENT ART
Restoration and Preservation

G. G. Scott, *Remarks on Secular and Domestic Architecture, Present and Future*, London, 1857, 229–32

G. G. Scott, *Personal and Professional Recollections*, ed. G. Gilbert Scott, London, 1879, 88

G. Stamp, *Gothic for the Steam Age: An Illustrated Biography of George Gilbert Scott*, London, 2015

1874 CARDIFF AND COCH CASTLES
Medievalism and Scholarship

The Architect, 14 March 1874, 146–7

W. Burges, The Castell Coch report, Dept of Art, National Museum and Gallery, Cardiff as quoted in D. McLees, *Castell Coch*, Cardiff, 1998, 20 (Cadw guidebook)

BIBLIOGRAPHY

P. Floud, *Castell Coch, Glamorgan*, London, 1954, 3
J. Mordaunt Crook, *William Burges and the High Victorian Dream*, London, 1981
M. Williams, *Cardiff Castle and the Marquesses of Bute*, London, 2019

1899 KENILWORTH CASTLE
Mass Tourism

Photograph Country Life Picture Library / *c.* 1899
J. Leland, *The Shakespeare Country*, London, *c.* 1899
H. James, *English Hours*, Cambridge, MA, 1905, 198–201
S. Thurley, *Men from the Ministry*, New Haven and London, 2013

1911 TATTERSHALL CASTLE
Saving Britain's Heritage

The Late Marquis of Curzon of Kedleston and H. Avray Tipping, *Tattershall Castle, Lincolnshire: A Historical and Descriptive Survey*, London, 1929, 142–3
Hansard, House of Lords Debate, 30 April 1912, vol. 11, 871–2
The Marquis of Curzon of Kedleston, *Bodiam Castle, Sussex: A Historical and Descriptive Survey*, London, 1926, 143–5
S. Thurley, *Men from the Ministry*, New Haven and London, 2013
A. de Moubray, *Twentieth Century Castles in Britain*, London, 2013

1921 FARLEIGH HUNGERFORD
State Restoration

H. A. Peto, a letter, *Country Life*, 5 November 1921, 593
H. A. Tipping, 'The Castle of Farleigh Hungerford and its Preservation', *Country Life*, 5 November 1921, 692–6
S. Thurley, *Men from the Ministry*, New Haven and London, 2013, 261

1923 BLANDINGS CASTLE
The Castle as Idyll

P. G. Wodehouse, *Leave it to Psmith*, Harmondsworth, 1923, Chapter 11
T. Brittain-Catlin, *The Edwardians and their Houses*, London, 2019
M. Hall, *The English Country House*, London, 1994
A. Tinniswood, *The Long Weekend: Life in the English Country House, 1918–1939*, London, 2016

1925 ST DONAT'S CASTLE
Purchasing History

Anon., Leader, *Country Life*, 22 August 1925, 271
C. Aslet, *The Edwardian Country House*, 2nd edn, London, 2012, 185–98
J. Harris, *Moving Rooms: The Trade in Architectural Salvages*, New Haven and London, 2007

BIBLIOGRAPHY

1930 CASTLE DROGO, DEVON
A New Ancestral Seat

Photograph Country Life Picture Library / 1945
J. Goodall, 'Lambay Castle, Co. Dublin', *Country Life*, 19 October 2016, 50–57
G. Stamp, *Edwin Lutyens: Country Houses*, London, 2001, 117–49
C. Hussey, *The Life of Sir Edwin Lutyens*, London, 1950

1940 WORLD WAR II
An Explosive Miscalculation

National Archives 14/1524 as quoted in M. McCarthy, H. Summerson and R. Annis, *Carlisle Castle*, English Heritage Archaeological Report, 18, London, 1990, 267
The Letters of Evelyn Waugh, ed. M. Amory, London, 1980, 160–61
J. Coad, *Dover Castle*, London, 1995
J. M. Robinson, *Requisitioned: The British Country House in the Second World War*, London, 2014

1949 GODSEND AND COURANTSDAIR CASTLES
Decay, Neglect and Obscurity

Dodie Smith, *I Capture the Castle*, London, 1948, 1
O. Lancaster, *The Saracen's Head*, London, 1948, 7 and 67
D. Cannadine, *The Decline and Fall of the English Aristocracy*, New Haven and London, 1990
R. Strong et al., *The Destruction of the Country House*, London, 1974
G. Worsley, *England's Lost Houses*, London, 2002

1969 CAERNARFON CASTLE
The Investiture of the Prince of Wales

https://www.princeofwales.gov.uk/speech/speech-hrh-prince-wales-replying-loyal-address-sir-ben-bowen-thomas-president-university
A. F. Jones, 'King Edward I's castles in North Wales – Now and Tomorrow' and A. Wheatley, 'Caernarfon Castle and its Mythology', in *The Impact of the Edwardian Castles in Wales*, ed. D. M. Williams and J. R. Kenyon, Oxford, 2010, 198–202 and 129–39
C. Kightly, *A Royal Palace in Wales*, Cardiff, 1991, 12–14

1997 WINDSOR CASTLE
The Rebuilding of St George's Hall

Photograph Mark Fiennes / Royal Collection copyright HM The Queen / 1997
S. Brindle and J. Marsden, 'Modern Times, 1945 to the Present Day', in *Windsor Castle: A Thousand Years of a Royal Palace*, ed. S. Brindle, London, 2018, 454–62
A. Nicolson, *Restoration: The Rebuilding of Windsor Castle*, London, 1997
M. Girouard, *Windsor: The Most Romantic Castle*, London, 1993
G. Worsley, 'Windsor Castle, Berkshire', *Country Life*, 21 January 1993, 30–33
G. Worsley, 'Windsor Competition Results', *Country Life*, 15 July 1993, 52–7

BIBLIOGRAPHY

1997 HOGWARTS CASTLE
The Modern Gothic Castle

J. K. Rowling, *Harry Potter and the Philosopher's Stone*, London, 1997

2009 DOVER CASTLE
Recreating the Past

Photograph Country Life Picture Library / Will Pryce / 2010
S. Brindle and P. Pattison, 'The Great Tower Project: An Evocation of the Angevin Royal Palace at Dover', in *The Great Tower of Dover Castle, History, Architecture and Context*, ed. P. Pattison, S. Brindle and D. M. Robinson, Swindon, 2020

2012 LANCASTER CASTLE
An Empty Prison

Photograph Country Life Picture Library / Paul Barker / 2012
J. M. Robinson, 'Georgian Courts of Lancaster Castle', *Country Life*, 9 December 2015, 30–35
J. Goodall, 'Lancaster Castle', *Country Life*, 20 February 2013, 55–7

EPILOGUE
The Disney Castle . . . and the Future

For a sequence of forty-five opening sequences to Disney films, see https://www.youtube.com/watch?v=6KyFeG7kfTM

ILLUSTRATION CREDITS

page 15 Bamburgh Castle, Northumbria. Paul Barker/Country Life Picture Library.

21 Bayeux Tapestry. Musée de la Tapisserie, Bayeux, France/Bridgeman Images.

23 Lincoln Castle. Paul Highnam/Country Life Picture Library.

26 Tower of London. Author.

29 Richmond Castle, Yorkshire. Paul Barker/Country Life Picture Library.

36 Hereford Cathedral. Paul Highnam/Country Life Picture Library.

39 Gatehouse of Sherborne Castle, Dorset. Author.

43 Interior of the great tower of Castle Hedingham, Essex. Paul Highnam/Country Life Picture Library.

45 Durham Castle and Cathedral. Paul Barker/Country Life Picture Library.

55 Dover Castle, Kent. Will Pryce/Country Life Picture Library.

66 Caerphilly Castle, Glamorgan. Dr David Robinson.

72 Ruins of Flint Castle. Paul Barker/Country Life Picture Library.

77 The great hall at Winchester Castle. Dr John Crook.

79 Beaumaris Castle, Anglesey © Crown copyright (2021) Cymru Wales.

82 Seal of Rochester. Society of Antiquaries of London.

84 Caerlaverock Castle, Dumfries. Author.

88 Conwy Castle. Author.

92 The Castle of Love from the Luttrell Psalter. Mss Add. 42130, f.75v. British Library, London, UK © British Library Board. All Rights Reserved/Bridgeman Images.

103 Gatehouse vault at the Tower of London. Author.

107 Stafford Castle. Author.

111 Ivory panel from a casket. Accession Number: 2003.131.2. The Metropolitian Museum of Art, Cloisters Collection, New York, 2003.

115 Rubbing of the funerary brass of Bishop Wyville of Salisbury, by Derrick Chivers. Author.

117 The gatehouse of Saltwood Castle, Kent. Paul Highnam/Country Life Picture Library.

128 Conwy Castle, North Wales © Crown copyright (2021) Cymru Wales.

132 The great tower of Warkworth, Northumbria. Paul Barker/Country Life Picture Library.

139 The great tower of Tattershall, Lincolnshire. Paul Barker/Country Life Picture Library.

143 View of Richmond Castle from a fifteenth-century manuscript. Cotton MS Faustina B VII, f.85v. British Library, London, UK © British Library Board. All Rights Reserved/Bridgeman Images.

151 Detail from the *Rous Roll*. Mss Add. 48976 ff.15-19. British Library, London, UK © British Library Board. All Rights Reserved/Bridgeman Images.

155 The hall at Durham Castle. Paul Barker/Country Life Picture Library.

159 Carew Castle, Pembrokshire. Paul Barker/Country Life Picture Library.

163 Detail from a sixteenth-century painting of the Field of Cloth of Gold. Universal History Archive/UIG/Bridgeman Images.

167 Thornbury Castle, Gloucestershire, by J. C. Buckler. Artokoloro/Alamy Stock Photo.

174 Drawing of a 'Castle in the Downes'. Cotton MS Augustus I i 20. British Library, London, UK/Bridgeman Images.

179 Wressle Castle, Yorkshire. Author.

182 Framlingham Castle, Suffolk. Author.

191 Drawing of Pontefract Castle. TNA MR1/16/1, The National Archives, UK.

197 The south front of Wollaton, Nottinghamshire. Paul Highnam/Country Life Picture Library.

205 Naworth Castle, Cumbria. Paul Highnam/Country Life Picture Library.

208 Ludlow Castle, Shropshire. Author.

215 Scarborough Castle. Dr David Robinson.

219 Engravings of Kenilworth Castle, by Wenceslaus Hollar. Sir William Dugdale, *The Antiquities of Warwickshire*. Author.

222 Skipton Castle, Yorkshire. Author.

225 *The Battle of Medway*, by Willem Schellinks. SK-C-1736. Rijksmuseum Amsterdam.

228 Capheaton, Northumberland, by Peter Hartover. Private Collection. Paul Highnam/Country Life Picture Library.

232 The guard chamber at Hampton Court, Surrey. Will Pryce/Country Life Picture Library.

235 Doubting Castle from *The Pilgrim's Progress*. Author.

241 Warwick Castle, by Canaletto. Accession Number: 2019.141.7. The Metropolitian Museum of Art, New York, Bequest of Mrs Charles Wrightson, 2019.

244 Blenheim Castle. Engraving from *Vitruvius Britannicus* (1715); Author's photo.

247 Engraving of Newark Castle, Nottinghamshire, by Samuel Buck. Author.

249 Engraving of Wentworth Castle, Yorkshire, by Thomas Badeslade. Author.

251 Plan for Inverary Castle, by Dugal Campbell. By kind permission of the Duke of Argyll.

ILLUSTRATION CREDITS

261 Engraving of Bodiam Castle, Sussex. Author.

265 Dinefwr Castle. William Gilpin, *Observations on the River Wye*. Author.

268 Lough Cutra Castle, Co. Galway. Paul Highnam/Country Life Picture Library.

273 Belvoir Castle, Leicestershire. Paul Highnam/Country Life Picture Library.

277 Lowther Castle, Cumbria. Paul Highnam/Country Life Picture Library.

279 Sketch of Hawarden Castle. Country Life Picture Library.

281 The keep of Conisbrough Castle, Yorkshire. Dr David Robinson.

285 Gwrych Castle. Paul Highnam/Country Life Picture Library.

287 Windsor Castle, by Wyatville. RCIN 918431. Royal Library, Windsor, Berkshire, UK Royal Collection Trust © Her Majesty Queen Elizabeth II, 2021/ Bridgeman Images.

291 Benington Lordship, Hertfordshire. Paul Highnam/Country Life Picture Library.

295 Detail of the Great Drawing Room ceiling at Taymouth Castle, Perthshire. James Brittain/Country Life Picture Library.

302 Peckforton Castle, Cheshire. RIBA Collections.

307 The keep of Alnwick Castle, Northumbria. Author.

311 Cardiff Castle, Glamorgan. Paul Barker/Country Life Picture Library.

315 Kenilworth Castle, Warwickshire. Country Life Picture Library.

322 Farleigh Hungerford, Somerset. Author.

328 Telegram from William Randolph Hearst. Country Life Archive.

330 Castle Drogo, Devon. Country Life Picture Library.

332 Kelburn Castle, Ayrshire. John Millar/Country Life Picture Library.

339 The investiture of the Prince of Wales at Caernarfon Castle © Crown copyright (2021) Cymru Wales.

342 The screen and armour of the King's Champion in St George's Hall, Windsor Castle. Private Collection © Mark Fiennes Archive/Bridgeman Images.

348 The interior of the keep at Dover Castle. Will Pryce/Country Life Picture Library.

350 Lancaster Castle. Paul Barker/Country Life Picture Library.

ACKNOWLEDGEMENTS

This book aims to use the voices of past generations to illuminate the story of the castle to the present, step by step, as it has unravelled. I am intensely conscious, therefore, of the enormous debt I owe to those whose work I have quoted, living and dead. Also, where appropriate, to their translators, whose labours give contemporary voice and immediacy to their words.

I am also grateful to the many private and institutional owners of castles and houses across the country who have given access to properties – and often their archives as well – for the purposes of producing articles for *Country Life*. In the process they have inadvertently laid the foundations for this book. Also to the many contributors to the architectural pages of the magazine who have fed my own enthusiasm with their insights and knowledge, notably Clive Aslet, William Aslet, Marcus Binney, Steven Brindle, Nicholas Cooper, John Crook, Kathryn Ferry, Michael Hall, Richard Hewlings, Rosemary Hill, Edward Impey, Mary Miers, Jeremy Musson, Tim Richardson, David Robinson, John Martin Robinson, the late Gavin Stamp, Simon Thurley and Roger White. No less important has been the magazine's editorial team at large, including Mark Hedges, Kate Green, Paula Lester, Octavia Pollock, James Fisher, Heather Clark, Lucy Ford, Emily Anderson and Cindie Johnston and all those who directly contribute to – and improve – the architecture pages every week. Also to recent former colleagues Melanie Bryan and Paula Fahey. Particular thanks must go to the photographers, whose hard work illustrates them (and most of this book) so beautifully, Paul Highnam, Will Pryce and the late Paul Barker.

Beyond the magazine, I would also like to express my gratitude to Jeremy Ashbee, Alixe Bovey, Derrick Chivers, Jonathan Coad, Jeremy Cunnington, Ptolemy Dean, Anna Eavis, Chris Jones-Jenkins, Anna Keay, Con Manning, John McNeill, Linda Monckton, Richard Plant, Bronwen Riley, Warwick Rodwell, Tim Tatton-Brown and Abigail Wheatley. Special thanks must also go to Stuart Hay, who has discussed the text at length and written penetrating, unsparing and (occasionally) hilarious criticisms of it. All faults and errors, however, remain my own.

The team at Yale University Press have made possible the production of this book and I am grateful to Heather McCallum for commissioning it. Also to Katie Urquhart, Felicity Maunder, Percie Edgeler, Stuart Weir and Lucy Buchan for helping bring it to fruition. Two anonymous readers refined the text and purged it of many errors.

Finally, this book could not have been written without the support of both the Goodall and Campbell families at large. Several of them, including my mother, sister and brother-in-law, commented on the text. Additional thanks, however, must go to my wife and children, who, during the trials of the pandemic, tolerated my writing

ACKNOWLEDGEMENTS

much of the text. Their company set my work in proper proportion, kept me happy and proved beyond reasonable doubt that, in our house at least, 'home schooling' is an oxymoron.

We are grateful to the following for permission to reproduce copyright material: Extracts from *The Anglo-Saxon Chronicles*, translated and edited by Michael Swanton, Orion Publishing Group Limited, 2000, pp. 173–4, 199, 216, 230–1, 264–5. Reproduced with permission of the Licensor through PLSclear; extracts from *Gesta Stephani*, translated by R. H. C. Davis, ed. K. R. Potter, University Press, 1976. Reproduced with permission of the Licensor through PLSclear; an extract from *Jordan Fantosme's Chronicle*, translated by J. C. Johnston, Oxford University Press, 1981, pp. 86–97, 102–13, 130–5. Reproduced with permission of the Licensor through PLSclear; an extract from *Matthew Paris, Chronica Majora*, published in 'The Western Entrance to the Tower of London, 1240–1241' by Edward Impey, translated by Jeremy Ashbee in *Transactions of the London and Middlesex Archaeological Society*, vol. 48, 1998, p. 66. Reproduced with permission from LAMAS, http://www.lamas.org.uk/; an extract from *The History of the King's Works*, vol. 1, ed. R. A. Brown, H. M. Colvin and A. J. Taylor, HMSO, 1963, pp. 398–9. Licensed under the Open Government Licence v3.0; an extract from *The Chronicle of Geoffrey le Baker of Swinbrook*, translated by E. Preest, ed. R. Barber, Boydell & Brewer, 2012. Reproduced with permission of the Licensor through PLSclear; an extract from 'Master John Burcestre and the Castles of Stafford and Maxstoke' by M. J. B. Hislop and A. M. Hislop in *Transactions of the South Staffordshire Archaeological and Historical Society*, vol. 33, 1993, pp. 14–20. Reproduced with permission of the publisher; an extract from *Sir Gawain and the Green Knight* translated by Michael Smith, first published in the UK by Unbound, copyright © Michael Smith, 2018. Reproduced with permission of the publisher; extracts from *The Chronica Maiora of Thomas of Walsingham, 1376–1422*, translated by D. Preest, Boydell & Brewer, 2005. Reproduced with permission of the Licensor through PLSclear; an extract from 'The Building Accounts of Tattershall Castle, 1434–72' by W. D. Simpson, *Lincoln Record Society*, vol. SS, 1960, pp. 25, 56, 32, 73, copyright © Lincoln Record Society. Reproduced with permission; extracts from *The Vita Mariae Angliae Reginae of Robert Wingfield of Brantham*, ed. Diarmaid MacCulloch, Camden Miscellany, 28, 4th series, vol. 29, Cambridge University Press, 1984, pp. 255–65. Reproduced with permission of the publisher through Copyright Clearance Center; extracts from *The White Tower*, ed. Edward Impey, Yale University Press, 2008, pp. 338, 163–5. Reproduced with permission of the Licensor through PLSclear; an extract from *The Memoirs and Memorials of Sir Hugh Cholmley of Whitby, 1600–57*, ed. Dr Jack Binns, Yorkshire Archaeological Society Record Series, vol. 153, 1997–8, pp. 154–7. Reproduced with permission of Yorkshire Archaeological and Historical Society; an extract from 'The Life of Me Lady Anne Clifford' in *Anne Clifford's Autobiographical Writing, 1590–1676*, ed. J. L. Malay, Manchester University Press, 2018. Reproduced with permission of the Licensor through PLSclear; extracts from 1667 contract for the construction of Capheaton. Reproduced with permission from private collection; extracts from *The Diary of John Evelyn, Kalendarium*, vols 3 and 4, ed. Esmond Samuel De Beer, Oxford University Press, 1959. Reproduced with permission of the Licensor through PLSclear; letter from Bowyer Edward Sparke to the Duke of Rutland, July 10, 1801. Reproduced with permission from Belvoir Castle Archive; extracts from British Library Add. MS. 17398, ff. 103–26, published in *Sussex Depicted, Views and Descriptions 1600–1800*, ed. John Farrant, Sussex Record Society, Lewes 2001. Reproduced with permission; extracts from *The History of the*

ACKNOWLEDGEMENTS

King's Works, vol. 6, 1782–1851, ed. J. Mordaunt Crook and M. H. Port, HMSO, 1973, pp. 381–3. Licensed under the Open Government Licence v3.0; extract from *Leave it to Psmith* by P. G. Wodehouse. Copyright © The Estate of P. G. Wodehouse. Reproduced with permission of the Estate c/o Rogers, Coleridge & White Ltd., 20 Powis Mews, London W11 1JN; letter from Evelyn Waugh Letter, May 31st 1942, copyright © 1942, The Estate of Laura Waugh, used by permission of The Wylie Agency (UK) Limited; extract from 'A speech by HRH The Prince of Wales replying to the Loyal Address by Sir Ben Bowen Thomas, President of the University College of Wales, Aberystwyth, The Investiture of The Investiture of The Prince of Wales, Caernarfon Castle, North Wales, 1st July 1969'. Reproduced with permission; and an extract from *Harry Potter and the Philosopher's Stone*, copyright © J. K. Rowling 1997. Reproduced with permission.

INDEX

INDEX

INDEX

Stirling Castle, 86–7
stone
  Castle Hedingham, 43–4
  early stone towers, 14, 26–8, 41
  Normal stone castles, 25, 26–8
  Rievaulx Abbey, Yorkshire, 49
  Roger of Salisbury's buildings, 39, 41
Sudbury, Archbishop, 119, 120
Sudeley Castle, 272, 310

Tattershall Castle
  brick-built, 139–42
  great tower, 139, 271
  restoration, 318–20, 322
Taymouth Castle, 295
Thomas of Walsingham, 117–19, 120,
  121–2
Thornbury Castle, 167–70
Tipping, Henry Avray, 322–4
tourism
  Belvoir Castle, 273–5
  Chirk Castle, 304–6
  Conisbrough Castle, 281–4
  Dinefwr Castle, 265–7
  Dover Castle, 69–71, 348–9
  Eglinton Castle, 295–8
  Kenilworth Castle, 315–17
  Pevensey, Hastings and Bodiam
    Castles, 261–4
  Tower of London, 199–201, 234,
    315–16
  Warwick Castle, 152, 241–3
  Wressle Castle, 179–81
tournaments
  Carew Castle, 162
  Edward III, 102, 104, 162
  Eglinton Castle, 295–8
Tower of London
  animal sculptures, 103, 105
  Beauchamp Tower, 68
  construction of, 26
  escape of Roger de Mortimer, 94–6
  garrisons, 117
  gatehouse, 68
  gunpowder and, 188–90, 199–201
  Henry III's fortification of, 66–8
  Knights of the Bath, 188–90
  national significance, 28
  Peasants' Revolt, 117–20
  as a prison, 27, 66, 68, 94–6
  rectangular style, 27

  a sixteenth-century tour of,
    199–201, 234
  Small Armoury, 234
  tourism, 199–201, 234, 315–16
  White Tower, 82, 188–90, 199, 201
towers
  Beauchamp Tower, 68
  Berkeley Castle, 101
  Clifford's Tower, 58
  of Continental castles, 14
  Dublin Castle, 61
  early stone towers, 14, 26–8, 41
  of Norman architecture, 27–8
  Pontefract Castle, 191–2
  as prisons, 27, 51
  rectangular style, 27
  Rochester Castle, 63–5, 225–7
  Scarborough Castle, 215–18
  Tattershall Castle, 139, 271
  of timber on mottes, 14, 22
  Warkworth Castle, 132
Trollopp, Robert, 228–31
Tynemouth Castle, 33, 34, 35
Tynemouth Priory, 35

Vanbrugh, Sir John, 245–6
Venerable Bede, 15–16, 17
Verrio, Antonio, 238, 239
Vitruvius Britannicus, 244, 249

Wales
  Beaumaris Castle, 79–81
  Caernarfon Castle, 74, 339–41
  Caerphilly Castle, 66, 68
  Cardiff Castle, 50, 311–13
  Carew Castle, 159–62
  Chirk Castle, 74, 304–6
  Conwy Castle, 1, 74, 88–91, 128–31
  Denbigh Castle, 74
  Dinefwr Castle, 265–7
  Edward I in, 72–4
  Flint Castle, 72–3, 124–7
  Gwrych Castle, 285–6
  Harlech Castle, 74
  Holt Castle, 74
  rebellions against the English,
    128–9
  St Donat's Castle, 328–9
Walpole, Horace, 114, 201, 255–7,
  298
Walter of Exeter, 84–5, 94

391